The
Garland Library
of
War and Peace

The
Garland Library
of
War and Peace

Under the General Editorship of

Blanche Wiesen Cook, *John Jay College, C.U.N.Y.*

Sandi E. Cooper, *Richmond College, C.U.N.Y.*

Charles Chatfield, *Wittenberg University*

Social Progress
and the Darwinian Theory

A Study of Force as a
Factor in Human Relations

by

George Nasmyth

with an introduction by

Norman Angell

with a new introduction
for the Garland Edition by

Catherine Ann Cline

Garland Publishing, Inc., New York & London
1973

Library of Congress Cataloging in Publication Data

Nasmyth, George William, 1882-1920.
  Social progress and the Darwinian theory.

  (Garland library of war and peace)
  Reprint of the 1916 ed. published by Putnam, New
York.
  1. Social change. 2. Evolution. 3. War.
I. Title. II. Series.
HM106.N3 1973   301'.0424   73-147479
ISBN 0-8240-0271-7

Introduction

It is ironic that the outbreak of World War I was preceded by one of the most hopeful periods in the history of the peace movement in the United States. Peace organizations multiplied, their memberships increased, and generous financial support for their activities was provided.[1] The vigorous efforts of these groups appeared to have a substantial impact both on government officials and on public opinion. Arbitration treaties between the United States and other nations were concluded. Opposition to the steadily-increasing naval appropriations began to make itself felt in Congress. The bellicose spirit that had characterized the American public during the war with Spain ebbed, and the enthusiasm for imperial adventures evaporated. Even the fruitless international peace conferences at the Hague were viewed by the pacifists as encouraging first steps toward international machinery for the elimination of war.[2] As a lieutenant in the peace movement George Nasmyth (1882-1920) shared in, and contributed to, the easy optimism of those years. His career provides a case study of the response of one pacifist to the shattering of those hopes.

Nasmyth was born on July 9, 1882 in Cleveland, Ohio, of Scotch-Canadian parentage. After attending

5

public schools in New York City and Buffalo, he entered Cornell University. After his graduation in 1906 he remained at Cornell serving as an instructor in physics while pursuing graduate study in that field. In 1909 he received his doctorate, and the results of his research published between 1908 and 1911 suggest that his career in science was proceeding smoothly.[3]

It was through membership in the Cosmopolitan Club at Cornell that Nasmyth's interest in the peace movement, which was soon to lead him to abandon his scientific pursuits, was first aroused. The Cosmopolitan Clubs, which sprang up on American campuses between 1903 and 1914, reflected the belief, widely held both in the United States and abroad, that the exchange of university students could be a powerful force for international understanding. The sympathy of students, who would be the leaders of the future, was considered of crucial importance for the success of the peace movement, and their devotion to scholarship, which tends to ignore national boundaries, was thought to predispose them in favor of international good will. Thus the decision of the Chinese government to use the Boxer indemnity returned to it by the United States to provide scholarships for Chinese students at American universities was acclaimed as an effective step toward the improvement of relations between the two countries. The establishment, at about the same time, of Rhodes scholarships and the Kahn Travelling

INTRODUCTION

Fellowship, which required its recipient to visit Europe, America, and the Far East, were likewise designed to strengthen friendship and further understanding among the nations involved.

Stimulated by what appeared to be a general trend toward foreign study, the leaders of the Cosmopolitan Clubs sought to build a peace movement by promoting contacts between American and foreign students and faculty on American campuses. In terms of their ambitious hopes their program seems limited indeed. Most Club meetings consisted of "National Evenings" during which foreign students entertained with the songs and dances of their respective countries, or gave talks on their customs and institutions. This was known as "cultivating the international mind," and it was believed that those who participated would come to recognize that "the other fellow is animated by the same high ideals" as themselves, and that they would henceforth be "apostles of international good will." Proceeding on the assumption that international "misunderstandings" resulted from "mutual ignorance," the Cosmopolitan Clubs, which took no official position on various proposals for mechanisms for the settlement of disputes between nations, pursued world peace through the strategy of building personal friendships across national boundaries.[4]

In the years between 1906 and 1914 the Clubs prospered in the United States and extended their contacts abroad. Cosmopolitan Clubs were estab-

lished on thirty American campuses, on some of which residences were built or purchased. The World Peace Foundation, impressed with the possibilities of the organization, furnished an annual subsidy in support of its activities. In 1911 the Clubs affiliated with Corda Fratres, *a European student organization that drew most of its membership from Italy and France, and* Liga de los Estudiantes, *a group representing South American students. The importance of the Cosmopolitan Clubs was recognized when Nasmyth was named president of the new international federation.[5]*

By the time Nasmyth assumed his new post in 1911, the American peace movement was strong enough to undertake missionary activity. It was agreed that, with the financial support of the World Peace Federation, he would spend the following year in Europe, keeping in touch with the leaders of existing student groups and attempting to extend the Cosmopolitan Club movement. Germany was selected as the logical focus of his activity. Student organizations with internationalist or pacifist ideals, common at other Continental universities, were completely absent from that nation. Nasmyth regarded it as "the center of gravity in Europe,"[6] and he believed furthermore that hopeful internal political developments made this the "critical hour"[7] for the German peace movement. The German universities likewise provided an ideal location for his simultaneous pursuit of advanced study in physics.

8

INTRODUCTION

Despite Nasmyth's zeal, the ideals of the Cosmo-politan Clubs were not easily transplanted to Germany. Whereas the exotic Chinese had been hospitably received on American campuses, Germans fiercely resented the Russian Jews who constituted the most numerous group of foreign students in Germany. His success in recruiting Russian members simply insured that the organization would be shunned by Germans. [8] *Such amiable Club customs as learning the national anthem of each member of the group were unsuited to a country where the speaking of a foreign language at a public meeting might lead to the arrival of the police.*

The atmosphere of Wilhelmian Germany seems to have convinced Nasmyth that a more "scientific" appeal must be substituted for the vague good will which had hitherto characterized his organization's approach to world peace. For this purpose the doctrines of Norman Angell, the British author of The Great Illusion *(1910), seemed admirably fitted. Angell, whose work had attracted wide attention both in Britain and abroad, was the proponent of the view that under modern conditions war constituted an economic catastrophe for the victor as well as the vanquished. This "new pacifism" attempted to build anti-war sentiment on grounds of enlightened self interest rather than on lofty sentiments of brotherhood.*

At Nasmyth's invitation, Angell, in February 1913, undertook a lecture tour of the German universities

9

under the auspices of the Cosmopolitan Clubs. An intensive campaign preceded his appearances. With the financial help of the Carnegie Endowment for International Peace, 40,000 copies of an "Open Letter to German Students" were distributed explaining the essentials of his argument. Over 2,000 copies of the German translation of The Great Illusion *were sent to selected faculty and students. Forewarned, the members of the "corporations," the dueling fraternities, appeared at the lectures in force, objecting loudly to the presentation of "international ideas" "which could only endanger the fatherland." On one occasion Angell's talk was delayed when protesters, outraged by his lecturing in English, summoned the police who had to be persuaded that all proceedings would be immediately translated into German. Other meetings degenerated into violent confrontations between two sections of the audience.*[9]

Despite such hostility, Nasmyth insisted, both at the time and subsequently, that his efforts in Germany were beginning to bear fruit. He was less surprised by the opposition his activities aroused than by the degree of sympathy and cooperation which he encountered. Following Angell's stormy tour, Nasmyth reported bravely to his supporters in the United States that the lectures had created "a great intellectual ferment" which would ultimately strengthen the peace forces, and he noted that in the extensive comment surrounding the meetings the Liberal press argued that the thesis of The Great Illusion *should not be rejected unexamined.*[10] *Likewise he based hope for the future of the student movement on the popularity enjoyed by Americans attending the universities. He had discovered strong supporters among second-generation German-Americans, some with family ties to the liberal exodus of 1848, who could serve as a "bridge" between German and foreign students.*[11] *It should be noted that Norman Angell, who was free of the professional optimism which tends to afflict workers in any movement, shared Nasmyth's favorable estimate of the impact of the peace effort in the universities. Given five more years, he later observed, it would have "diluted Prussianism sufficiently as to have rendered it much less dangerous."*[12]

Nasmyth's stay in Germany lengthened into two and one-half years, broken by occasional visits to the United States and brief trips to other European countries. While he regarded peace work in Germany as most crucial for the present, he advised that future effort should be concentrated on Russia "where great changes are impending."[13] *He found students at St. Petersburg eager to participate in the peace movement, which provided an outlet for their frustrated political idealism. Throughout Scandinavia, Poland, Austria-Hungary, and the Balkans he made special efforts, as he had in Germany, to contact the numerous Russians studying outside their own country.*

INTRODUCTION

The height of the prewar international student movement was reached at a meeting held at Cornell in the summer of 1913. Nasmyth arrived proudly with thirty-five students representing the seven Cosmopolitan Clubs established at German universities. Delegates from thirty countries were in attendance. Deeply impressed by their lengthy discussions with such figures as Norman Angell, the participants entrained for Washington where they were addressed in sympathetic terms by both President Wilson and Secretary of State William Jennings Bryan. [14]

By 1913 the peace movement had become for Nasmyth an all-consuming interest. After long talks with Angell he determined to forsake physics in order to devote his total energy to international affairs. In notifying Edwin Mead of the World Peace Foundation of his decision he wrote:

> A new era in human history is dawning — the era of the unity of the world. . . . I feel that I must travel the length and breadth of America preaching this great doctrine of humanity and pleading for the organization of a great missionary movement which will send peace workers out to all countries, and that I must go through the world, rousing the students to the significance of the coming dawn. . . [15]

Despite his evangelical tone, Nasmyth did not regard commitment to peace work as a rejection of science. What the peace movement needed, in his judgment, was a "rational and scientific basis." [16] *He*

12

was confident that such a foundation could be provided by a science of international relations, and he resolved to contribute to the establishment of such a discipline. He was thus, in his own view, simply transferring his technique of scientific inquiry into the field of most urgent need. In pursuit of this goal he plunged into the study of economics while still in Germany, arranged to take appropriate courses at Harvard, and, under Angell's tutelage, acquainted himself with European works on economics, politics, and social philosophy which were little known in the United States.[17]

Thus, by 1914 Nasmyth's future plans were fully formulated. He would continue to work to extend student peace organizations, while attempting to provide the peace movement with a more "scientific" approach. The outbreak of the war in Europe and the disintegration of the European peace movement for which he had labored so diligently in no way dampened his enthusiasm. "The breakdown of civilization in Europe this year," he maintained, "has brought to many students, as to myself, a new consecration to the cause of peace and world organization."[18] Throughout the years of America's neutrality, he strove to carry out the program he had set for himself in more promising days.

The most immediate task was to prevent the entrance of the United States into the conflict. Nasmyth became president of the Federation of International Polity Clubs, a successor of the Cosmo-

politan Clubs, which took an official stand against intervention.[19] *In an effort to correct the excesses of Allied propaganda he produced a pamphlet designed to present a more balanced picture of the mood in Germany.*[20] *Alarmed by the growing demand for "preparedness," he attacked the proposals for universal military training, disputing the need for a large army in a nation protected by two oceans and a strong navy. As for the secondary benefits claimed for conscription by its proponents, his years in central Europe had convinced him that conscription had proved itself neither a democratizing force in Germany nor a unifying element in Austria-Hungary.*[21]

Whereas Nasmyth felt constrained to attack what he regarded as "militarism," he was more at ease in the constructive task of building public support for the establishment of an international organization after the war. From the outset he gave strong support to the League to Enforce Peace, an organization including both interventionists and noninterventionists who were determined that machinery for collective security should be part of the peace treaty. Through his close ties with Angell he served as a link between the League and the Union of Democratic Control, a British group working along similar lines.[22]

While engaged in these day-by-day tasks of propaganda, Nasmyth was preparing a work designed to destroy the underlying philosophical assumptions of

14

militarism. Since the last decades of the nineteenth century, advocates of force in the United States and elsewhere had claimed the authority of science in support of their position. In Social Progress and Darwinism *(1916), he attempted to meet these arguments on their own scientific ground.*

The object of Nasmyth's attack was social Darwinism, the social philosophy which drew its rationalization, though not its origin, from Charles Darwin's theory of natural selection. Certain concepts such as "competition," "survival of the fittest," and "struggle for existence" used by Darwin to explain the evolution from lower to higher forms of life were seized upon by thinkers like Herbert Spencer eager to justify prevailing economic and political institutions and practices. Transferring Darwin's theory from the physical to the social world, they argued that struggle, in which the fittest survived and the unfit perished, was the sole path for man's economic, social and political improvement as it had been for his physical development. Thus proposals to protect the weak by regulating capitalism or halting imperialism were pictured as futile, and even harmful, interferences with natural law.

Despite the dominance exercised by social Darwinism over American thought after 1870, it had been subjected to criticism from the beginning. Thinkers like Lester Ward, arguing that the physical and social worlds were fundamentally different, simply rejected the crude biological analogy. Some clergymen denounced its indifference to the fate of the weak as antithetical to the Christian gospel. Socialists, while they might borrow selectively from social Darwinism to bolster their theories of class struggle, found its extreme individualism at odds with their own "scientific" projection of the future. Thus, in attacking this philosophy in 1916, Nasmyth was confronting a system of social theory which, whatever its hold on the popular mind, had been undermined by decades of critical thought.[23]

While earlier American critics of social Darwinism had relied heavily on the writings of such British thinkers as Thomas Huxley, Continental works on the subject had been relatively neglected. Nasmyth's purpose in Social Progress and Darwinism *was to make available to American readers a critique of this philosophy developed by Russian scientists and social scientists. The ideas presented by Nasmyth were first adumbrated in 1880 by a zoologist, Professor Kessler, in a lecture before a congress of Russian naturalists. His argument was elaborated with a wealth of supporting scientific evidence by Prince Kropotkin in his work* Mutual Aid *(1902).*[24] *Jacques Novicow, a Russian sociologist living in Paris, likewise produced a voluminous body of writings attacking, as had Kessler and Kropotkin, the foundation in physical science claimed by theorists who advocated a society based on struggle and competition.*[25]

Nasmyth's work, which follows closely the analysis of Novicow's La Critique du Darwinisme Sociale

16

INTRODUCTION

(1910), makes no claim to originality.[26] *Novicow's criticism as presented by Nasmyth did, however, introduce into the American discussion of social Darwinism an approach which hitherto had been relatively unexplored. Whereas earlier critics had, for the most part, questioned the logic or wisdom of transferring the laws of the physical universe into the social world, Nasmyth argues that the social Darwinists had misread the findings of science. The struggle for survival, he insists, was a struggle, not among individuals of the same species, but rather of the species with the environment. Cooperation has contributed to group survival, while physical conflict has had indifferent or deleterious effects.*

Despite these criticisms, Nasmyth was no less a social Darwinist than those whom he attacked. There could, he believed, be no "break" between "the cosmic process and human society" (pp. 270-71). Darwinian theory provided a "clear guiding principle" for the social sciences as Newton's law of gravity had provided a "vitalizing organization and system" for the physical sciences in the seventeenth century. That principle, as Nasmyth had demonstrated to his own satisfaction, was cooperation. Thus, he concludes, "the federation of the world becomes ... in the Darwinian sense, the ultimate goal of human evolution" (pp. 301-02). Whatever may be thought of the scientific or logical validity of his argument, his attempt to bring social theory into harmony with physical science had at least produced a far more

17

agreeable vision of the future than earlier efforts.

The subsequent history of Social Progress and Darwinism *provides a curious and illuminating episode in American intellectual history. It is evident that Nasmyth intended his study as a serious contribution to the discussion of social theory rather than as a piece of propaganda designed to influence the current debate concerning intervention. It contains, to be sure, some passages highly critical of German militarism, which he considered a particularly shocking example of the effect of a "false" social Darwinism (pp. 41-2). The work was produced, however, when he was still involved in efforts to prevent the entrance of the United States into the war, and his disapproval of the annexationist aims of the Allies is equally clear (p. 226). It is, therefore, surprising to find him, after America's declaration of war, reporting to his publisher that he found a growing interest in the work "as a war book" that revealed the theory "which is back of Germany's program of world domination," and even suggesting that it should be advertised as an exposé of "the fallacies of the Prussian philosophy of force."[27] The public response suggests that social Darwinism had become hateful to Americans, and Merle Curti is doubtless correct in assigning Nasmyth part of the credit for "putting the finishing touches to the work of demolishing [it]."[28] The paradoxical consequence of this rejection of ideas justifying struggle was, however, America's participation in a war against the*

18

nation which was thought to embody these evil beliefs.

Nasmyth's willingness to allow his book to be presented as an anti-German tract suggests the ambiguities of his position after American entrance into the war. On the one hand he clung firmly to a determination to refuse to fight. He confided to a friend that if the draft was extended to his age group

> ... The only position which my conscience and a lifetime of work for international peace in half the countries of the world will permit me to take is that of a conscientious objector to war and while I am willing to stand up against the wall and be shot if necessary, I cannot, as a follower of Jesus Christ and a believer in the religion of humanity, kill my fellowmen ... [29]

This personal decision was clearly influenced by his ties with the Society of Friends which extended back to 1913. On the other hand, he had come to regard an Allied victory as the best hope for an improved world order. As early as 1915, in commenting on the plan of a group working for the establishment of an international organization after the war, he confessed that it seemed "pregnant with such possibilities that I would almost wish for a break with Germany if this program would result."[30] Thus he took no public stand in opposition to the war after America's intervention. Indeed he cooperated with the war effort by serving on commissions dealing with the economic problems created by America's participa-

19

tion.[31] *Meanwhile he worked energetically to build public support for the establishment of an international peace-keeping organization at the end of the war.*

In the two years which remained to Nasmyth after the close of the war he witnessed the wreckage of his most cherished hopes. Returning to Europe with the intention of reconstructing the international student movement, he found scarcely a trace of the results of his earlier work. The mood at the German universities was "more jingoistic and reactionary" than in the prewar period, and the treatment of foreign students, never gracious, had become harsh.[32] Throughout eastern Europe xenophobia among students was, if possible, even more pronounced.[33]

If the atmosphere in Europe was dismal, the situation in the United States was no less alarming. Like many American pacifists, Nasmyth had assumed that his nation would be the mainstay of the new international organization. Indeed his ambivalent attitude toward the war had been the consequence of that expectation. By January 1920 he was deploring "the tide of American provincialism and isolation which is threatening to create such havoc in the world."[34] Two months later this new temper manifested itself in the Senate's rejection of membership in the League of Nations.

INTRODUCTION

A person less sanguine than Nasmyth might, at this point, have retreated to the physics laboratory. The summer of 1920 found him in Europe, however, still deeply engrossed in peace work. As the representative of the World Alliance for Promoting International Friendship through the Churches, he traveled throughout the Continent attempting to mobilize religious groups in support of the League of Nations. It was an uncomfortable and dangerous journey. In Poland he wandered behind the shifting Bolshevik lines, and extricated himself only by assuming a disguise. In the Balkans he contracted typhoid fever which led to his death in Geneva on September 20, 1920 at the age of thirty-nine.

The pleasant "National Evenings" of the Cosmopolitan Clubs in the prewar years and that final fatal trek across war-torn Europe were both incidents in Nasmyth's gallant search for an effective approach to the problem of international conflict. If the solution eluded him, he must at least be credited with having contributed to a deepened understanding of the problem of war. Beginning with a naive faith in personal good will as the means for eliminating international tensions, he turned to economics, biology, and social science in his quest for a more realistic foundation for the peace movement. The value of the "scientific" ideas which he attempted to popularize was chiefly negative: war does not pay,

21

INTRODUCTION

natural law does not dictate that society must be based on struggle. The elimination of such myths was insufficient to prevent war, but it served as a necessary clearing of the ground.

Catherine Ann Cline
History Department
Catholic University of America

INTRODUCTION

NOTES

[1] *The World Peace Foundation and the Carnegie Endowment for International Peace were both established in 1910. The former had an initial endowment of $1,000,000, the latter $10,000,000.*

[2] *On the prewar peace efforts see Merle Curti,* Peace or War: The American Struggle, 1835-1936 *(New York, 1936), Chapter VII.*

[3] *George William Nasmyth,* The Frequency of the Singing Arc *(New York, 1908), and* "Experiments in Impact Excitation," Physical Review, XXXII *(1911), 69-117.*

[4] *The Cosmopolitan Club movement was described by one of its leaders, Louis Lochner, in* Advocate of Peace, LXXII *(April, 1910), 88-89,* The Cosmopolitan Club Movement *(New York, 1912), as well as in his autobiography,* Always the Unexpected *(New York, 1956), Chapter IV.*

[5] *In 1911 the organization assumed the name "Corda Fratres, International Federation of Students"; in 1913 it was changed to "Corda Fratres, Association of Cosmopolitan Clubs."*

[6] World Peace Foundation: Its Present Activities *(Boston, 1913), p. 34.*

[7] World Peace Foundation: Its Present Activities *(Boston, 1912), p. 22.*

[8] *Nasmyth to Edwin Mead (Copy), July 29, 1912, Peace Collection, Swarthmore College.*

[9] *On Angell's tour see Nasmyth's unexpurgated draft report, dated March 14, 1913, Norman Angell Papers, Ball State University, and the account in Angell's autobiography,* After All *(New York, 1951), pp. 171-72.*

[10] World Peace Foundation: Its Present Activities *(Boston, 1913), p. 32.*

[11] *Nasmyth to Edwin Mead (Copy), July 29, 1912, Peace Collection.*

NOTES

[12] *Angell, op. cit., p. 172.*

[13] World Peace Foundation: Its Present Activities *(Boston, 1913), p. 34.*

[14] *For an account of the meeting see Lochner,* Always the Unexpected, *p. 42, and Angell, op. cit., p. 173.*

[15] *Nasmyth to Edwin Mead (Copy), April 24, 1913, Peace Collection.*

[16] *Nasmyth to Angell, June 11, 1914, Angell Papers, Ball State University.*

[17] *Angell to Nasmyth (Copy), April 28, 1913, Angell Papers.*

[18] World Peace Foundation: Its Present Activities *(Boston, 1914), p. 35.*

[19] World Peace Foundation: Its Present Activities *(Boston, 1915), p. 12.*

[20] *Nasmyth,* What I Saw in Germany *(London, 1914?), as cited in Curti, op. cit., pp. 231 and 351.*

[21] *Nasmyth,* Universal Military Service and Democracy *(Washington, 1917).*

[22] *See the correspondence between Nasmyth and Angell in the Angell Papers, and Nasmyth's correspondence with E. D. Morel in the Peace Collection.*

[23] *The standard work on social Darwinism in the United States is Richard Hofstadter,* Social Darwinism in American Thought *(2nd ed., Boston, 1955).*

[24] *Prince Peter Kropotkin (1842-1921) based his work on scientific observations conducted during a geographical expedition to Manchuria when he was a young man. Much of his later life was spent in anarchist-nihilist activities. Because* Mutual Aid *was published in English, it was better known in the United States than the work of other Continental theorists who were developing similar theories.*

[25] *Jacques Novicow (1849-1912) was Vice President of the International Institute of Sociology. His works were, for the most part, published in French.*

[26] *The chief difference between Nasmyth and Novicow lies in the former's claim that Darwin shared the Kropotkin-Novicow-Nasmyth view of the social implications of his theory. While Darwin was not a thorough social Darwinist, his position was not as clear-cut as Nasmyth*

24

NOTES

suggests. See the exchange in Science and Society, *VI (1942), pp. 71-78.*

[27]*Nasmyth to G. P. Putnam's (Copy), August 6, 1918, Peace Collection.*

[28]*Curti, op. cit., p. 121.*

[29]*Nasmyth to the Reverend Harry Hodgkin (Copy), Sept. 9, 1918, Peace Collection.*

[30]*Nasmyth to Angell, March 29, 1916, Angell Papers.*

[31]*He served as secretary of the Commission on the price of the 1917 wheat crop and as head of the administrative division of the U.S. Fuel Administration, 1917-19.*

[32]*Nasmyth to the Reverend Edward Cummings (Copy), June 4, 1920, Peace Collection.*

[33]*Nasmyth to Paul Dubi (Copy), July 28, 1920, Peace Collection.*

[34]*Nasmyth to Lucia Ann Mead (Copy), Jan. 14, 1920, Peace Collection.*

Social Progress

and the

Darwinian Theory

A Study of Force as a Factor in Human Relations

By

George Nasmyth, Ph.D.

With an Introduction by

Norman Angell

G. P. Putnam's Sons
New York and London
The Knickerbocker Press
1916

The Knickerbocker Press, New York

CONTENTS

INTRODUCTION

THIS book is the outcome of a suggestion which I once made to my friend George Nasmyth, to the effect that Novikov's work on the application of Darwinism to social problems was not known to the English-speaking world as it ought to be. Such a presentation could not be a mere work of translation. For one thing, Novikov had a mind that saw so many sides of his subject and saw his arguments so completely that some of his books run into unmanageable lengths. Now no wise man lightly shoulders a labour of condensation, even if the raw material is his own. To take a man like Novikov, condense him, and still deliver his full message means knowing the subject better than he knew it himself and knowing his mind better than he did. That is a large order. What happens, of course, in such a case is that the interpreter has to write a new book, and that is what Nasmyth has done.

This book has to do with one or two of the few really fundamental questions which concern men condemned to live together in society—as all men are. Yet a book of this character is more likely to be read about and talked about than read; just as an earlier generation read about Darwin instead of reading him.   The process by which in the modern world we undermine error seems to be something like this: A Spencer or a Darwin gives his life to the statement of a certain truth; a fractional part of that truth—distorted—is taken by some chatter-merchant, as the modern journalist has been called, put into a paragraph, or worse still, into a head line, and that for the mass of us is what we know of the life-work in question.   Thus for twenty years Darwinism, to the great public, was summed up in the question, "Were men once monkeys?"; and this distortion, this failure to grasp the real meaning of Darwin's message, did not affect only the Philistine and the multitude.

The social implications of Darwin's message have been discussed by at least some scientists, by men of learning and cultivation, who, almost certainly—astounding as the assertion may seem —did not trouble to read any one of his books through.   The world has fixed upon an interpretation of Darwinism in applying it to social phenomena which Darwin feared they would give it, against which he expressly warned them, and concerning which he declared in advance that such an interpretation was not his.   His warning does not seem to have had the least effect.   Such phrases as "the struggle for existence," "survival of the fittest," and "the rôle of conflict and force" have been seized upon by reactionary politicians and sociologists and applied to their own problems and Darwin has been made to deliver a message which was the direct contrary of the message which it was his intention to deliver. One of the pathetic "situations" of the history of literature is to find Darwin towards the close of his life, as he watched the growing misinterpretation of his message, saying, with a disconsolate sigh: "I am beginning to despair of ever making the majority understand my notions. . . . I must be a very bad explainer."

A like fate in some measure, of course, may possibly await such ideas as those with which this book deals. The author has attempted to disentangle a certain truth touching the science of society, the truth, namely, that the vast and complex co-operative partnerships of human association do not work towards efficiency by one of the parties—groups within the nation or national groups themselves—exercising compulsion or coercion upon the other, but by free co-operation based upon an intelligent recognition of mutual interest in such co-operation. Now it is very difficult to realize how and in what manner that principle works in society; and it is partly because it is so difficult that society often works so badly and breaks down so disastrously. Therefore, says the average social critic, "Don't let us trouble about seeing it at all. Speaking broadly, social amelioration in the widest and deepest sense (such sense not being limited, that is, to municipal wash-houses and straight streets) depends upon

our getting clear the true principles of co-
operation.   Therefore, don't let us study them."

   That, quite simply and briefly, is the attitude
generally adopted towards discussion of the subject dealt with in this book.   One can foretell pretty
well the kind of criticism which this book will provoke.   It will be along some such lines as these:

The attempt to base society upon anything but
force is an idealistic effort, a counsel of perfection
worthy of all praise, but not having much relation to
practical affairs.   Human nature being what it is,
men and nations will only yield to the argument of
the big battalion.   The human elements which at
bottom render an army necessary are those which at
bottom render a police force necessary.   When human
nature has been improved out of existence, men may
be guided by sweet reasonableness, and the element of
force and compulsion may disappear from human
affairs.   But until that happy millennium arrives, the
ultima ratio regum will still be, both as regards the
king's subjects and the king's enemies, what it always
has been.   Society is too complex a thing and human
nature too wayward a thing for either to be guided
by a simple theory, or by a formula.   From generation
to generation, whether in Aristotelian or Platonic
Greece, in a Palestine looking for a new kingdom, in a
France of the eighteenth century which sees in democratic government the birth of a new heaven and a
new earth, in Chartist England improving on the
dream, men have hatched these theories, but always
do we find them breaking down in the crude fact of
the policeman and the soldier.

Such, with variations and adaptations, will be the "criticism" to which books of this character are subjected.

It is not necessary, of course, to read a book to dismiss it in this manner; it suffices that it is supposed to have an idealistic tendency. And yet one has only to vary the formula a little to see how this sort of criticism stands self-condemned. Let us make a variation and see the result:

Man is a blood-thirsty and unthinking creature. His civilization is but skin-deep, and beneath this thin varnish lie impulses of animalism reaching back to an ancestry which stretches over æons of time. This savage is only held in check by perceptions, understandings, and second thoughts so frail and dubious that at any moment he is likely to get the better of them and destroy the moral labour of toiling generations. Don't let us therefore bother to strengthen those things. It is only by virtue of understanding, of clearly realizing certain truths of human co-operation that we can make our civilization secure; therefore, do not let us trouble to understand those truths. It is not practical. The practical thing is to have plenty of "force"—and to place its employment in the hands of men who don't realize in the least how it should be used. Men are at bottom illogical, unseeing, incapable of weighing the result of their acts; in that case don't worry with sobering and rationalizing influences; the practical thing is to place unrestrictedly at their disposal force of immeasurable destructiveness. Civilization will then be secure.

These conclusions of the "practical" man, who is so sure that he is talking sense and is so sure that he is not erecting theories or laying down dogmas, could be extended indefinitely. And I am disposed to think that the next real step in civilization will be the discovery of the "practical" man that he is drawing from certain undoubted facts such as the complexity of society, the frailty of human wisdom and reason, the uncertainty and mysteriousness of our impulses, conclusions which are the exact contrary of the true ones.

Such a result would be in keeping with the process of most human advancement; to be able to reason correctly concerning those facts of existence visible to all is of more worth than to possess an intimate knowledge of phenomena only available to specialists. The civilization of Greece or Rome had some claims to consideration in comparison with (say) that of Prussia. Yet that intimate knowledge of the properties of matter which gives the Prussian such efficiency in its control was *terra incognita* to the ancient civilizations. But the slight knowledge of physics possessed by the ancients did not exclude a deep understanding of certain essential facts in human society (their legacy to us in law and civics is evidence of that) which sufficed to construct a civilization now, after twenty centuries, still feeding the roots of our own. So far as the earlier civilization was built on a knowledge of the more complex facts of physics it was a knowledge not

used mainly for material ends at all. The real
importance of astronomy for long lay not in its
services to navigation or civil engineering, which
in its beginnings were perhaps small, but in its
effect on the moral conceptions, in its creation in
the minds of men of a sense of ordered law in the
world. Its real service was to enable them to
think clearly about the universe and men's relations to it and to one another. For Americans,
perhaps above all others, is it important to grasp
the real meaning of the facts hinted at here. For
it is perhaps roughly and broadly true to say that
while we have successfully established general
laws in the field of mechanics, which have given
us to a marvellous degree the material conquest
of nature, while the laws of the physical world
are being revealed to us in increasing measure,
there is no corresponding development of understanding in the field of human relationship, in our
conception of human right and obligation, the
laws of the social world, the nature of the social
organism, the mechanism of human society. In
all that we are hardly more advanced than the
Greeks or the Romans, or, for that matter, the
Egyptians and the Chaldeans. We have covered
the earth with a marvellous mechanism which will
carry our thought and understanding to the utmost
corners; with the invisible waves of wireless
telegraphy, with post-offices, railroads, *hôtels de
luxe*, and cinematograph shows, but we cannot
cover it with a system of law. We can analyse

all human food and we know most of the mysteries
of its growth and composition, but we cannot so
distribute it as to give every child a cup of milk.
We can blow a town to pieces with a handful of
dust, but we cannot destroy the monstrous pile
of misery which every great city connotes. Wherever, leaving material things, our management
touches human relations, the things of the mind,
it fails.

Our advance during the last century in the
material conquest of nature has been blinding in
its rapidity, but can any man say that in the
understanding of the laws of human relationship
we are much beyond the Romans from whom we
still take our jurisprudence, or the Greeks from
whom we still take our philosophy? In the
mechanical reproduction of the written word, for
instance, in the mechanism of our modern newspaper, we have material instruments that would
have seemed to Socrates and to Aristotle achievements of the gods themselves. But what of the
mind revealed in these documents, the mere
material substance of which implies such mechanical marvels; what of the ideas which find expression in them? It would be rather cruel to push
the comparison. But let the reader make for himself, with some detachment, the comparison of the
present-day newspaper discussions in Paris, Berlin,
London, or New York, with the general discussions
of the Greek capital two thousand years ago.
Would it be very unjust to say that the under-

standing of the essentials of human intercourse revealed by the men capable of these modern mechanical wonders (which would have seemed miraculous to the ancient world) is not very much better than that of the desert tribesmen who gave us our proverbs and our psalms, and whose mechanical conquest of nature was hardly more advanced than that of the men to whom the manufacture of a stone axe represented the highest achievement of human engineering?

Now, all our advance on the material side threatens to be of no avail in the really vital and fundamental things that touch mankind, because our understanding of the nature of human associations has not kept pace with our understanding of matter and its control. Of what avail is our immense increase in wealth production if we do not know how to distribute it in the order of our most vital needs—if the total net result of our discovery and achievements is to give still more to those who have already too much and to render the underworld still more dependent, their lives still more precarious? What should we say, asks Shaw, of the starving man who, on being given a dollar, forthwith spends it all on a bottle of scent for his handkerchief? Yet that is what the modern world does, and it is, we are told, incapable of doing anything else, so intellectually bankrupt are we to assume it. So immense is the failure on this side that responsible students of the comparative condition of men seriously question

whether the mass in our society are in essentials
either morally or materially better off than those
of the thirteenth century.

Evidence enough remains, as one good historian
points out, to show that there was in ancient Rome
as in London or New York today, a preponderat-
ing mass of those who loved their children and
their homes, who were good neighbours, and
faithful friends, who conscientiously discharged
their civil duties. Even the Eastern Roman
Empire, that not many years ago was usually
dismissed with sharp contempt, is now recovered
to history, and many centuries in its fluctuating
phases are shown to have been epochs of an established state, with well-devised laws well admin-
istered, with commerce prosperously managed, and
social order conveniently worked and maintained.

And one remembers, of course, the sad doubt of
Mill:

It is questionable if all the mechanical inventions
yet made have lightened the day's toil of any human
being. They have enabled a greater population to
live the same life of drudgery and imprisonment, and
an increased number to make fortunes. But they
have not yet begun to effect those great changes in
human destiny which it is in their nature and in their
futurity to accomplish.

So that unless we can make some equivalent
advance in the understanding of the laws and
principles of human association, in the manage-

ment of society, all our advance on the material side, the management of matter, may go for nothing, or conceivably even worse than nothing.

It is conceivable, for instance, as an ingenious novelist has suggested, that our researches in radio-activity might give us the secret of atomic disintegration so as to make a cent's worth of rock equivalent in value as a source of energy to a train load of coal—to multiply the wealth of the world a thousand times—and the result of it to be merely more poverty of the many, and luxury and dangerous power on the part of the few.

The great need, therefore, is an understanding of the nature and mechanism of human association, a realization of its more fundamental laws. It does not help us to take the position that the present defects of society are the result of a "plot" on the part of a powerful few and that if their rule be broken, a new earth would come into being next Tuesday morning. If we ask ourselves, "What would happen if the reins of government were seized by a group of very radical and advanced Socialists or Syndicalists, or other social reformers?" we are obliged to reply that nothing at all would happen; things would go on very much as usual. It has occurred more than once in Europe that wild revolutionaries have achieved power and they generally end by accomplishing less than their more conservative colleagues and becoming more reactionary.

They were obliged to realize that society,

because it is an organism, cannot stop breathing while experiments are made with its internal mechanism. The mere possession of power does not give control either over a complex machine or a complex organism. If the mechanism of your motor car works imperfectly, it serves no purpose that you have a crow-bar which will smash the whole thing in pieces. You must "know how" or you are helpless, since the power of destruction serves no purpose at all.

And the revolutionaries who have from time to time "arrived" have not "known how." For the social organism is even more complex than a motor car, and its general control is in the hands not of experts but of all of us.

Can we ever hope that "the general mind" will rise to effective knowledge fitting men for the control of their own social destiny? In these complex matters where the experts differ, is there any hope that the mass will ever achieve sufficient capacity to enable social progress to equal the advances made in those material sciences which are in the hands of experts?

Many would answer that question in the negative, although a negative answer involves a paralysing pessimism which one is glad to think is no part of the American genius.

But I do not think that a negative answer need be given. I will appeal to an analogy that I have used elsewhere.

In the sixteenth century Montaigne, who did

not believe in witchcraft and saw the evil that it
brought, wrote to this effect:

The day will never come when the common ruck
of men will cease to believe in witchcraft. If the
lawyers and judges of our modern sixteenth-century
France, men trained to sift evidence and learned in
science, can be so far deceived as to send thousands of
victims to their deaths for impossible crimes, how can
we ever hope that the common man will avoid these
errors?

Yet, ask a ten-year-old boy of our time whether
he thinks it likely that an old woman would or
could change herself into a cow or a goat, and he
will almost always promptly reply: "Certainly
not." (I have put this many times to the test of
experiment.) What enables the unlearned boy
to decide right where the learned judge decided
wrong? You say it is the "instinct" of the boy.
But the instinct of the seventeenth-century boy
(like the learning of the sixteenth, or seventeenth-
century judge) taught him the exact reverse.
Something has happened. What is it?

It is probably the unconscious application on
the part of the boy, of the inductive method of
reasoning (of which he has never heard, and could
not define), and the general attitude of mind
towards phenomena which comes of that habit.
Again, to quote myself: "He forms by reasoning
correctly (on the prompting of parents, nurses, and
teachers) about a few simple facts—which impress

him by their visibility and tangibility—a working hypothesis of how things happen in the world, which, while not infallibly applied—while, indeed, often landing the boy into mistakes—is far more trustworthy as a rule than that formed by the learned judge reasoning incorrectly from an immense number of facts."

Such is the simple basis of this very amazing miracle, the great fact which is at the bottom of the main difference between the modern and mediæval world, between the Western and Eastern civilizations.

It has two outstanding lessons for us: it shows the incalculable service that the correction of a fundamental misconception or wrong principle may achieve; and it shows that such correction of general principle may be the unintended but inevitable by-product of the correction of error in some special case.

For the revival of the inductive method and all that it has involved was in large part the unintended result of the religious reformation. And it has had these immense results because, like the views which the author of this book is urging, it was a readjustment of ideas concerning the place of force in certain activities of life.

A further and very profound readjustment of those same ideas followed upon the work of one man, Charles Darwin. But his work and message have, as he himself so pathetically declared, been misinterpreted and misunderstood even by his own "disciples." Darwinism has come to stand for a social doctrine which Darwin himself repudiated. And now, after fifty years, we may well take stock of the social conceptions (or misconceptions) which have grown up around "Darwinism" and see what aid biological laws, half a century after Darwin, give us in the framing of social principles. It was a work which direly needed doing; and all students of those subjects which really do represent the social foundations will be grateful to Dr. Nasmyth for having contributed to it.

NORMAN ANGELL.

ITHACA, NEW YORK,
    June 30, 1915.

PREFACE

THIS book is the outcome of a study, commenced several years before the outbreak of the war, with the object of making available for English readers some of the important results of recent researches on the applications of Darwin's theory to human society. This subject is of course much broader than the single question of war; in fact, as I have tried to show, especially in Chapter VIII., the philosophy of force has affected the entire structure of society. But it frequently happens that it is through the discussion of some special and critical problem that the human race establishes general principles which serve for the solution of a larger group of social problems, and this is the consideration which has led me to devote a large amount of attention to the special question of war, in this general study of the social applications of the Darwinian theory.

It is a significant commentary on the strength of the deeper social and democratic currents in modern Russia that the most important contributions in this field have all been made by Russian scientists. The rediscovery of Darwin's social message may be dated from a lecture before a congress of Russian naturalists in January, 1880, by the eminent Russian zoölogist, Professor Kessler, formerly dean of the University of St. Petersburg. Like so many valuable contributions to science published only in the Russian language, however, it remained almost entirely unknown to the outside world, and it was not until the next decade that one of his disciples, Prince Kropotkin, developed his ideas and made them available for English readers in a series of remarkable articles in the *Nineteenth Century*, afterwards reprinted in book form as *Mutual Aid a Factor of Evolution*. Later, the subject was still further developed by another Russian thinker and worker of genius, Novikov (French: Novicow), formerly vice-president of the International Institute of Sociology, whose score of volumes on social theory mark the beginning of a new epoch in the social sciences. Unfortunately, Novikov, unlike his predecessors Kessler and Kropotkin, did not realize that he had the authority of Darwin upon his side, and includes him in the crushing criticism which he directs against the distorted "social Darwinism" that has come to represent the social applications of the theory of evolution so largely in modern thought.

The misunderstanding of Darwin's social theory is so widespread, and his writings on the subject are so little known, that I have thought it desirable to state his theory of social progress as far as possible in his own words, and to include in the present volume a large number of representative

Preface

quotations from *The Descent of Man.* I have also
drawn largely upon Novikov's works, especially
La Critique du Darwinisme social and *La Justice
et l'expansion de la vie.* If this introduction should
lead to an increased interest in Novikov's writings,
to a wider study of his epoch-making contributions to a more scientific social theory, and to a
renewed discussion of the whole question of the
application of Darwin's theory to human society,
my chief purpose in publishing this book will
have been realized.

GEORGE NASMYTH.

CAMBRIDGE, MASS.,
January, 1916.

PART I

THE PHILOSOPHY OF FORCE

CHAPTER I

THE PHILOSOPHY OF FORCE

WHAT object does human society set before itself? What is the purpose for which the State—our State—exists?

No problem of sociology can be discussed effectively without raising this fundamental question. Sociological discussion usually comes to it at the last; obviously it should raise it at the beginning.

In the first place, it is of course impossible to test the value of any instrument or method as a means to an end unless we realize clearly what that end is. Otherwise, when we do come to grapple with the question of "what it is all for," we shall find ourselves trying to make the end fit the means, the task fit the tool, and not choose our tool to fit our task.

We could find no better illustration of what I mean by this than the social and moral story of Prussia—indeed, of Europe—and the meaning of the war which began in August, 1914.

Until a generation or so ago German thought and moral influence were undoubtedly working towards ends which Christendom as a whole pronounced "good": Kant and Fichte, Goethe and Schiller stood for moral values upon which Christendom as a whole was agreed.

But as an incident of the protection of German society from outside aggression—as a mere detail of military protective measures—certain political and military devices were introduced into the German State; a certain tool was adopted. At the time of their introduction these changes were not expected to alter the "ends" for which Germans lived their lives; nor was it anticipated that they would lead to any reconsideration of moral values.

But the introduction of those changes—that tool—has recast the moral values of German society from top to bottom and seems in a fair way to recast the moral values of European society as a whole—including our own. In other words, the danger which Mommsen foresaw for Prussia is a danger which now menaces all Western civilization. A generation ago Mommsen said:

Have a care lest in this country, which has been at once a power in arms and a power in intelligence, the intelligence should vanish and nothing but the pure military State should remain.[1]

Those things for which Kant and Fichte, Goethe and Schiller stood have been rejected or profoundly revised by this kind of process:

[1] Quoted by Professor Hicks in the *Hibbert Journal*, October, 1914. *Cf.* also W. H. Dawson, *Modern Germany*, p. 3.

At a given stage of political development in Germany, German rulers urged that in order to protect the moral and intellectual heritage of Germany, such and such measures had to be taken. They were taken and then developed. It was then seen that their use and development made it necessary to discard or sacrifice the moral and intellectual possessions which it had been the original object of the measures to protect.

I am not discussing for the moment whether the tool used was good or bad; I am only pointing out that its use—whether for good or ill—transforms all social and moral values, even the most fundamental. I want to make clear that force is not merely a tool—that it is a root of moral ideas, that its use colours all human values and determines the nature of society.

The importance therefore which any social instrument may assume makes it necessary to submit it to close scrutiny. What follows is an attempt to submit one such instrument—force—which mankind has used in the process of evolution, to critical examination; to probe scientifically the philosophy upon which the use of this tool is based.

The philosophy of force is the theory of society which is based on the belief in the effectiveness and inevitability of the use of force in human relationships to advance those ends, economic, social, and moral, for which men live and strive. In international relations its modern name is militarism.

The Philosophy of Force

The philosophy of force claims to find its scientific foundation in the application of Darwin's theory of natural selection and the struggle for existence to human society.

If, then, we are to understand this instrument, we must begin our study with the foundations of its philosophy in the Darwinian theory.

The current view of the Darwinian theory in its relation to human association is summarized by one of the foremost exponents of the theory of evolution as follows:

The theory of selection teaches that in human life, as in animal and plant life, everywhere and at all times, only a small and chosen minority can exist and flourish, while the enormous majority starve, and perish miserably and more or less prematurely. . . . The cruel and merciless struggle for existence which rages throughout living nature, and in the course of nature *must* rage, this unceasing and inexorable competition of all living creatures is an incontestable fact; only the picked minority of the qualified fittest is in a position to resist it successfully, while the great majority of the competitors must necessarily perish miserably. We may profoundly lament this tragical state of things, but we can neither controvert nor alter it. "Many are called, but few are chosen." This principle of selection is as far as possible from democratic; on the contrary it is aristocratic in the strictest sense of the word.[1]

[1] Ernst Haeckel, *Freedom in Science and Teaching*, p. 93.

This view of the theory of selection is not an isolated interpretation; on the contrary it is the view held by the great majority of the authorities on the Darwinian theory, with a few exceptions, as well as by the immense body of popular opinion which follows the view of these authorities. We live in a world of struggle, and man is a fighting animal, say the adherents of this view.

We must therefore resign ourselves to the fact of struggle as one of the laws of life, as one of the hard facts of existence in a world governed by the law of the survival of the fittest, where the weakest goes to the wall and all life is but a life of battle. War is held to be a part of this great law of evolution, which runs throughout the universe, and however much we may regret the horrors and the suffering which it brings in its train, we must recognize that war is the cause of social progress.

The eminent Russian sociologist, Novikov, has defined "social Darwinism" as "the doctrine that collective homicide is the cause of the progress of the human race." The name, as we shall see later, is unjust to Darwin. A more accurate description of this doctrine would be "distorted social Darwinism." But the doctrine itself, which Novikov defines in such paradoxical terms, is a basic part of the teaching associated with the names of some of the most eminent sociologists.

Before beginning the critical study of the doctrine, it may be well to show by quotations from the writings of scientific men, sociologists, and

philosophers of all countries how universal is the
belief that war is the cause of social progress.
Thus Herbert Spencer,[1] writing in 1876, has
developed his sociology on the basis of the struggle
for existence:

As carried on throughout the animate world at
large, the struggle for existence has been an indispensable means to evolution. Not simply do we see
that, in the competition among individuals of the
same kind, survival of the fittest has from the beginning furthered the production of a higher type; but we
see that to the unceasing warfare between species is
mainly due both growth and organization. Without
universal conflict there would have been no development of the active powers. . . .

Similarly with social organisms. We must recognize the truth that the struggles for existence between
societies has been instrumental to their evolution.
Neither the consolidation and re-consolidation of
small groups into large ones; nor the organization of
such compound and doubly compound groups; nor the
concomitant developments of those aids to a higher life
which civilization has brought; would have been possible without inter-tribal and inter-national conflicts.
Social co-operation is initiated by joint defence and
offence; and from the co-operation thus initiated all
kinds of co-operations have arisen. Inconceivable as
have been the horrors caused by the universal antagonism which, beginning with the chronic hostilities
of small hordes tens of thousands of years ago, has

[1] *Principles of Sociology*, vol. ii., part 5, "Political Institutions,"
p. 241.

ended in the occasional vast battles of immense nations, we must nevertheless admit that without it the world would still have been inhabited only by men of feeble types sheltering in caves and living on wild food.

If the world were still inhabited by men seeking a shelter in caves, and if the great societies of nations had never been formed, the progress of the human race would not have taken place. Progress, therefore, according to Herbert Spencer, is due to war,—that is to say, to collective homicide.

A possible objection that war and collective homicide are not synonymous is met by Novikov by an appeal to the actual facts:

What takes place in war? The combatants of the two armies come together. They commence to kill each other with swords, rifles, and cannons. A battle is a series of homicides, accomplished in the same way and at the same time; therefore a collective assassination. The fact that the two adversaries may have equal chances and attack each other openly does not make any change in the essential nature of the action. In an individual duel the struggle may be accomplished also, not only with complete fairness, but even with a great display of courtesy. This does not change the fact that when one adversary or both of them lose their lives the duel is only, in fact, a homicide. In war incidentally, it is not at all believed that one is obliged to fight fairly. Surprises and ruses are practised continually.[1]

[1] *La Critique du Darwinisme Social*, p. 4.

The philosophy of force has been thoroughly developed by a German sociologist, G. Ratzenhofer,[1] who maintains that the formation of the States can be brought about only by violence.

The formation of the States did not result from the play of free interests as did the formation of the horde, of tribes, of parties, and of associations in general; no, it arose from antagonistic interests and as a consequence it is a coercive organization. . . . All evolution is the result of competition, but in the case of the State, violence itself is the agent which has created it. Since this violence follows the path of social necessity, since it acts in the direction of true natural interests, this is the criterion by which we can judge that the State realizes its mission in the social life. Every time we disregard this fundamental conception of the State, every time we admit the opinion that the State could proceed as a simple effect of civilization, of a pacific union, or of any other combinations of this nature, we enter into contradiction with the teaching of sociology and we prepare the way for political experiences which terminate in a most lamentable fashion.

The eminent American sociologist, Professor Lester F. Ward, who has been largely influenced by the work of Ratzenhofer, and of the Polish sociologist, Ludwig Gumplowicz,[2] traces the origin of the entire system of industrial production to

[1] *Die Sociologische Erkentniss*, Leipzig, Brockhaus, 1898, pp. 233-34.
[2] *Der Rassenkampf.*

conquest and war. He traces the analogy between biological and industrial evolution thus:

Just as organic evolution began with the metazoic stage, so social evolution began with the metasocial stage. So, too, as the metazoic stage was brought about through the union of several or many unicellular organisms in a multicellular organism, so the metasocial stage was brought about by the union of two or more simple hordes or clans into a compound group of amalgamated hordes or clans. . . . Two groups thus brought into proximity may be, and usually are, utterly unknown to each other. The mutual encroachment is certain to produce hostilities. War is the result, and one of the two groups is almost certain to prove the superior warrior and to conquer the other. The first step in the whole process is the conquest of one race by another. . . . The greater part of the conquered race is enslaved and the institution of slavery begins here. The slaves are compelled to work, and labour in the economic sense begins here. The enslavement of the producers and the compelling them to work was the only way in which mankind could have been taught to labour, and therefore the whole industrial system of society begins here.[1]

In his treatise on *Pure Sociology*, Professor Ward has generalized the influence of war as follows:

It is impossible in dealing with this subject to avoid the bearing of war and peace on human progress. All civilized men realize the horrors of war, and if

[1] *American Journal of Sociology*, March, 1905, p. 594.

sociology has any utilitarian purposes one of these certainly is to diminish or mitigate these horrors. But pure sociology is simply an inquiry into the social facts and conditions and has nothing to do with utilitarian purposes. In making this objective inquiry, it finds that, as a matter of fact, war has been the chief and leading condition of human progress.

This is perfectly obvious to any one who understands the meaning of the struggle of races. When races stop struggling, progress ceases. They want no progress and they have none. For all primitive and early, undeveloped races, certainly, the condition of peace is a condition of social stagnation. We may enlarge to our soul's content on the blessings of peace, but the facts remain as stated, and cannot be successfully disproved.[1]

The philosophy of force is found not only among the men of science but is widely held by the philosophers in all nations. Thus, in France, Ernest Renan[2] has given the doctrine wide currency:

If the stupidity, the negligence, the laziness, the improvidence of states did not have as a consequence to make them fight, it is difficult to say to what degree of abasement the human species might descend. War is in a way one of the conditions of progress, the cut of the whip which prevents a country from going to sleep, forcing satisfied mediocrity itself to leave its apathy. Man is only sustained by effort and struggle. . . . The day on which humanity becomes a great

[1] P. 238.
[2] *La Réforme Intellectuelle et Morale*, Paris, 1871, p 111.

Roman Empire, pacified and not having any more external enemies, will be the day on which morality and intelligence will run the greatest dangers.

In England, Ruskin has held war to be the source of all the arts. In an address on war delivered at Woolwich Arsenal, he said[1]:

> . . . War is the foundation of all the arts . . . of all the high virtues and faculties of men. . . . There is no great art possible to a nation but that which is based on battle. . . . All great nations learned their truth of word, and strength of thought, in war; they were nourished in war and wasted by peace; taught by war and deceived by peace; trained by war and betrayed by peace.

In Germany Nietzsche has given the philosophy of force almost classic expression. In Nietzsche we find the same idea as in Renan; that peace leads to stagnation, war to progress:

> Ye shall love peace as a means to new wars, and the short peace better than the long.
> I do not advise you to work, but to fight. I do not advise you to conclude peace, but to conquer. Let your work be a fight, your peace a victory!
> One cannot be silent and sit still unless one hath bow and arrow. Otherwise one talketh and quarreleth. Let your peace be a victory!
> Ye say, a good cause will hallow even war? I say unto you: a good war halloweth every cause.[2]

[1] *The Crown of Wild Olive.*
[2] *Thus Spake Zarathustra:* I. "Of War and Warriors."

The intellectual and moral glorification of war which characterizes the militaristic school of all nations is derived from the sociologists and philosophers who have distorted the social teachings of Darwin. But in applying the philosophy of force to practical life the men of action have discarded all the qualifications with which the scientific men have surrounded their statements. Thus, although Herbert Spencer bases his entire theory of social evolution on struggle, he hastens to qualify his theory by the statement that this does not apply to the future[1]:

Mark now, however, that while this merciless discipline of Nature "red in tooth and claw," has been essential to the progress of sentient life, its persistence through all time with all creatures must not be inferred. The high organization, evolved by and for this universal conflict, is not necessarily forever employed to like ends. The resulting power and intelligence admit of being far otherwise employed. . . .

But now observe that the inter-social struggle for existence which has been indispensable in evolving societies will not necessarily play in the future a part like that which it has played in the past. Recognizing our indebtedness to war for forming great communities and developing their structures, we may yet infer that the acquired powers, available for other activities, will lose their original activities. While conceding that without these perpetual bloody strifes, civilized societies could not have arisen, and that an adapted form of human nature, fierce as well as intelligent, was

[1] *Principles of Sociology*, vol. ii., p. 242.

a needful concomitant, we may at the same time hold that such societies having been produced, the brutality of nature in their units which was necessitated by the process, ceasing to be necessary with the cessation of the process, will disappear.

Thus his final judgment is clearly rendered:

From war has been gained all that it had to give. . . . Only further evils are to be looked for from the continuance of militancy in civilized nations.[1]

No such qualifications disturb the conclusions of the militarists.   Shortly after Ernest Renan wrote the passage cited above, Marshal von Moltke wrote, in a letter to Bluntschli which has become famous:

Perpetual peace is a dream, and not even a beautiful dream.   War is an element of the order of the world established by God.   The most noble virtues of men are developed in it. . . .   Without war the world would stagnate and lose itself in materialism.

The philosophy is held by statesmen as well as militarists.   In his book on *Weltstadt und Friedensproblem*, Prof. Baron Karl von Stengel, a jurist who was one of Germany's delegates at the first Hague Peace Conference, has a chapter entitled, "The Significance of War for the Development of Humanity," in which he says:

War has more often facilitated than hindered progress.   Athens and Rome, not only in spite of, but

[1] P. 664.

just because of their many wars, rose to the zenith of civilization. Great states like Germany and Italy are welded into nationalities only through blood and iron.

Storm purifies the air and destroys the frail trees, leaving the sturdy oak standing. War is a test of a nation's political, physical, and intellectual worth. The State in which there is much that is rotten may vegetate for a while in peace, but in war its weaknesses are revealed.

Germany's preparations for war have not resulted in economic disaster, but in unexampled economic expansion, unquestionably because of our demonstrated superiority over France. It is better to spend money on armaments and battleships than luxury, motor mania, and other sensual living.

In America ex-President Roosevelt is the most distinguished exponent of this philosophy of force. In *The Strenuous Life*, written after his military experiences in the Spanish-American War had greatly modified his social theories, we find many echoes of this philosophy, of which the following will serve as an illustration:

In this world the nation that has trained itself to a career of unwarlike and isolated ease is bound, in the end, to go down before other nations which have not lost the manly and adventurous qualities.[1]

These quotations could be multiplied by hundreds from the literature of all nations, but all of

[1] P. 6.

them repeat the same idea in different forms, and enough have been given to show the justification for Novikov's definition of the distorted "social Darwinism" as "the doctrine that collective homicide is the cause of human progress." Without war the world would still be inhabited by men seeking a shelter in caves, and the great societies of nations would never have been formed, according to Herbert Spencer. The formation of a State is impossible without violence, that is to say without war, according to Mr. Ratzenhofer. Without war humanity would never have learned to work, according to Professor Ward, and the system of industrial production would have been impossible. Without war no great art would have been possible according to Ruskin. Without war the virile qualities would decay; the moral fibre of the nations would rot; the world would stagnate and lose itself in materialism, according to Renan, von Moltke, and Roosevelt. Novikov sums up the evidence thus:

The idea that war has been the cause of the progress of our species is almost universal in the minds of the great public. The number of persons who do not share this belief is very limited and the persons who are imbued with it are to be found in the first ranks of the social hierarchy and among those who have the greatest political influence. All those persons who pretend to be *practical* and *realistic*, who do not wish to be ridiculed or to be accused of being idealists, affirm categorically that homicide serves progress.

The philosophy of force[1] has been admirably interpreted by Professor William James[2] in the following passage:

The war party is assuredly right in affirming and re-affirming that the martial virtues, although originally gained by the race through war, are absolute and permanent human goods. Patriotic pride and ambition in their military form are, after all, only specifications of a more general competitive passion. . . . Pacificism makes no converts from the military party. The military party denies neither the bestiality, nor the horror, nor the expense; it only says that these things tell but half the story. It only says that war is *worth* them; that, taking human nature as a whole, its wars are its best protection against its weaker and more cowardly self, and that mankind cannot *afford* to adopt a peace economy. . . . Militarism is the great preserver of our ideals of hardihood, and human life with no use for hardihood would be contemptible. . . . This natural sort of feeling forms, I think, the innermost soul of army-writings. Without any excep-

[1] For other militaristic expressions of the philosophy of force see Admiral Mahan, *The Place of Power in International Relations*, in the *North American Review* for January, 1912, and such books as Professor Spenser Wilkinson's *The Great Alternative, Britain at Bay, War and Policy;* see also the recent work of an American, General Homer Lea, *The Valor of Ignorance*, with its introduction by another American soldier, General John J. P. Storey. In German see S. R. Steinmetz, *Philosophie des Krieges;* Clauss Wagner, *Der Krieg als Schaffendes Weltprinzip;* and in French, Colonel Arthur Boucher, *La France Victorieuse dans la Guerre de Demain*, and M. Keller, *La Guerre de Demain*.

[2] *The Moral Equivalent of War* (Am. Assn. for International Conciliation, February, 1910).

tion known to me, militarist authors take a highly
mystical view of their subject, and regard war as a
biological or sociological necessity. . . . Our ancestors have bred pugnacity into our bone and marrow
and thousands of years of peace won't breed it out of
us.

Despite the apparent plausibility of the philosophy of force, it is founded, as we shall see later,
upon a profound misreading of the biological
analogy, upon a deep-seated misunderstanding of
the facts of human relationships, and upon a gross
distortion of Darwin's own theory of social progress. In spite of its immense success, as we shall
see in the succeeding chapters, this distorted
"social Darwinism" is nevertheless completely
false in theory. It contains errors so numerous
that it is impossible to treat them all. It is
necessary to make a selection and to speak solely
of the most important.

When we discover how gross are the errors of
this distorted "social Darwinism" we are compelled
to ask with astonishment how they could last so
long, not only in popular belief, but even among
the men of enlightenment. The only reply is that
the favour which the mystical belief which is called
"social Darwinism" has enjoyed, shows in a striking
fashion how undeveloped is the science of sociology
and how formidable is the power of ancient routine
nourished by a traditionalist spirit.

CHAPTER II

CAUSES OF THE SUCCESS OF THE PHILOSOPHY OF FORCE

WHAT are the causes of the success of the philosophy of force, and how did the distorted form of "social Darwinism,"which it claims for its scientific foundation, gain its almost universal acceptance?

In seeking the answer to this question we shall come upon a surprising series of facts.

We shall discover that the doctrine known as "social Darwinism," which finds the cause of social progress in war, universal competition, and the rôle of struggle and force in human relations, was not created by Darwin; but that he based his whole theory of social progress on the moral law and the social instincts.

We shall find that this doctrine was repudiated in its application as a law of human society by the co-discoverer of the theory of evolution, Wallace; and by Darwin's intimate friend and chief disciple, Huxley.

We shall find that the misapplication of Darwin's biological theory to human society, which is current in the modern world, did not emerge as the result of the thorough discussion of a subject which recent events have shown to be one of the most important questions in applied social science —that is, the place of struggle and force as a factor in human associations. On the contrary, it grew up almost unnoticed, and as an unconscious by-product of a debate between some of the greatest minds of the age, over an entirely irrelevant, and, as the modern world has largely come to regard it, a socially unimportant subject—the theological implications of the Darwinian theory as they shaped themselves in the warfare between science and traditional theology around the issue of evolution *vs.* special creation.   Instead of subjecting it to the searching analysis demanded by its practical social importance, the intellectual world and public opinion has accepted "social Darwinism" uncritically and by almost unanimous consent as an integral part of the theory of evolution.

The causes of this almost miraculous success are to be found largely in three factors: (1) the universality of the appeal which "social Dar-winism" makes to the human spirit, enlisting both the highest aspirations toward perfection and justice and the lowest instinct of selfish greed and brute force; (2) the intellectual environment in which the social applications of the theory of evolution were developed, and (3) the influence of historical events, especially the Franco-Prussian war, and the rapid growth of Imperialism

among all the Western civilized Powers since
1870.

The universality of the appeal made by the
evolutionary ethics of the philosophy of force, has
been pointed out by an historian of modern
political thought, as follows:

Darwinism has been pressed into political service by
very different parties. Militarists have appealed to
the ideas of struggle for existence and selection of the
fittest, in order to justify the selective agency of war.
Individualists have appealed to the same ideas in
order to find justification for an internal policy of
laissez-faire, which shall not interfere with the selective activity of the "beneficent struggle." It is in
truth an easy procedure to steal Darwin's theory of
the natural world, and to apply it, without remember-
ing *mutare mutanda*, to the spiritual world of human
relations. It is easy to argue "Nature sets her children
to compete; let the State set its citizens to do the
like: Nature recognizes the strongest species as
the right species; let the human world recognize the
strongest nation as the right nation."[1]

But the breadth of its appeal is not limited to the
militarist and the individualist, widely as these are
separated. Its appeal is to the free-thinker, the
positivist, and the monist on the one hand, and to
the mystic, the idealist, and the dualist on the
other. It satisfies not only the conservatives, who
rely wholly on brute force, but also the liberals,

[1] Ernest Barker, *Political Thought in England from Herbert
Spencer to the Present Day*, 1915; p. 146.

who are devoted to the idea of justice. Since its doctrines were acceptable to natures having the most diametrically opposite aspirations, we can understand one of the reasons, at least, why the distorted "social Darwinism" had such an enormous and rapid success. It is interesting to trace the influence of these two groups upon the success of the philosophy of force, and to try and understand the peculiar appeal which it made to each.

The favour of the most enlightened and most liberal spirits of the time was assured to the philosophy of force, partly because of its association with the triumph of true Darwinism.

The first day of July, 1858, marks the division between two epochs of human thought; for on this day two papers, one presented by Charles Darwin, and the other by Alfred Russel Wallace, were read before the Linnæan Society at London, and with the reading of these papers, the doctrine of evolution by natural selection was born. On November twenty-fourth of the following year, Darwin published the first instalment of his thought in its fuller development,—his book on *The Origin of Species by Means of Natural Selection*. This was the fruit of thirty years of work and thought by a worker and thinker of genius, and it at once commanded the world's attention by the transparent honesty and judicial fairness with which it presented its wealth of facts, gathered from a world-wide observation; compared with almost infinite patience; and woven into a theory which revealed one of the great unifying principles of the cosmic order.

Darwin had found one of the great secrets at the heart of the evolutionary process for which a long line of investigators from the days of Aristotle had sought in vain,—the thin red line which was to guide him, and after him all workers in the natural sciences, through the labyrinth of the infinite variety of the facts of Nature. The work undoubtedly marks one of the most important events in the history of the human race. Not only was it epoch-making because with its publication Nature re-entered upon a grand and magnificent unity. It was important, too, because it marked the enfranchisement of the human spirit from a mediæval theology, from outworn traditions, from ancient routines, and the ignorance and superstitions of a barbarous past. Man raised his head; he felt himself master of the world; he saw infinite horizons opening before his eyes, with no authority which henceforth could arrest him in his conquest. We can understand with what enthusiasm this definite liberation of the human mind would be received by the thinkers of a purely scientific spirit.

It would be difficult to exaggerate the changes which have come about in all departments of human thought, as the result of the theory of natural selection. During the past half century, all the sciences, from astronomy to sociology, have been profoundly influenced by Darwin's discovery

of evolution. In historical and in political thinking especially, the philosophy of force was greatly
strengthened by the discovery of such apparently
scientific foundations.

In *The Origin of Species*, Darwin did not apply
his theory to human relationships, but confined
himself to the field of biology. The only reference
which he makes to man is at the end of the book,
where he says that in the future "much light will
be thrown on the origin of man and his history."
Darwin's theory of social progress is contained in
The Descent of Man, which was not published until
twelve years later. During these twelve years
Darwin was patiently at work on the application
of his theory to human society, and as early as
1864 he wrote to A. R. Wallace:

> The great leading idea is quite new to me viz., that
> during late ages, the mind will have been modified
> more than the body; yet I had got as far as to see with
> you that the struggle between the races of man de-
> pended entirely upon intellectual and moral qualities.[1]

But the followers, and especially the popularizers of Darwin's theory could not wait for his
own application of the theory of natural selection
to social progress. The publication of *The Origin
of Species* had acted as a great liberalizing influence upon the minds of men, and the flood of
new thought pouring over the world stimulated
and nourished research and reasoning in every

[1] *Life and Letters of Charles Darwin*, vol. iii., p. 89.

land.　Edition after edition of the book was called for and it was translated even into Japanese and Hindustani.　A vast army of young men took up every line of investigation, and epoch-making books appeared in all the great nations.　Spencer, Wallace, Huxley, Galton, Tyndall, Tylor, Lubbock, Bagehot, Lewes, in England, and groups of strong men in Germany, Italy, France, and America, published important works in every department of biology.　Under these conditions it was inevitable that Darwin's theory should be applied to man.

In order to trace the distortion which Darwin's theories suffered in this application to human society, it is necessary to understand the intellectual world into which they were born, and the philosophical doctrines current in the aristocratic intellectual circles in which they were discussed and developed.

On the one hand can be traced the influence of teachers like Carlyle, Kingsley, and Ruskin, who have done so much to foster the belief in a "divine right" of force.　Ruskin's view of the value of war for civilization and art we have already noticed. Charles Kingsley had defended the Crimean War as "a just war against tyrants and oppressors," and had eloquently advocated such a war as in accord with the highest teachings of Christianity and the Bible.　The direction of Carlyle's political teachings, which were in accord with his hero worship and "will to power" philosophy, may be judged from the following summary:

Carlyle condemned democracy, which he identified with laissez-faire, as "a self-cancelling business," a government which only achieved the negation of any government. Representative institutions, a free and broad electorate, in a word all the paraphernalia of democracy, were in his eyes a matter of mere palaver and ballot boxes—"nothing except emptiness" and zero. To get governance, men must turn to those who are able to govern, the silent few, standing aloof and alone in their wisdom, who are nature's appointed Hero-Kings. . . . Wise, and in their wisdom also virtuous, they must guide and even drill their lesser fellows, who shall find in obedience their chief end and highest pleasure.

. . . Guidance, regulation, drill became his ideals: military metaphors recur in his writings. He even advanced to the military doctrine that might is the measure of right. If a man be able, wise of heart, strong of will, firm in his resolution to do his duty among his fellows, he must govern according to the measure of his strength, and his right over his fellows is according to his might. "The strong thing is the just thing": rights are "correctly articulated mights."[1]

To men holding this philosophy, "social Darwinism" made an especially strong appeal; it proclaimed the idea of the survival of the fittest; it strengthened their faith in the triumph of the best; it affirmed that Nature practices an incorruptible justice,—that the idea of justice is found even in the biological realm. Thus the philosophy

[1] Ernest Barker, *Political Thought in England from Herbert Spencer to the Present Day*, p. 184.

of force enlisted in its service the highest aspirations of the human soul, man's passionate desire for justice and perfection. "Man has an inextinguishable thirst for justice," says Novikov; "it could not be otherwise, because justice is life; injustice death."

On the other hand, Darwin's biological theories were applied to human society in an intellectual world dominated by individualistic scientists like Spencer and by conservative lawyers like Sir Henry Maine.

One of the chief influences in the rise of the philosophy of force was the contribution of Spencer's social philosophy. As early as 1851 we find him recognizing, in *Social Statics*, the

stern discipline of nature which eliminates the unfit and results in the maintenance of a constitution completely adapted to the surrounding conditions.

And we find a prophecy of the modern "social Darwinism" in the fact that Spencer attacked the system of poor relief in the name of this discipline.

Spencer never became a Darwinian. The first draft of his *Synthetic Philosophy* was made in the beginning of 1858, a few months before Darwin published his first paper, and no essential change was made on account of the publication of the Darwinian theory. Whenever biological principles were needed for his sociology, Spencer adapted to his system the principles which had been suggested by Lamarck as early as 1800. Lamarck had held,

(1) that external environment acts on living beings (in adapting this principle, Spencer was undoubtedly much fortified by Buckle's *History of Civilization*, which was published in 1856); (2) that living beings adapt their structures and functions to the external environment, and (3) that such acquired characteristics are inherited (a belief on the basis of which Maine and others defended the hereditary principle of the House of Lords). Darwin, on the other hand, did not believe in the doctrine of purposive adaptation to environment, but he did believe in accidental variations, and that those accidental variations which suited the environment were perpetuated by inheritance. Nevertheless, Spencer's sociological theory, based on struggle, became incorporated as an integral part of the popular understanding of the theory of evolution. There is even some justification for the view that Spencer was more responsible than Darwin himself for the "social Darwinism" which has come to represent the Darwinian theory in public opinion ever since. It is largely through Spencer's contributions that the extreme individualism of an age chiefly under the influence of Adam Smith and Bentham, and in revolt against governmental interference in economic affairs, fell into "social Darwinism." This strong tendency toward the laissez-faire doctrine which was dominant in the aristocratic intellectual atmosphere in which Spencer wrote, was reinforced by Spencer's strong abhorrence to actual government

and its ways, a feeling which Spencer says he brought from his "dissenting family, antagonistic to arbitrary control." Thus Spencer's philosophy (and with it the philosophy of force), instead of being established on a scientific basis, had a strong bias of *a priori* conceptions of individual rights and laissez-faire doctrines from the beginning. As Barker says:

He did not really approach politics through science, without preconceptions drawn from other sources, and with the sole idea of eliciting the political lessons which science might teach; on the contrary, he was already charged with political preconceptions when he approached science, and he sought to find in science examples or analogies to point a moral already drawn and adorn a tale whose plot was already sketched.[1]

As Spencer and the sociologists brought to the philosophy of force at the same time a distortion and a reinforcement through their interpretation in social and biological terms of the spirit of the age, so Sir Henry Maine and the lawyers brought to the philosophy of force distortion and reinforcement from the side of political theory.

Maine's *Ancient Law* was published in 1861, two years after Darwin's *Origin of Species*. In this work Maine popularized Savigny's conception of law as a continuous historical development, and the connection between this theory and the doctrine

[1] *Political Thought in England from Herbert Spencer to the Present Day*, p. 85.

of evolution is clear. Sir Frederick Pollock has expressed the connection thus: " If the doctrine of evolution is nothing else than the historical method applied to the facts of nature, the historical method is nothing else than the doctrine of evolution applied to human institutions."

The final outcome of this historical method as embodied in Maine's *Popular Government*, published in 1884, in which he aims a blow at the foundations of the Benthamite faith in democracy, is a somewhat melancholy conservatism. We find a significant foreshadowing of the Nietzschean and other "will to power" philosophies in this book, in which Maine defends aristocracy and the English House of Lords, and makes it a part of his indictment of democracy that the multitude evidently dislikes the doctrine of the struggle for existence, to which he refers as

that beneficent private war which makes one man strive to climb on the shoulders of another and remain there through the law of the survival of the fittest.

Such was the intellectual atmosphere in which Darwin's biological theory was applied to human society. The process of distortion which occurred in this application has been traced by Kropotkin (who has been called the only true Darwinian in England), as follows:

It happened with Darwin's theory as it always happens with theories having any bearing upon

human relations.   Instead of widening it according to
his own hints, his followers narrowed it still more.
And while Herbert Spencer, starting on independent
but closely allied lines, attempted to widen the inquiry
into that great question, "Who are the fittest?"
especially in the appendix to the third edition of the
Data of Ethics, the numberless followers of Darwin
reduced the notion of struggle for existence to its
narrowest limits.   They came to conceive the animal
world as a world of perpetual struggle among half-
starved individuals, thirsting for one another's blood.
They made modern literature resound with the war-
cry of "*Woe to the vanquished*" as if it were the last
word of modern biology.   They raised the "pitiless"
struggle for personal advantages to the height of a
biological principle which man must submit to as well,
under the menace of otherwise succumbing in a world
based upon mutual extermination.   Leaving aside the
economists who know of natural science but a few
words borrowed from second-hand vulgarizers, we
must recognize that even the most authorized exponents of Darwin's views did their best to maintain
those false ideas.[1]

Even Huxley, who was one of the most powerful
protagonists of Darwin in the battle which raged
between science and traditional theology, and who
is considered to be one of the ablest exponents of
the theory of evolution, has been quoted in support
of the philosophy of force, by those who assume
that definite biological analogies can be applied
to human society.   Thus in his essay on *The*

[1] Kropotkin, *Mutual Aid a Factor of Evolution*, p. 3.

Struggle for Existence in Human Society he wrote:

From the point of view of the moralist the animal world is on about the same level as a gladiator's show. The creatures are fairly well treated, and set to fight— whereby the strongest, the swiftest, and the cunningest live to fight another day. The spectator has no need to turn his thumb down, as no quarter is given.

And as among animals so among primitive men:

. . . the weakest and stupidest went to the wall, while the toughest and shrewdest, those who were best fitted to cope with their circumstances, but not the best in another sense, survived. Life was a continual free fight, and beyond the limited and temporary relations of the family, the Hobbesian war of each against all was the normal state of existence.[1]

But when he begins to apply the theory of evolution to human relations, Huxley turns away from the idea of mutual struggle and shows that a new set of factors enter into play. Thus in the same essay he says:

. . . society differs from nature in having a definite moral object; whence it comes about that the course shaped by the ethical man—the member of society or citizen—necessarily runs counter to that which the non-ethical man—the primitive savage, or man as a mere member of the animal kingdom—tends to

[1] Huxley, *Evolution and Ethics*, pp. 199, 204.

adopt.   The latter fights out the struggle for existence
to the bitter end, like any other animal; the former
devotes his best energies to the object of setting
limits to the struggle.[1]

But Huxley's emphasis upon the ethical factors
in human society, like Darwin's own theory of
social progress, was entirely neglected by those
who found in natural selection the justification for
the philosophy of force.   The tide of opinion in
favour of the distorted "social Darwinism" had
set in so strongly that attention was paid only to
those parts which were favourable to this doctrine
—parts which rest upon errors due, as Kropotkin
and Novikov have since shown, to a one-sided
misreading of the biological struggle and a misconception of the primitive life of man.

On the one hand, then, we have as one of the
causes of its success, the appeal which the new
doctrine made to some of the most enlightened
spirits of the age.   On the other hand, there came
to it the support of an entirely different group of
men, because the philosophy of force responded to
the archaic instincts of brutality so deeply em-
bedded in the nature of the traditionalist, the
routinist, and the ignorant, who still form, unfortunately so large a proportion of the human
race.   After the Darwinian theory had been
announced, Marshal von Moltke could write with
a semblance of scientific authority that war

[1] Huxley, *Evolution and Ethics*, p. 203.

"conforms to the order of things established by God," because the "order established by God" corresponds perfectly to the "law of nature" of which the sociologists and the "social Darwinians" made use.

Although it has received renewed popularity from the immense success of Darwin's work, this brutal aspect of the philosophy of force is of course much older than Darwin. Its roots go back to the sixth century before our era, when the famous Greek philosopher, Heraclitus of Ephesus, gave the philosophy of force a classic expression in the famous dictum "war is the father of all things,"— πόλεμος πατήρ πάντων.

At the beginning of the sixteenth century Machiavelli (1469–1527) based his science of statesmanship upon the philosophy of force, which he found dominant among the aristocratic ruling classes of his time, and in *The Prince* laid down rules which have affected the orthodox diplomacy of the European nations ever since. Machiavelli was seeking a remedy for the discord and anarchy of Italy, and he found it in the tyranny of Cesare Borgia, imposing his despotic will without regard to moral scruples. Machiavelli holds that the State is essentially non-moral, and in this view we find a significant foreshadowing of a theory which has not entirely disappeared from the modern world. Any crime may be committed in its name, he contends. The State knows no law higher than necessity. Since mankind is totally depraved, it must be beaten into order by any means, and the only effective instrument is an unlimited will. There is no authority above the Sovereign to impose rules of action upon him. He may find religion and morality useful instruments, but for him they are only agencies, not authorities. Everything must be sacrificed to the unity, strength, and growth of the State.[1]

The period of deep unrest, conspiracy, and private warfare of the latter half of the sixteenth century, culminating in the horrors of St. Bartholomew's Day evoked another great book, *De la République* by Jean Bodin (1530–1596), which has since held its place, as the foundation of nearly all subsequent political thought, with Machiavelli's *The Prince*. Bodin did not consider it sufficient merely to analyse the existing institution of monarchy, as Machiavelli had done; he considered that an abstract theory of the State must be created, founded on axioms of reason, which could serve as a new foundation for the monarch's throne, and thus put an end to the anarchy of the Wars of Religion. Bodin found the corner-stone for this theory of the State in the conception of "sovereignty" which he describes as being "absolute, indivisible, inalienable." Since it is absolute it admits of no limitation; since it is indivisible, it cannot be shared or partitioned; since it is

---

[1] See *Il Principe*, Burd's edition, Oxford, 1891, and also the admirable discussion of Machiavelli's doctrines in Villari, *The Life and Times of Machiavelli*, London, 1898, vol. ii., pp. 89, 184.

inalienable, it cannot be lost or taken away. This conception of sovereignty, which has proved to be the most serious theoretical obstacle to the organization of the world under a system of justice, lent itself directly to the distortion of the philosophy of force. Bodin's conception of the State places it in the category of Might, and not in the category of Right. If the State is absolute, has no superior, and is subject to no law, there must remain forever as many ungoverned, ungovernable, and purely arbitrary entities as there are sovereign States, thus ensuring perpetual anarchy in the realm of international relations.

This idea of the State was developed further by Thomas Hobbes (1588–1679). His contributions form so important a part of the modern philosophy of force that it is worth while to examine them in some detail. Hobbes, like Machiavelli and Bodin, was greatly influenced by the conditions of the time in which he wrote and drew from the Thirty Years' War the picture of nations living "in a condition of perpetual war and upon the confines of battle," as representing the permanent reality with which the statesman and the political philosopher have to deal.

Hobbes, who was strongly in sympathy with the aristocratic ruling class of the Royalists, deduced his social philosophy from an imaginary man, whom he assumes to be naturally self-seeking, egotistic, and nothing more. In a state of nature, where selfish characteristics rule unrestrained, according to Hobbes, the result must be a continuous warfare in which every man's hand is raised against his neighbour. Hobbes is a realist to the core, and declares in his pitiless frankness that the life of man, while he continues to live in a state of nature, will doubtless always be "solitary, poor, nasty, brutish, and short," but nevertheless, he says, "this is his natural condition."   In his *Leviathan* he points to the facts as he sees them:

> In all places, where men have lived by small families, to rob and spoil one another has been a trade, and so far from being reputed against the Law of Nature, the greater spoils they gained, the greater was their honour.

And he applies his realistic social theory to the State with logical consistency:

> As small families did then, so now do cities and kingdoms, which are greater families, for their own security, enlarge their dominion upon all pretences of danger and fear of invasion . . . endeavouring, as much as they can, to subdue by open force or secret arts, for want of other caution, justly; and are remembered for it in after years with honour.[1]

Thus war, from being universal and perpetual in a "state of nature," is suppressed within the State for the benefit of its subjects, but will continue its course naturally, and, as Hobbes does not hesitate to say, quite "justly," between States,

[1] Hobbes, *Leviathan* (1651), chapters xiii. and xvii.

which have no "compact" with a superior power to preserve them from its evils. The State being in its essence merely a mutual benefit association, according to this theory, the subject is best served by the success of the State as a predatory enterprise by which others are despoiled. Law and order, therefore, end with the particular State, according to Hobbes, and internationally, since society is founded upon "interests" and not upon "rights," war will continue indefinitely, because there is no way of stopping it, and that nation will be the best off, which, being the strongest, can most despoil the rest.

The dominance of the teachings of Machiavelli, Bodin, and Hobbes in the aristocratic intellectual circles and among the ruling classes of all countries in Darwin's time contributed greatly to the success of the distorted application of his theory to human society. The new "social Darwinism" was seized upon with enthusiasm by all the men of violence because it permitted them to raise the basest instincts of greed and vandalism to the height of a universal law of nature. Since the feeblest must pèrish necessarily in the battle for existence, since this is the immutable principle of the living world, then the *vae victis* was of all that one could imagine the most rational and most legitimate course.

We can imagine the effect which this distorted social Darwinism would have upon a man of power like Bismarck. H. Lichtenberger, analysing his character, says:

Bismarck had in a rare degree the love of force, the joy of exercising and expanding his power and that of his people. He constantly put into practice this "agonistic" conception of existence without remorse and without scruple, without pity for the feeble, and without generosity for the vanquished.[1]

Men of Bismarck's type found in the new doctrines complete justification for their tendencies, a kind of superior sanction for a policy of blood and iron. Political theory in all Europe was based on the new "social Darwinism," and it was proclaimed that might always makes right. Bismarck was the leader of the school in Germany; in England, Chamberlain; in the United States and elsewhere the Imperialists proclaimed with the Iron Chancellor that force alone is noble, beautiful, and respectable. Banditism was raised upon a superb pedestal by the sovereigns, the ministers, and the statesmen with the instinct of conquest.

The historical events of the second half of the nineteenth century contributed greatly to the spread of the philosophy of force as a theory of international relations. Novikov[2] has traced with fine insight the way in which the idea of the struggle for existence and the survival of the fittest was applied to nations under the influence of these historical events.

The development of the Darwinian ideas had been especially marked in Germany, where the

[1] *L'Allemagne moderne et son évolution.* Paris, 1907, p. 113.
[2] *La Critique du Darwinisme social*, pp. 12-15.

first edition of *The Origin of Species* was published in 1860. As early as 1861, Darwin wrote, "my book seems to be exciting much attention in Germany, judging from the number of discussions sent me," and his son, Francis Darwin, writes, "in a few years the voice of German science was to become one of the strongest of the advocates of evolution.[1]

In the midst of all this discussion came the war of 1870, exerting a profound influence in popularizing the theory of "social Darwinism" as the arbiter of national destiny. It is easy to understand the effect of the war upon the victorious Prussians, and through them upon a large part of the German people, for Prussia had now gained the leadership in the newly-formed German Empire.

Intoxicated by their brilliant victories, they were easily converted to the adoration of brute force. They proclaimed on high that it took precedence of law. They found it entirely natural that it menaced the world. They claimed that the vanquished had no right to protest, that they ought simply to submit to their fate. All the benefits which came from the unity of the German states were ascribed to the victorious war. The great expansion of economic life, following the transition from an agricultural to a predominately industrial state which had set in in the previous decade, was also credited to the war and it was felt that the principle of natural selection could

[1] *Life and Letters of Darwin*, p. 150.

be directly observed at work in the German nation.

It is not surprising that victory should have contributed greatly to the success of the philosophy of force in Germany, but it seems paradoxical that the war of 1870 should have increased the popularity of "social Darwinism" also in *France!* It would seem that this country, having been defeated and subjected to a flagrant violation of its rights, ought to have found force hateful and justice admirable, but nevertheless it did not so happen. How can this apparent contradiction be explained? Novikov has unravelled the complicated causes as follows:

After the defeat of 1870 French public opinion might have followed either of two different directions. The French could have said: "We have suffered a hateful injustice; it is necessary therefore to do everything in our power to insure that such international deeds as this may never be repeated. We must attempt to suppress injustice; in other words we must work for an international union. Might is wrong; Right alone is beautiful. Down with Force; long live the Law!"

But another conclusion was also possible: "The military power of Prussia has inflicted upon us the deepest humiliation and the most cruel torment. If force had been upon our side it is we who would have tasted the sweets of triumph, and the Prussians who would have drained the dregs

of defeat. Nothing is more useful than power.
Down with Law! Long live Force!"

For many centuries France had been a formidable nation, belligerent, proud, and intoxicated with success. Twice she had exercised
an incontestable dominance in Europe, under
Louis XIV. and under Napoleon. France had
used and abused force. She could not resign
herself to defeat. From this we can trace the
rise of a *revanche* party and the success of "social
Darwinism" in France and we can understand
also the growing disfavour which befell "Idealism"
—that is to say the political philosophy of justice—in the years immediately following 1870.

The same circumstances explain the dominance
of the philosophy of force in Italy as in France.
When at the epoch of the *Risorgimento* the different
states of Italy were finally formed into one nation, they suffered, blow after blow, the bitterness
of defeat—at first at Custozza (1866) and then
at Lissa. In their period of "juvenile efferves-
cence," as Novikov calls it, the Italians had an
eager desire to make for themselves a place equal
to the other powers of Europe. Not being able
to obtain this, they were filled with bitter regret,
and the possession of force appeared to them also
to constitute the apex of human felicity. They
felt that a victory would exalt them as much as
a defeat had discouraged them. They believed
that after one or two brilliant victories they could
occupy immediately a position of the first rank

as a Great Power. They were deprived of this profound joy and saw themselves condemned to modesty. All this gave an extraordinary prestige to force and favoured the popularity of the Darwinian doctrine. The Italians had inaugurated a new era in the history of the world—the formation of a great State, not by massacre on the field of battle, but by the unanimous plebiscite of her citizens. They had the supreme glory of being the first nation founded upon law. Yet they attributed to this fact a mediocre importance. They would have greatly preferred a victory gained through bloodshed and wholesale slaughter, to the most wonderful victory gained in the domain of ideas, and all these exaltations of brute force aided in the triumph of the distorted Darwinian doctrine.

The other nations of Europe were also influenced by the current of ideas which had established themselves in Germany, France, and Italy. England, the cradle of true Darwinism, was naturally very sympathetic toward this distorted "social Darwinism" which was reflected from the continent especially because she had an immense colonial empire founded upon force and in parts still sustained by force.

From Europe the philosophy of force spread to the rest of the world. The South American countries received the doctrine from France and Italy. The Imperialists of America imported their ideas from the Imperialists of England. The strong feudal traditions of Japan, the influence of German ideas upon Japanese education, the victory of the Japanese over the Chinese in 1896 and over the Russians in 1906, have combined to augment the prestige of the philosophy of force and the popularity of this distorted Darwinian doctrine in Asia. Even China, with its centuries-old traditions of pacifism handed down from her great philosophers and teachers, Confucius and Lao-Tse and Mo, has felt the influence of the doctrine brought back by her students from the universities in Japan and Europe.

Among all the Western nations the unprecedented growth of modern Imperialism, which finds its scientific defence in the application of the Darwinian theory to the struggle between races, has given an immense impulse to the philosophy of force. The leading characteristic of international relations since 1870 has been the competition of rival empires. From 1870 to 1900 Great Britain added to its domains an area of 4,754,000 square miles, with an estimated population of 88,000,000—about forty times the area and double the population of the mother country. The close of the Franco-Prussian war marked the beginning of a new colonial policy for France, and a little later, for Germany, and this policy began to assume practical form after 1880. Since 1880 France has acquired an area of more than 3,500,000 square miles, almost all of it tropical or subtropical, with a native population of about

37,000,000. During the fifteen years following
1884, when Germany entered upon her Imperialist
career with a policy of African protectorates and
the annexation of Oceanic islands, she acquired
an area of about 1,000,000 square miles, with an
estimated population of 14,000,000. Almost the
whole of her added territory was tropical, and the
white population numbered only a few thousands.

Italy, Portugal, and Belgium entered directly
into the competition of the new Imperialism
between 1880 and 1884. Russia's expansionist
policy, though more in the nature of a regular
colonial policy of settlement for the purposes of
agriculture and industry than the new Imperialism,
comes definitely into competition with this in Asia,
as in Persia and Manchuria, and has been assuming increasingly an Imperialist nature.

The annexation of Formosa by Japan following
the victory over China, and of Korea following the
Russo-Japanese war, showed that this rising and
progressive Oriental Empire adopted Imperialism with the other characteristics of Occidental
civilization.

The entrance of the United States of America
upon an Imperialistic career by the annexation of
Hawaii, and later, of the Philippines, marks the
extension of the competition to the Western
Hemisphere.

This unprecedented growth of Imperialism
among all the great powers contributed powerfully
to the spread of the philosophy of force. On the

one hand, "social Darwinism" was enlisted to justify the methods of force which were used so extensively in this process of conquest and subjugation; on the other hand, the results of Imperialism were pointed to as the proofs of the process of the survival of the fittest and the inevitable dominance of the higher civilization, thus contributing to the spread of the pseudo-scientific doctrine.

Even sociologists have shown themselves eager in some cases to accept the philosophy of force as the sufficient justification of Imperialism, and to apply it to defend the necessity, the utility, and even the righteousness of continuing the physical struggle between races and types of civilization to the point of complete subjugation or extermination. Thus Professor Karl Pearson maintains that a constant struggle with other groups or races is demanded for the maintenance and progress of a race or nation. If you abate the necessity of struggle, the vigour of the race flags and perishes. It is to the real interest of a vigorous race, he says, to be

kept up to a high pitch of external efficiency by contest, chiefly by way of war with inferior races, and with equal races by the struggle for trade routes and for the sources of raw material and of food supply. This is the natural history view of mankind, and I do not think you can in its main features subvert it.[1]

[1] *National Life from the Standpoint of Science,* 1901, p. 44.

By others, who take a wider, cosmic view, the argument has been put on the ground of "social efficiency." "Human progress," so runs the argument, "requires the maintenance of the race struggle, in which the weakest races shall go under, while the 'socially efficient' races survive and flourish; we are the socially efficient race; therefore our nation must take up the 'white man's burden' and enter upon an Imperialistic career." The principle of social efficiency is described as being "as indisputable as the law of gravitation" by Edmund Demolins, who enunciates it as follows:

When one race shows itself superior to another in the various externals of domestic life, it *inevitably* in the long run gets the upper hand in public life and establishes its predominance. Whether this predominance is asserted by peaceable means or feats of arms, it is none the less, when the proper time comes, officially established, and afterwards unreservedly acknowledged. I have said that this law is the only thing which accounts for the history of the human race and the revolutions of empires, and that, moreover, it explains and justifies the appropriation by Europeans of territories in Asia, Africa, and Oceania, and the whole of our colonial development.[1]

The gospel of Imperialism, as embodied in the career of Hubert Hervey of the British South African Chartered Company, has been summed up by his fellow-adventurer, Earl Grey, as follows:

[1] *Boers or British*, p. 24.

Probably every one would agree that an Englishman would be right in considering his way of looking
at the world and at life better than that of the Maori
or Hottentot, and no one will object in the abstract
to England doing her best to impose her better and
higher view on those savages. But the same idea will
carry you much farther. In so far as an Englishman
differs in essentials from a Swede or Belgian, he believes
that he represents a more perfectly developed standard
of general excellence. Yes, and even those nations
nearest to us in mind and sentiment—German and
Scandinavian—we regard on the whole as not so
excellent as ourselves, comparing their typical characteristics with ours. Were this not so, our energies
would be directed to becoming what they are. Without doing this, however, we may well endeavour to
pick out their best qualities and add them to ours,
believing that our compound will be superior to the
foreign stock.

It is the mark of an independent nation that it
should feel thus. How far such a feeling is, in any
particular case, justified, history alone decides. But
it is essential that each claimant for the first place
sho ld put forward his whole energy to prove his
righ This is the moral justification for international
stri and for war, and a great change must come
over the world and over men's minds before there can
be any question of everlasting universal peace, or the
settlement of all international differences by arbitration. More especially must the difficulty caused by
the absence of a generally recognized standard of
justice be felt in the case of contact between civilized
and uncivilized races. Is there any likelihood of the
gulf between the white and the black man being

4

bridged within any period of time that we can foresee?
Can there be any doubt that the white man must, and
will, impose his superior civilization on the coloured
races?   The rivalry of the principal European countries in extending their influence over other continents should lead naturally to the evolution of the
highest attainable type of government of subject
races by the superior qualities of their rulers.[1]

This is an excellent statement of the scientific
basis of Imperialism, including in its survey the
physical struggle between white races, the subjugation of lower races by the white race, the necessity and the utility of this struggle and this
subjugation, and finally the right of domination
based upon this necessity. The white man believes
he is a more excellent type than any other man; he
believes he is better able to assimilate any special
virtues others may have; he believes that this
character gives him a right to rule which no other
can possess.   Thus, starting from natural history,
the doctrine soon takes on the outer garments of
ethical and even religious sanctions, and we soon
reach the elevated atmosphere of "Imperial
Christianity," the "mission of civilization," in
which our nation is called upon to teach the "arts
of good government," the "dignity of labour."
And not only our nation; Mr. Hervey admits that
the patriotic Frenchman, the German, the Russian, feels in the same way his own sense of superi-

[1] *Memoir of Hubert Hervey*, by Earl Grey (1899), quoted by
J. A. Hobson, in *Imperialism, a Study*, pp. 138–39.

ority, and the rights it confers on him. So much the better, he says, agreeing with Professor Pearson, for this cross-conviction and these cross-interests insure the survival and the gradual perfection of the fittest through international strife and war.

Here we have "social Darwinism" in its final consummation, transformed from its lowly beginnings of struggle in the animal world to its apotheosis in the mighty conflicts of rival empires. In the history of modern Europe, in the ententes and alliances of the "balance of power"; in the reciprocal and cumulative preparations "for defence only" while these rival aggressive policies of Imperialism were being steadily pursued, we can follow the inevitable development of a system of international anarchy based on doctrines of mutual antagonism and destructive competition. And finally, if the pragmatic test, "By their fruits ye shall know them," is to be applied to the logical results of social and political theory, the philosophy of force is self-condemned by the breakdown in August, 1914, of the civilization founded in so large a measure upon this philosophy.

It is not sufficient, however, to know that a social philosophy is unsound, as shown by the fact that it breaks down in practice. If the truer theory of human relations by which we hope to replace it is not to run the danger of having the same or similar weaknesses, we must apply to the outworn system a searching criticism; we must find out by careful analysis just where it is wrong, and what are its errors. In the next chapter, therefore, we shall proceed to the consideration of the biological errors of the philosophy of force.

CHAPTER III

THE BIOLOGICAL ERRORS

THE primary error[1] of those who have distorted Darwin's theory beyond all recognition is one of stupendous magnitude. It consists in ignoring completely the existence of the physical universe! The cause of progress is assumed to be, not the struggle of man with his environment, from which he gets food, clothing, shelter, and all other necessities, but the struggle of man with man, a struggle which is by its nature unproductive and fruitless.

The infinite error involved in forgetting entirely the existence of the physical universe is due, first, to a common defect of the human mind, which tends to overlook the most commonplace

[1] Novikov's analysis (*La Critique du Darwinisme social*, chapters ii.–xx.) of the errors of "social Darwinism" into three groups—(1) errors of the biological order; (2) general errors of the sociological order, and (3) special errors of the sociological order—has been followed in this and the two succeeding chapters of the present work. Those desiring a more detailed criticism than is given in the present summary are referred to Novikov's larger work, in which a separate chapter is devoted to each of the seventeen most important errors.

and obvious facts of existence in favour of the unusual and abnormal; and second, to a misunderstanding of the terms "struggle for existence" and "survival of the fittest" as used by Darwin.

Those who believe in the distorted form of "social Darwinism," obsessed by the idea of struggle, forget entirely the greatest struggle of all, the struggle of man against his physical environment, because it is so common and so omnipresent. The relations of men to the universe are infinitely closer than those of men to each other. A man may live for years without contact with other men, like Alexander Selkirk, whose experiences have been given literary form in Defoe's *Robinson Crusoe*, but the necessity for adaptation to the physical universe is constant. Man, in common with all animals, is compelled to engage in a continual effort to maintain a constant temperature. He cannot live more than a few minutes without air, or a few days without water, or a few weeks without food. The danger from disease germs is always present. The greatest waste of the philosophy of force and the war system consists in the fact that, having accustomed us to consider collective homicide as the source of all civilization, it diverts our energies and our attentions from the real struggle against the external universe and the common enemies of mankind to the destructive struggle against the artificial enemies whom we create, on account of false ideas, out of other parts of the human race.

The struggle against the physical environment is the most important labour which occupies our species as well as all other species.   Consider, for example, the struggle against the physical universe involved in maintaining the proper difference of temperature between ourselves and the surrounding atmosphere.   We take infinite pains to provide ourselves with clothing, dwellings, and with complicated heating systems in cold climates, and cooling systems in hot climates. The necessity for providing air which is sufficiently pure in a chemical sense constitutes an ever-present problem, especially in large cities, where, in the case of tenements, it is far from being solved.   To get air which is sufficiently pure in a biological sense is a matter even more urgent and gives rise to the whole system of modern sanitation, from the extensive sewage systems of modern cities to the institutes for the research and cure of tuberculosis.   To get an abundant supply of pure water for drinking purposes immense aqueducts are built, at great cost, to the sources of an adequate and pure supply in the springs and watersheds of the mountains.   The necessity of struggle for an adequate food supply occupies a large part of the energies of men.   It gives rise to the great industries of agriculture, stock-raising, fishing, and hunting, as well as to the derived industries and manufactures of all kinds, such as meat-packers, butchers, bakeries.   The struggle against the physical environment gives rise to the whole complicated system of distribution and transportation, to the manufacture of agricultural instruments, the building of railroads and ships, stockyards and canals. It has led to the process of specialization and the division of labour. First man, gathers the fruits which he eats directly, then he makes a tool with which to reach the fruits, then he makes a second tool with which to manufacture the first, and so on through an infinite number of inventions to all the wonders of modern scientific research and discovery.

It is difficult to imagine a more colossal error than is committed by the philosophy of force when it disregards all this infinite struggle of man against his physical environment and concentrates all its attention upon the struggle of man against man. The biological error involved is like that which was committed by the old political economy, which considered solely the secondary phenomena of exchange between men, and left out of account all considerations of the primary phenomena of production and of the adaptation of the environment to man's needs.

When this "immemorial warfare of man against Nature,"[1] is brought to the attention of the "social Darwinists," they go so far as to deny that the relations between man and his physical environments can be described by the word *struggle*. Thus Mr. E. d'Eichthal protests against applying

[1] William James, *Memories and Studies*, p. 288.

the word struggle to the process of adapting the
physical universe to the needs of man:

> This is a real abuse of words. Struggle ought always
> to imply the intention to destroy one another. No
> struggle can take place between or against inanimate
> bodies; this becomes a simple metaphor.[1]

To say that the relations between man and his
physical environment are not a struggle and to re-
serve this term uniquely for the relations between
men is to fail to see ninety-nine one hundredths
of our activity.   Mr. d'Eichthal is perfectly right
in saying that the action of one inanimate body on
another can only be described as a struggle by a
metaphorical use of the word, but the relations
between man and the physical environment, which
includes the entire world—mineral, vegetable, and
animal, is a real struggle in the literal sense of the
terms.

As a matter of fact struggle never has for its
object the destruction of the adversary. Its
object is always to transform the environment
so that the individual may survive. When a
farmer plucks the weed of a field in order to sow
wheat, it is not for the purpose of harming the
weed, but in order to have bread. When the
microbes of tuberculosis are killed by a disinfect-
ant, it is not done for the sake of destroying the
microbes, but with the object of saving the life
of a human being. The "social Darwinists"

[1] *Guerre et paix internationales*, Paris, 1909, p. 7.

who would exclude the warfare with nature from the conception of struggle and confine its interpretations to the narrow sense of battle, from the hand-to-hand combat of individuals to the collective homicide of great wars, have not read Darwin's works, but have obtained their opinions of the meaning of his terms at second hand from the popularizers who have distorted his theory. Darwin, who complains bitterly in his letters against the misrepresentations of his ideas,[1] tried to guard expressly against the misinterpretation of the word "struggle" which has occurred in the philosophy of force. In a section headed, "The Term Struggle for Existence Used in a Large Sense," he says:

I should premise that I use this term in a large and metaphorical sense, including dependence of one being on another, and including (which is more important) not only the life of the individual, but success in leaving progeny.[2]

He then proceeds to illustrate the term in words which leave no doubt that it includes as one of its most important elements the struggle against the universe. Thus

a plant on the edge of a desert is said to struggle for life against the drought, though more properly it

---

[1] In a letter to C. Lyell he wrote:
"I am beginning to despair of ever making the majority understand my notions . . . I must be a very bad explainer."—*Life and Letters of Darwin*, vol. ii., p. 111.

[2] *The Origin of Species*, 6th edition, p. 56.

should be said to be dependent on the moisture. A plant which annually produces a thousand seeds, of which only one of an average comes to maturity, may be more truly said to struggle with the plants of the same and other kinds which already clothe the ground. . . . When we reach the arctic regions, or snow-capped summits, or absolute deserts, the struggle for life is almost exclusively with the elements.[1]

The "social Darwinists" claim to find the basis of their theories in biological facts, but the biologists follow Darwin in refusing to disregard completely the most fundamental facts of life. Thus, Felix Le Dantec says:

The life of a living being results from two factors: the being and the environment. At each instance the vital or functional phenomena do not reside in the being alone, nor in the environment alone, but in the actual relations which exist between the being and the environment.[2]

The same author says in another place:

It was considered formerly that the living being existed by itself within its limiting surface independently of the surrounding environment, but this idea contains a manifest error derived from the old vitalistic theories, in which it was supposed that a vital principle animated the living body and was localized in it. In reality the living being is the result of a struggle between two factors: the substance localized

[1] *The Origin of Species*, pp. 56, 61.
[2] *Revue scientifique*, 1908, November 14, p. 610.

within the surface of the animal—the body of the animal—on the one side; and on the other side, the surrounding environment. . . . Life is the struggle itself between the body of the being and the surroundings. . . . The immediate phenomena of the struggle take place between the individual and its surroundings much more often than between one individual and another individual. The direct struggle is the struggle of man against his environment; this struggle is life.[1]

Thus the science of biology, on which the philosophy of force relies for its proof that war is a biological necessity, decides not for it but against it. Biology, in demonstrating that life is the struggle against the physical environment, teaches us to see in this struggle the principal phenomenon, while the struggle between individuals of the same species is an accessory phenomenon of subsidiary importance. Biology thus restores things to their proper proportions. It obliges sociology to consider before everything else the relations of man with his physical environment, and forces it to rid itself of the social myopia that has fallen upon the "social Darwinists." It compels it to recognize at the threshold of its task, that there is an external world, infinite in extent, the study of which ought to take the precedence over all other considerations.

The same disregard of the existence of the universe leads to a misinterpretation of the term

[1] *La lutte universelle*, Paris, 1906, pp. 73, 283.

"Survival of the Fittest." In the philosophy of force "fittest" means "strongest," often indeed "most brutal." In Darwin's work and in biology "fittest" means "best adapted" to the physical environment. In the chapter on "Natural Selection; or the Survival of the Fittest," Darwin says:

Let it also be borne in mind how infinitely complex and close-fitting are the mutual relations of all organic beings to each other and to their physical conditions of life; and consequently what infinitely varied diversities of structures might be of use to each being under changing conditions of life. . . . This preservation of favourable individual differences and variations, and the destruction of those which are injurious, I have called Natural Selection, or the Survival of the Fittest.[1]

We shall best understand the probable course of Natural Selection by taking the case of a country undergoing some physical change, for instance, of climate. The proportional numbers of its inhabitants will almost immediately undergo a change and some species will probably become extinct. . . . In such cases, slight modification, which in any way favoured

[1] In a letter to C. Lyell, in which Darwin complained of the way in which his work was misrepresented and misunderstood, he wrote: "I suppose 'Natural Selection' was a bad term; but to change it now, I think, would make confusion worse confounded; nor can I think of a better. 'Natural Preservation' would not imply a preservation of particular varieties and would seem a truism and would not bring man's and nature's selections under one point of view."—*Life and Letters of Darwin*, vol. ii., p. 111.

individuals of any species, by better adapting them to their altered conditions, would tend to be preserved; and natural selection would have free scope for the work of improvement.[1]

The struggle against the physical universe, which is so completely disregarded in the philosophy of force, constitutes what is usually called economic production.   This struggle is continuous: it is being waged every minute and indeed every second.   The disproportion between the days of labour given to this struggle against the surroundings and the days of labour given to the struggle between men is simply enormous.   Some people such as the Swedish people, for example, have not had either a war with a foreign nation or a civil war for a century.   The number of days used in combating their own kind has been 0 during this period.   But the number of days devoted to the struggle against the physical environment, on the basis of an average working population of three million people during the 36,500 days of the century is 109,500,000,000 at least.   The proportion of zero to 109 billion is infinite.   But Sweden has made enormous progress during the nineteenth century and ranks among the highest and most civilized nations in the world.   Yet all this progress has been made without the aid of a single war.   How can it be affirmed then that collective homicide is the cause of pro-

[1] *The Origin of Species*, pp. 69–71.

gress? Since the struggle against the physical environment is the most constant struggle which the individual has to endure, it is natural that the amount of happiness should be in direct proportion to the importance of the victory attained in this field. But this victory is the adaptation of the environment to the needs of the individual. Adaptation is obtained by economic work. To say that progress results from collective homicide is equivalent to affirming that the well-being of man does not result from the adaptation of his environment to his needs. This disregard of the existence of the universe constitutes the most profound deception imaginable in the realm of social science.

The importance of labour as the real struggle of the human race is recognized increasingly by all students of social problems. One of them sums up the case against the first error of the philosophy of force as follows:

Labour is the great Conqueror. Not War but Work, is the great Educator; and the essential watchword of all permanent advance. . . . It is not the men that give up fighting, who lose stamina and virility, but the men who give up work. The most "unfit" are they who least co-operate in the great struggle of their race against whatever in its environment obstructs real progress and development. And of all such obstacles War is the greatest, as may at any time clearly be seen from the condition of those peoples who chiefly occupy their time in conflict, either with their neighbours or among themselves.[1]

[1] W. L. Grane, *The Passing of War*, p. 61.

William James comes to the same conclusion and finds a moral equivalent for war and a remedy for existing injustice in the idea of compulsory industrial service. Instead of military conscription, he advocates a conscription of the whole youthful population to form for a certain number of years a part of the army enlisted against *Nature*.[1]

The second error of the philosophy of force is that in which struggle is confused with the extermination of fellow-creatures. A typical example of this confusion may be quoted from Spencer[2] who maintains that without the collective homicides of the past ten thousand years the world would still be inhabited only by cavemen of a feeble type:

... to the unceasing warfare between species is mainly due both growth and organization. Without universal conflict there would have been no development of the active powers. ... Among predatory animals death by starvation, and among animals preyed upon death by destruction, has carried off the least-favourably modified individuals and varieties. Every advance in strength, speed, agility, or sagacity, in creatures of the one class, has necessitated a corresponding advance in creatures of the other class; and without the never-ending efforts to catch and to escape, with loss of life as the penalty of failure, the progress of neither could have been achieved. ...

[1] *The Moral Equivalent of War*, p. 17.
[2] *Principles of Sociology*, 2d edition, vol. ii., p. 240.

Similarly with social organisms. We must recognize the truth that the struggle for existence between societies has been instrumental to their evolution.

The first objection which presents itself is a biological one. It is strange that Spencer did not realize that his argument was inconsistent. The unceasing warfare between species, he says, is the cause of both growth and organization, that is, of the appearance of more perfect types. Since the Paleozoic Age all the species, without exception, have been subjected to the pressure of the struggle for existence. Why is it then that certain species have evolved to a being as high as man, while others have remained at a more rudimentary stage of life? The struggle for existence cannot be the sole cause of the evolution of species. There must be other causes which we do not know.

From the point of view of sociology, however, it is not this biological objection which is of the greatest interest. It is the immense leap which Spencer makes in applying the definite analogy to human society. He speaks of the struggle between animals and then, without any transition or explanation, says: "Similarly with social organisms." It is astonishing to find an eminent philosopher making such an elementary error. This is an example of the kind of errors of which Darwin complains in one of his letters, in which he said: "How curious it is that several of my re-

5

viewers should advance such wild arguments
. . . and should bring up the old exploded doctrine
of definite analogies. . . ."[1]

In this case Spencer has not exactly forgotten
the existence of the universe but he has disregarded
one of the most widespread facts which can be
observed in it,—that living beings exist in it in
relationships of a most extraordinary complexity,
ranging from the most irreducible antagonism
to the most absolute solidarity. To jump from
the conclusion that since certain relations are
established between animals of different species,
the same relations ought to be found without any
modification whatsoever between societies of the
human race, is to make an assumption which is
not supported by science or reason. Spencer makes
two chief conclusions which render his comparison
entirely false.

1.   He compares the struggle between individuals
of *different* species with the struggle between individuals of the same species;

2.   He compares the struggle between individuals
to the struggle between collectivities.

1.   The struggle between individuals of different species is not of the same character as those
between individuals of the same species and cannot be grouped under the same law without
further examination. If we consider examples
of the struggle between individuals and different

[1] *Life and Letters of Darwin*, vol. ii., p. 111.

species, as in the case of the microbe which preys upon plants and animals, or carnivorous animals which prey upon herbivorous animals, we see that there is an irreducible antagonism and perpetual hostility between individuals of such different species. The life of the predatory animals can only be maintained by the death of their prey. But between individuals of the same species, we often have relations which are diametrically opposite, relations of alliance and association. To proceed from the struggles of microbes and men, of herbs and cattle, of wolves and sheep, to the struggle between man and man, without further justification than the statement "similarly with social organisms" although characteristic of much of the distorted "social Darwinism," is opposed to the scientific spirit of Darwin's own work.

If Spencer had wished to compare the battles of animals with the battles of human beings, he should have compared the combats of men with the combats between animals of the same species. The combat between a tiger and a bull is not comparable with a duel between two men, because the tiger and the bull are individuals of two species which are not associable and are indeed naturally antagonistic, while the duellists are individuals of the same species. The comparison would have been more exact if Spencer had compared the relations between men with the relations between tigers. In this case he would have been dealing with animals, not indeed associated in any permanent fashion, but at least of the same species. But as soon as we approach the concrete reality we see that tigers do not eat each other and that the relations between individuals of the same species are not the same as those between individuals of different species. Since animals of the same species do not massacre each other, Spencer has no justification from the biological analogy for affirming that human progress would have been impossible if men had not exterminated each other.

A closer analogy would be to compare the relations between men with the relations between individuals of a species capable of association such as bees, apes, beavers, monkeys, etc. But when we come to the real analogy the scene changes entirely. Not only do we see that the individuals of species capable of association do not devour each other, but on the contrary they unite for common work; they exchange services, and as a result they create the group of a higher degree of evolution which is called a society.

2.   The second great error of Spencer is to compare the struggle between individuals of the same species or of different species, not with that of human individuals but with human societies. The fight between two pugilists of different races might be likened in some manner to a combat between a lion and a bull, but the war between the English and Zulus, between the Russians and the Japanese, cannot be likened in any definite manner

to a combat between a lion and a bull or even to a combat between two lions. The combat between two individuals (the lion and the bull for example) remains in the domain of zoölogy. The combat between the Russians and the Japanese enters into the social domain, which presupposes the inter-action of an enormous number of facts—psychological, economical, political, and intellectual. Spencer's phrase "similarly with social organisms" constitutes a blind leap from the biological to the sociological realm which is not justified by any logic.

But collective combats do take place in the animal kingdom, say the "social Darwinists," and these combats have contributed to the advancement of the species. It is known that the ants wage war in good and due form. Since the ants wage war, collective combat is a fact of Nature, runs the argument, and it is useless to try to abolish war between human collectivities. In fact, it is worse than useless; it would be disastrous to civilization. So the popular advocates of the philosophy of force, following the sociologists, base their case on these "biological laws" and apply it to the modern relations between human collectivities. Thus Bernhardi says:

The knowledge, therefore, that war depends on biological laws leads to the conclusion that every attempt to exclude it from international relations must be demonstrably untenable. But it is not only a biological law, but a moral obligation, and, as such, an indispensable factor in civilization.[1]

The steps of logic which the "social Darwinists" disregard in making their definite analogies are astonishing. It is necessary to prove first that the evolution of species has been the result of the combats which they have waged against other species, a conclusion which is still subject to doubt. Second, it is necessary to prove that collective combats, as well as individual combats, have contributed to biological progress. Passing on then to the case of the ant, it is necessary to prove that they have bettered their organization and that they therefore have progressed as the result of warfare waged between colonies of ants. Finally it is necessary to demonstrate that what is true of the ants is literally applicable to man.

The ants of New Zealand cannot enter into communication with the ants of England, while, thanks to the telegraph, the New Zealanders are in communication with the English. Ants cannot exchange services and merchandise from ant colony to ant colony. A scientific discovery made in one colony is not communicated immediately to the other colonies of ants of the entire world. The intelligence of the ants may be so feeble that it is impossible for them to realize the interests which extend outside of their own colony, while men realize perfectly well the common

[1] *Germany and the Next War*, p. 24.

interests which exist between New Zealand or America and Europe. The ants distributed over the entire world cannot form a single association. Human collectivities spread over the entire world can do this very easily. There is an enormous gulf separating ants from men. The points of disagreement are much greater than those of agreement. Even if it were proved that the battles between ant colonies have improved the species of ants this would be far from demonstrating that the battles between nations have improved the human race. The wide breach between the animal world and human society presented in this concrete illustration makes the definite analogy of Spencer's phrase "similarly with social organisms" seem extremely superficial and arbitrary.

In the domain of zoölogy we think of the struggle for existence as an extermination between antagonistic species, such as that between the wolf and the sheep. In the case of the human species, however, the struggle is thought of solely as an extermination between fellow-creatures, Mr. V. de Lapouge states what is a common point of view as follows:

In civilized countries man has no more enemies to fear. All the dangers have disappeared and the formidable animals have been destroyed. He does not even have to take the trouble to search for food. He finds it at the grocery store. The struggle for existence is now only with his own kind, *Homo homini lupus.* It is carried on only by social acts, but because it has changed its methods and its name, it is none the less cruel and murderous.[1]

Mr. de Lapouge has overlooked enemies such as the microbe of tuberculosis and the bacilli of cholera and of typhoid fever, which men may fear even in civilized countries. Men find food at the grocery store on the condition that they have something to give in exchange to the merchant. The necessity of having this something to give in exchange is a source of constant care of which man can never rid himself.

Why is it considered that in the case of all other animals the struggle should take place only between members of different species, while in the case of man struggle takes place only between members of the same species? The reasons for this contradiction is found in a number of interesting psychological facts. In part, it is due to the dramatic character of war, which, being relatively rare, strikes the human imagination vividly, while the struggle against other species and the physical environment which goes on constantly comes to be considered so natural that we no longer think about it. Thus struggle becomes synonymous with the combat between men and between men alone, so much so that it is sometimes denied, as we have seen above, that this word may be applied to the efforts necessary to adapt the

[1] *Les sélections sociales*, Paris, 1896, p. 199.

environment to our needs. And in part the contradiction is due to a striking conflict between the social instincts and the growing intelligence of man.

Among the anthropomorphic apes there is nothing which resembles our wars of conquest and our armed peace. This is because the apes, possessing a very low order of intelligence, have not been able to create organizations so vast and perfect as ours. The association of apes has not passed the purely rudimentary phase of wandering troupes, while human association has arrived at the phase of the state, of nationality, and even of the group of civilizations. It is only because of his increased intelligence, therefore, that man has been able to wage wars of conquest and to establish the perpetual state of latent war called armed peace, between individuals of the same species.

If we ask why wolves do not eat each other, the answer is that if wolves were constantly attacking their own kind in order to devour them, the wolf species would have ceased to exist long ago. We do not know how instincts are transmitted by heredity, but we do know that hereditary instincts exist. When man developed from earlier forms he possessed necessarily the hereditary instinct which is the common law of the animal kingdom, and which prevented him from attacking his own kind. This instinct is found not only among the herbivorous and frugivorous animals, which cannot eat each other, but even among the carnivorous animals. This instinct must have existed in man, who commenced by being frugivorous. But in proportion as the intelligence of man developed, instinct atrophied, because it became less useful.

Thus we see that at the present time animals possess very valuable instincts which we unfortunately no longer possess, or which unfortunately are not strong enough. There must have been an epoch in which the first man who dared to attack his fellow-creatures committed a novel act requiring the greatest bravery, and this act was only possible on account of the enfranchisement of the human spirit, victorious in its revolt against the hereditary instinct. The man who committed this act was greatly deceived in this special case. In his real interest and in that of his descendants, it would have been a thousand times better if he had followed his own instinct, which would have surely led to happiness. The story of Cain and Abel in Genesis dramatizes a great tragedy which must have taken place at some time in the history of the human race. We do not know at what stage of his descent from the animal world it occurred, but in any case we can see that it is solely as a result of his superior intelligence that man has been able to attack his own kind.

This analysis shows that there is an enormous difference, and in fact an opposition, between the sequence of zoölogical phenomena and the sequence of social phenomena. Let us admit for the sake of argument that the struggle between individuals within the animal kingdom has resulted in the survival of the fittest and the perfection of the species. In this case war is the cause and perfection the effect. But in the human race the sequence has been diametrically opposite. Here intellectual perfection has rendered war possible between men. Here it is perfection which has been the cause and war the effect. Again we see that it is anti-scientific to compare, as Spencer does, phenomena which are completely different.

The struggle for existence and war between members of the same species cannot be considered as identical terms. To a certain extent they may even be said to be contrary and opposed. The real struggle is that against the physical environment, and this is true of animals as of men. This fact is apparent wherever we come into contact with the touchstone of real life and direct observation. Here is the evidence of Kropotkin,[1] a keen observer and careful student of the Darwinian theory:

Two aspects of animal life impressed me most during the journeys which I made in my youth in Eastern Siberia and Northern Manchuria. One of them was the extreme severity of the struggle for existence which most species of animals have to carry on against an inclement Nature. . . . And the other was, that even in those spots where animal life teemed in abundance, I failed to find—although I was eagerly

[1] *Mutual Aid a Factor of Evolution*, p. vii.

looking for it—that bitter struggle for the means of existence *among animals belonging to the same species*, which was considered by most Darwinists (though not always by Darwin himself) as the dominant characteristic of struggle for life, and the main factor of evolution.

The terrible snow-storms which sweep over the northern portion of Eurasia in the later part of the winter, and the glazed frost that often follows them; the frosts and the snow-storms which return every year in the second half of May, when the trees are already in full blossom and insect life swarms everywhere; the early frosts, and, occasionally, the heavy snow-falls in July and August, which suddenly destroy myriads of insects, as well as the second broods of the birds in the prairies; . . . and finally, the heavy snow-falls, early in October, which eventually render a territory as large as France and Germany absolutely impracticable for ruminants and destroy them by the thousand— these were the conditions under which I saw animal life struggling in Northern Asia. They made me realize at an early date the overwhelming importance in Nature of what Darwin describes as "the natural checks to over-multiplication," in comparison to the struggle between individuals of the same species for the means of subsistence, which may go on here and there to some limited extent, but never attains the importance of the former. . . .

Consequently, when my attention was drawn later on, to the relations between Darwinism and Sociology, I could agree with none of the works and pamphlets that had been written upon this important subject. They all endeavoured to prove that Man, owing to his higher intelligence and knowledge, *may* mitigate the harshness of the struggle for life between men; but they all recognize at the same time that the struggle for the means of existence, of every animal against all its congeners, and every man against all other men, was "a law of Nature." This view, however, I could not accept, because I was persuaded that to admit a pitiless inner war for life within each species, and to see in that war a condition of progress, was to admit something which not only had not yet been proved, but also lacked confirmation from direct observation.

It is easy to see that when terrible snow-storms take place those individuals would survive which are most capable of withstanding the cold (*i. e.*, those which are best adapted to the physical environment); that those least able to withstand cold would perish; and that thus a selection favourable to the species would take place. The number of individuals perishing as a consequence of the severe climate is much greater than the number perishing as the result of attacks not only by individuals of the same species, but even by individuals of different species. In the first place the herbivorous and the frugivorous animals cannot perish on account of attacks by individuals of their own species and the carnivorous animals do not eat each other, because of the law of universal application, that force follows the line of least resistance. The carnivorous animals prey upon animals more feeble than themselves,—cats upon mice, tigers upon sheep and cattle, etc. It is therefore a fallacy for "social Darwinism" to assign to the struggle between individuals of the same species the chief rôle in evolution.   In reality this rôle is zero in a great number of cases (among the herbivorous and frugivorous animals for example) and is a very subordinate rôle in almost all cases.

The law holds true for men as well as for animals. Its application in human society is made clear by another illustration from Kropotkin:

. . . A number of villages in South-East Russia, the inhabitants of which enjoy plenty of food, . . . have no sanitary accommodation of any kind; and seeing that for the last eighty years the birth-rate was sixty in the thousand, while the population is now what it was eighty years ago, we might conclude that there has been a terrible competition between the inhabitants.   But the truth is that from year to year the population remained stationary, for the simple reason that one-third of the new-born died before reaching their sixth month of life; one-half died within the next four years, and out of each hundred born, only seventeen or so reached the age of twenty.   The newcomers went away before having grown to be competitors.[1]

What is the significance of the expression "the inhabitants have no sanitary accommodation of any kind?"   It means simply that they do not know how to struggle against the unfavourable conditions of their physical environment.   The

[1] *Mutual Aid a Factor of Evolution*, p. 68.

enormous mortality of children at an early age is caused by the severity of the climate, or the microbes of disease. Although the men in this case are present in abundance, the competition between men exercises no influence whatever upon the mortality of the children. The proof that the high infant mortality is caused by unfavourable conditions of the environment is given by the fact that infant mortality is very greatly reduced in countries with healthy and temperate climates. From the point of view of mankind as well as that of animals, therefore, if the struggle for existence improves the species, it is the struggle against the physical environment and not the struggle between fellow-creatures.

A third important error of the philosophy of force is due to an analysis which is too simple and observations which are too superficial; struggle is confounded with the total death of the vanquished. This is the only result of struggle recognized in "social Darwinism" but the facts are infinitely more complex in Nature. To understand the phenomena we have to divide the results of struggle into those which lead to the total death of the vanquished, and those which lead to the diminution of vital power or partial death.. The struggle which leads to total death must be again divided into two subdivisions—absorption and elimination.

Absorption is the more rapid procedure and is

found more often in the animal kingdom. It consists in killing a being in order to absorb it, as when a lion kills and eats an antelope. The struggle of absorption is opposed to any association between the victors and the vanquished. The only relation which can exist between them, is that of an absolute and unchangeable antagonism. The struggle for existence by absorption is extremely rare between animals of the same species. Neither wolves nor tigers eat each other. Men could not do so as long as they were a fruit-eating species. When fire was invented it became possible to eat flesh and therefore to eat each other, but cannibalism was practised very rarely, as a consequence of the law that force follows the line of least resistance. Cannibalism was introduced into the human species at a later epoch, when the species had already arrived at a certain degree of political organization. Cannibalism has always been a sporadic and rare phenomenon. Neither the Egyptians nor the Babylonians nor the Assyrians were acquainted with it. Moreover, anthropology shows that cannibalism has been practised among men not so much from the physiological motive of hunger as in consequence of a mental attitude—for example, the belief that by eating the body of a vanquished enemy the conqueror would acquire certain of his qualities, such as courage.

In comparing the struggle between human associations, as for example a war between Ger-

many and Denmark, to the struggle by absorption,
such as the combat between a lion and a gazelle,
the philosophy of force becomes involved in
several fallacies. The chief one is that the Germans and the Danes can form an association while
the lion and the gazelle cannot form an association
from the nature of the combat. In order to
establish the analogy, however, the philosophy of
force falls into a still greater error. By a process
of mental abstraction it makes of all Germans a
single being equal to the lion and of all the Danes
a single being like the gazelle. But a combat
between Germany and Denmark is an impossibility. The combat can take place between some
Germans and some Danes in flesh and blood who
line up opposite each other and commence to
massacre each other. As soon as we descend
from general similes to consider the concrete
realities, it is evident that the analogy will not
stand criticism. If the struggle for existence
takes place between human societies it must be
accomplished by processes which have nothing
in common with physiological absorption between
individuals of different species in the animal
kingdom.

The process of elimination is practised most
often among plants. 'It consists in monopolizing
the necessities of life in such a way as to force
the rival to die of starvation. The struggle by
elimination takes place among trees which struggle
for light in a forest. The strongest overshadow

the weaker and take away their sunshine. This produces at first atrophy in some of the branches and finally the death of the entire plant. The struggle by elimination can also be practised among animals, not only among the herbivorous but among the carnivorous animals, when the stronger animals drive away the weaker from the food and force them to die of inanition.

The Darwinian theory has found in the process of elimination as applied in sexual selection, one of the agencies in the transformation of species, but the direct action of the process of elimination, both as regards foodstuffs and as regards reproduction, is of secondary importance in the human species. As regards reproduction, Darwin pointed out that the factor often works in the reverse direction, the largest number of children coming from the feeble-minded and lowest strata of society.[1]

The analogy which is often drawn between the struggle for existence by elimination in biology and the process of elimination in human society fails because in the one case the result is the total death of the conquered while in society the result is a diminution of vital power or partial death. This radical difference gives rise to an immense number of new social phenomena which constitutes a new social kingdom, so different is it from the animal or plant kingdom. The substitution of partial death for total death is one of the first

[1] See *The Descent of Man*, chap. v., p. 154.

processes by which social life is organized in Nature. When the result of a struggle between two beings is no longer a total death, even deferred, of the vanquished, but solely a certain diminution of enjoyment, the conqueror and the conquered can live alongside each other for the normal duration of their existence. As we shall see later, this process is not the only one. Another process, much more rapid for forming societies, is co-operation.

The scale of subordination in society ranges from the difference in regard to food supply to that of intellect or sentiment. In respect to food supply the victor can obtain a more abundant and refined nourishment while condemning the vanquished to a less abundant and coarser supply of food. This does not prevent the vanquished from living out the full term of his life. It may even add to his longevity. The same things may occur in regard to clothing and shelter. The conqueror may live in a splendid palace while the vanquished can only imperfectly shelter himself from the severities of the climate. However, the inhabitant of a hut may reach as ripe an old age as the inhabitant of a mansion. Finally we may have a difference of satisfaction in regard to pride. The conqueror may obtain the applause and the honours which are withheld from the vanquished. This may prove a privation to him but it does not prevent him from living out the full time of his normal life. It means that he must be content with the second rank instead of the first.

From the moment when partial death replaces total death as the result of struggle we have, moreover, a new element entering in,—the possibility of reversal. Thus a man who is beaten in the economic struggle by a competitor may be reduced from an income of $5000 a year to an income of $2000 a year, but he may discover another process which will enable him to regain his income of $5000 or even increase it. Nothing analogous to this is possible in the struggles where total death takes place, as in the case of the gazelle eaten by the lion or the tree cut off from the sunshine by the shadow of its neighbour. The analogy of the biological struggle of elimination, resulting in the total death of the conquered, in which all association is of course impossible, does not apply to the economic struggle of human society, resulting only in a diminution of vital powers, but in which association still continues possible and is indeed a normal condition.

If the "social Darwinists" had wished to make a true comparison between biological and social phenomena, they should have compared the struggles between human associations with the struggles within the same organism. Here we have numerous and more exact analogies. The discoveries of modern physiology, made possible by the perfection of the microscope, have shown us that the cells of our bodies engage in a desperate struggle. The combats between cells resemble the combats of two citizens within a well-organized state, and the result is not total death but partial death of the vanquished cells, *i.e.*, simply a lessening of vitality. The organ in which the cells secure a larger share of the blood supply increases in size, while the organ or the tissue which is vanquished is enfeebled; thus an athlete who constantly uses his arms develops very large biceps, whereas a man who uses his brain intensively employs most of his blood supply and energy to feed the brain cells, while his biceps remain feeble. Cells within an organism may be compared legitimately to men in human society. They are opposed to each other in a certain measure, but in a more important way they are allied to each other and depend upon each other. The significant thing is that the cells do not attack each other, and alliance in human society consists exactly in this modification of the process of struggle, the abandonment of attack against one's neighbour.

Another most instructive analogy between the phenomena within an organism and the phenomena of social life can be found in the researches on cell life by Metchnikov and other naturalists. These have shown that there are in the human body errant cells which have two principal functions: (1) that of combating the microbes of disease which we take in by respiration and in other ways; and (2) that of doing, we might almost say, the police work of our body, in destroying cells which are worn out and decomposed. The macrophages which perform this latter function employ the process of total absorption. This process of killing and destroying harmful cells is quite different, however, from the process of complete destruction between naturally antagonistic beings such as the wolf and sheep. The destruction performed by the macrophages resembles in certain aspects much more the execution of a criminal within the state. The total death of the decomposed cells, like that of the criminal, result in the maintenance of the association. It is an act of biological justice. Both biological justice and social justice, without being identical, are certainly analogous because they have the same object—the maintenance of the association.

We see then that there are certain forms of struggle which are normal in society,—those which operate, by the special nature of their processes, to maintain the association. If all struggles led to the destruction of the association, societies would never have been formed on the earth. Of course, the macrophages are not animated by a conscious desire to suppress the decomposed elements in order to maintain the health of the entire organism. Sometimes the macrophages are deceived and attack healthy cells, but these are strong enough to prevent the macrophages from conquering them, while the enfeebled cells succumb. By the complex play of these attacks and this resistance, a general equilibrium is obtained and the organism remains vigorous. If the equilibrium is lost the process of dissociation commences and results in death. In an analogous way the same phenomena are reproduced in human society. If the people prevent the ruling classes from abusing their power and if the governments are able to compel citizens to respect the rights of their fellow-citizens, the community remains healthy and vigorous. If the rulers become despotic, or the citizens anarchistic, dissociation commences and the collectivity easily becomes dislocated.

The militarists are therefore right in saying that struggle is a universal law of Nature. It takes place not only between the stars in the celestial spaces, but also between the cells in the human body and between men within society,—but the processes by which this universal struggle operates are immensely varied. If we wish to compare the processes in the different domains in which the phenomena take place, it is necessary to do so with scrupulous care and close attention not only to their points of resemblance, but also to their differences. To consider only the processes which result in total death, and to ignore those which result in partial death is an incomplete and unilateral view, and is therefore anti-scientific because science demands first the recognition of all the phenomena which are accessible to intelligence, and then their final generalization.

The fourth biological error of the philosophy of force consists in its blindness to the true nature of social struggles. According to this philosophy they are based uniquely upon physiological phenomena, such as collective homicide. This is never the case. All social facts, without exception, can be reduced to psychic facts. All political and social institutions are the results of ideas, and the struggle which goes on is a struggle between ideas. It is an illustration of how little social thinking, even of the most elementary character, is done by the human race, that so few persons have grasped the truth, one of the primary axioms in sociology, that the character of social institutions depends upon the character of social ideas.

Social life in the last analysis is a series of actions taken by a certain number of individuals. The genesis of social institutions is exactly the same as the genesis of individual action. In the case of the individual, to take a common illustration, suppose a man goes for a walk in Central Park. This is only possible on one condition, that he represents in his mind a picture of Central Park. If this does not take place the idea of going for a walk in the park does not come to him. Thus the physiological movements made in walking through the park can only be effected if they have been preceded by certain psychic movements. Everything which eventually becomes a reality in action has been first a mental representation, an ideal. In society the process may be illustrated by a change in political institutions. Suppose that at a certain moment a man pictures to himself a political condition, not yet existent, *e.g.*, parliamentary institutions in an absolute monarchy. This man carries through a certain series of measures and obtains the desired result. The country passes from an absolute régime to a constitutional régime. This change is impossible if at some given moment the constitutional régime has not existed in the state of an idea and a future representation in someone's mind. But a mental representation is a series of psychic changes. All institutions, then, are necessarily preceded by psychic changes, by ideas.

In the case of social or collective facts the psychic movements are complicated by another element— propaganda. It is not sufficient that a single individual in a State which is an absolute monarchy should conceive of constitutional institutions and desire to apply them. It is necessary that a large number of persons, the majority of the people or at least the majority of the ruling class, should desire these new institutions. The inventor of the constitutional idea then, if we may use the expression, must commence by communicating his ideas to those around him. This gives rise to a representation of a constitutional régime in other brains like that which he already possesses in his own. Then he must arouse a desire and a will to realize it. When the agreement of wills is put into operation the new institution becomes an accomplished fact. However, the means by which the inventor propagates his idea is a series of inter-psychic acts. The human institution is a series of similar individual movements of the second degree of complexity. The first phase consists in the internal representation of the new human institution, and this representation is then communicated from one individual to other individuals, in the second phase.

International actions are by definition only a modification of human institutions, and follow the same course as domestic political action. If Europe, which has been divided into twenty-five sovereign states, under a system of complete anarchy, in which any state may declare war at any minute, should be united into a federation, what would this signify? It would mean that the twenty-five European states would give a different organization to their mutual relations than that which has heretofore existed. But this different organization would be preceded by an ideal representation and by propaganda from one individual to another, as in the case of institutional changes within a nation: the law would be the same. Ideas, therefore, are the source of institutions.

It seems difficult to contest the truth of this social mechanism, but if this analysis is correct, the philosophy of force fails completely. How can it be maintained that the progress of the human race is caused by collective homicide when it becomes manifest that progress is caused by better social institutions, and that the institutions do not arise from the homicide but from psychic movements, from mental representations.

Suppose we have two groups of human beings arranged in opposing armies, who commence to massacre each other. If we take the imaginary case in which the mutual massacre is complete so that not a single survivor remains, it is evident that there would be no social progress, because there would be no society. If survivors remain, progress depends uniquely on the institutions which govern them. If these institutions are more perfect after than before the battle, there will be progress, but if they are less perfect, there will be retrogression.

After the first Balkan War the condition of the people of Macedonia had improved because they had been freed from the yoke of Turkey. After the second Balkan War their condition was made worse, with the whole country full of refugees and blackened with hatred. In the one case there was progress and in the other retrogression. It is a complete self-deception to consider the progress realized sometimes after war and to neglect entirely the retrogression which follows so often. The claim that collective homicide is the cause of progress is absolutely unsustainable. We must take account of the fact that collective homicide is followed sometimes by progress, sometimes by retrogression. However, if this is so, it is a pure piece of sophistry to maintain that collective homicide, in the case in which it is followed by progress, is the cause of that progress. In science one phenomenon is held to be the cause of the second only when it is always and everywhere followed by the second. Since collective homicide does not always and everywhere precede progress, collective homicide is not the cause of progress. On the contrary, since more perfect political institutions always precede progress, it is the more perfect political institutions which are the cause of progress. But political institutions are the result of certain cerebral movements; therefore it is these cerebral movements and not the muscular movements in the process of collective homicide, which assure progress.

The roundabout way by which the philosophy of force seeks to escape this conclusion is familiar. It is impossible to affirm that collective homicide is the *direct* cause of progress. In the evening after a battle when a hundred thousand men lie upon the ground, some of them killed, the others groaning in agony, it is difficult to pretend at that very moment that the slaughter and the suffering produces progress. Even the distorted "social Darwinism" does not sustain such a preposterous proposition, but the "social Darwinists" affirm that it is the *preparation* for this savagery which furthers progress, because the people which are the better prepared obtain the victory. The preparation for war, it is contended, requires a series of actions which refine the intelligence, therefore collective homicide refines intelligence and consequently makes progress. This neglects the principal consideration, that everything depends on what the conqueror does after the victory. If he establishes a better set of institutions, it is these institutions, and not the battle, which cause progress. Moreover if the sum of intellectual effort employed in preparing for war had been employed directly to better the condition of the human race, this betterment would have proceded more rapidly. The straight line does not cease to be the shortest path between two points when we enter into the domain of sociology.

The object of struggle is to better one's condition. Since the condition of the individual in society can only be bettered by perfecting institutions the struggle in the sociological domain can only take place by inter-psychic processes. Homicide, not being an inter-psychic relation, cannot enter into the category of *social* facts. Homicide is a *pre-social* fact. It is the natural and inevitable form of the struggle between individuals who have not yet formed an association or who are prevented by their organic constitution from associating (as in the case of the wolf and the sheep). From another point of view individual and collective homicide are both *anti-social*. They arrest the course of development of society, and the interrupted progress must be taken up after the battle. The actual setback to all social reform is only less injurious than the eugenic setback of the race caused by the reverse selection of war, which kills off the best of each nation. And most disastrous of all is the effect of war, both on the victors and the vanquished, in the increase of militarism, leading often to a form of despotism, which means a curtailment of the liberty and a contraction of the life of the individual.

It is often said that the struggle of political parties maintains social activities. Activity is life, therefore this struggle leads to progress. This is true but it is necessary to analyse the phenomena more accurately. The struggle of political parties means in the last analysis the existence of liberty, that is, the absolute respect by each citizen of the rights of his neighbour. In other terms it means the suppression of homicide and of violence. If the struggle of parties is of value, it is because this struggle substitutes an intellectual combat (propaganda, agitation, electoral activities, etc.) for the biological combats which consist in slaughter. If the parties recur to homicide, we no longer have a struggle of parties but a civil war. And no one affirms that civil war in general causes the progress of the human race.

Political struggles take place also between the government and the governed. As long as these remain in the intellectual field, they are fruitful. The party in power proposes one program and the opposition another. But as soon as the struggle

between the government and the governed takes
place by biological processes (shootings and hang-
ings on the side of the State, lynching and terrorism on the side of the citizens), life and progress
are arrested, savagery and misery advance at a
tremendous rate. The true nature of a social
struggle which leads to progress is intellectual, it
is the struggle of ideas.

The biological argument for war breaks down
therefore, as soon as we submit it to the test of
a critical analysis.

Let us see how the sociological theories of the
philosophy of force will bear the searchlight of
analysis and reason.

CHAPTER IV

THE GENERAL SOCIOLOGICAL ERRORS

MAN owes his dominant position in the universe to the fact of association. He has increased his productive power enormously by practising mutual aid and the division of labour. Language, literature, science, all civilization results from the fact that man is a member of society, that he co-operates with his fellow-men. The growth of communication and interdependence has bound the human race into one social organism.

But this great fact of association, fully as important and as universal as the fact of struggle, is entirely ignored by the philosophy of force. This is an error in the field of sociology which is as important as the error of ignoring the existence of the physical universe in the realm of biology. The consequences of co-operation are so important for any true theory of human relationships that an entire chapter[1] has been devoted to their consideration, and nothing further need be said at the present time of this colossal error of the philosophy of force.

[1] See Chapter **X.** on *Mutual Aid as a Law of Nature.*

The second great social error of the philosophy of force, is in regard to the limits of association. The cause of progress is held to be homicide between societies, but never homicide within societies. Thus General von Bernhardi says[1]:

The State alone, so Schleiermacher once taught, gives the individual the highest degree of life. . . . To expand the idea of the State into that of humanity, and thus to entrust apparently higher duties to the individual, leads to error, since in the human race conceived as a whole, struggle and, by implication, the most essential vital principle would be ruled out. Any action in favour of collective humanity outside the limits of the State and nationality is impossible.

The boundaries of a State are supposed to mark the limits of association. Within these limits struggle and collective homicide are harmful, but beyond these limits struggle and collective homicide constitute the causes of the progress of the human race. This makes it necessary to consider the nature of association and its limits.

The true nature of association can best be understood by studying it in its simple form in biology. The hydra or fresh-water polyp, for example, which has the form of a simple tube, is furnished with a set of vibrating cilia which force a current of water into the mouth of the tube, and from this water the cells in the interior derive their nourishment. This illustrates the most elementary form

[1] *Germany and the Next War*, p. 25.

7

of vital circulation.   The cells at the mouth of the tube transmit to those in the interior a raw product which has not undergone any change.   Higher in the biological scale the process is not so simple. The cells differentiate themselves more and more. They specialize upon widely different functions and exchange the products of their activities, but it is always the phenomena of exchange, the vital circulation, which constitutes association.

It is important to note that distance plays only a subordinate rôle; nearness may facilitate the vital circulation between the parts, but it is the vital circulation itself which is the essential of association.

Two living beings placed side by side without any vital circulation between them form separate individual organisms, and they might as well live on opposite extremities of the earth.   A bed of oysters, for example, does not form a society.

As we pass to the higher realm of the biological scale, vital circulation passes through innumerable forms and results in an ever increasing interdependence of parts so that in the highest forms the solidarity becomes so great that all parts suffer with the suffering of any one, and if the suffering of one part becomes too acute, the death of the entire organism necessarily results.

Biology and sociology form a single science divided into two vast provinces.   It is impossible to say at what precise point biological phenomena end and sociological phenomena begin.   The phenomena which are found in the association of cells are paralleled by the phenomena of the association of individuals. It is vital circulation which forms societies, just as it forms biological organisms.

Within the human species vital circulation consists in the exchange of services and takes on three principal forms—the displacement of men, the displacement of goods, and the transmission of ideas. The displacement of men is illustrated by the hundreds of thousands of tourists who go from America to Europe each year, and by the migratory labour which has become so striking a phenomenon of modern industrial life. The displacement of goods constitutes commerce. The transmission of ideas may take place through material objects (books, reviews, newspapers, letters), by means of men (preachers, lecturers, professors, etc.), or by means of electricity (telegraph, cable, telephone, wireless).

The limits of association are determined by the limits of interdependence, and these limits are determined by the vital circulation. From the point of view of concrete reality the whole world is a unity in modern times and the entire human race forms one social organism. The failure of the wheat crop in India or floods in China raises the cost of living all over the world. A scientific discovery or a cure for disease made in the universities of Germany or Japan becomes available almost instantly to the scientists of every nation.

The appearance of the bubonic plague in Asia compels every country of Europe and America to take precautions against its spread. When the first Balkan War broke out in south-eastern Europe in 1912 the scarcity of capital, the calling in of credits, and the stagnation of trade in Europe caused banks to fail in Brazil and other countries in South America, and unemployed men to walk the streets of Chicago and New York, so delicate is the financial nervous system of the modern world. The Austrian Archduke Ferdinand is assassinated in the capital of Bosnia and men begin to murder each other, not only all over Europe, but in the heart of Africa, on the shores of Asia, and on the islands of the Pacific. If the British Isles were cut off from the vital circulation for any considerable period of time, three-fourths of the British people would starve to death, since Great Britain produces foodstuffs enough to supply only one-fourth of her population.

In the face of these concrete realities it is impossible to contend that the limits of association are marked by the boundaries of the State. Moreover it can be shown that the State, far from corresponding to any concrete realities, is an abstract conception, clearly subjective in character. The boundaries of the State change so rapidly that a map of Europe, only a few years old is practically worthless. The distinctive characteristic of a State is sovereignty, but this is such an intangible quality that it is impossible in many cases to

decide whether a State is sovereign or not. Is
Canada, for example, a sovereign State? In
international law the question would be answered
in the negative, yet it is free to make its own tariff,
its own laws and conduct its own affairs, just as
though it were an independent State. Is Persia
an independent State? In accordance with the
answer to this question, which depends upon
subjective impressions, the boundaries of Russia
and of the British Empire enlarge or contract.
Yet according to these subjective impressions,
corresponding to no concrete realities, collective
homicide is in the one case the cause of progress
and in the other a disaster, since it constitutes in
one case a foreign war, and in the other a civil
war. What is the essential difference which
would make a war between England and Scotland
contribute to the advance of civilization before the
countries were united, but not afterward?

It is because the philosophy of force ignores the
existence of the universe and the fact of association
based on concrete realities that the artificial and
oftentimes subjective limits of the State are falsely
considered to be the limits of association instead
of the true limits, which are marked by interdependence and the vital circulation. It is the
struggle against the physical environment which
impels men to associate themselves whether in the
town or city, where they desire to have paved
streets, electric lighting, and proper sanitation, or
in the larger units of the province and State, where

they associate in order to obtain better communications, justice, and the security which will enable them to carry on their activities more effectively. The philosophy of force fails to realize that vital circulation, the division of labour and association are advantageous in proportion to the extent of the association, and that the human race would reach its highest possible degree of happiness and prosperity if the limits of association were extended to include all mankind and to coincide with the objective realities, vital circulation and interdependence,—instead of stopping at the artificial and subjective boundaries of the State.

The great war itself has contributed towards the breaking down of the old idea of States as sovereign and independent units. It has been found that no nation in Europe can rely for its security and defense upon its own military and naval forces, but must depend upon alliances, ententes, and agreements which it makes with other nations, surrendering in the process a large part of its sovereignty in the questions of war and peace. Even the old fiction of the philosophy of force that association within the States is limited by natural antagonisms has been shown to be false. On the side of the Allies, for example, English, French, and Russians, Indians, Turcomen, Egyptians, Algerians, Japanese, Bengalese, every possible combination of race, language, and religion, white, yellow, brown, and black skins have been fighting side by side. England has made common cause with its hereditary enemy France and its great autocratic rival Empire of Russia, despite a century of antagonism with the one and the Crimean War to prevent access to warm waters by the other, while the Russians and Japanese, less than ten years after their great conflict in Asia, have been allied in the same war. In the face of these outstanding facts the theory of the limits of association as marked by natural antagonisms falls to the ground.

If we examine the other grounds which are given as marking the natural limits of association, all turn out to be untenable. The theory that geographical contiguity marks the limit of association is refuted by the British Empire, with England and New Zealand on opposite sides of the globe. The theory that it is a common language which marks the limits of association disappears, when we examine the case of Switzerland, where the French, German, and Italian speaking peoples form a single association; and of Canada where French and English speaking populations live happily together in close association. The theory of common racial derivation shatters on the fact of North America, where people of all races and births have no difficulty in forming a single association almost continental in extent.

We are forced to conclude then that the apparent limits of human association are conventional to a very great degree and that these limits are constantly varying. But this fact ruins the philosophy

of force. It affirms that collective homicide produces civilization only when it takes place at the
exterior of groups; but this exterior is a subjective
error of our minds. Such an exterior does not
exist. From the point of view of realities, all
humanity forms a single association, since the vital
circulation is now established between all the individuals who inhabit the earth. The struggles
which have taken place between men since antiquity have always taken place in the interior of
association, because the very fact itself that the two
societies have entered into contact shows that the
vital circulation was established between them and
therefore that they formed a single social group.
All collective homicides since the commencement
of history have been, from the biological point of
view, civil wars, because the distinction between
a civil war and a foreign war is not in any concrete
reality, but solely in the purely arbitrary conceptions of men's minds. Since, according to the
philosophy of force, progress is only realized by
foreign wars, progress would never have taken
place, because speaking properly, there have never
been any foreign wars.

Another error of the philosophy of force is its
failure to recognize the true nature of war, to
which it ascribes such important results. War is in
reality a process of dissociation. It corresponds
to disease, which is a rupture of equilibrium in
biology. The nature of war as a process of dis-

sociation is universally conceded in the case of civil war, as when the North and South fought in 1861. It is equally true but less generally realized that war is equally a process of dissociation when it occurs on the outside of political groups. It is a dissociation in this case precisely because it *prevents* association. The economic and intellectual bonds which unite the nations of Europe in the twentieth century are much more intimate than those which united the provinces of France, for example, in the seventeenth century, but the French provinces in the seventeenth century did not consider that it would serve any useful purposes to wage war with one another, although the European nations do consider it useful in the twentieth century. From the political point of view, therefore, the association between the European nations in the twentieth century is less intimate than that between the French provinces at the time of Louis XIV. Without war Europe would have been united. As a result of war, it is disunited. Therefore war is a process of dissociation at the exterior of the political organization as well as in the interior. Without war, there would have been only the fact of association between human beings. The political unity of the human race, the establishment of justice between all the nations of the earth, and the suppression of war, are all equivalent statements.

War and dissociation are therefore synonymous terms. Herbert Spencer and others have affirmed that war has been the cause of civilization because it alone has rendered possible the formation of the great nationalities like France and England. Exactly the opposite is the truth. War has always retarded the formation of great collectivities because it has created hatreds and bitterness. It was the wars between Scotland and England which prevented the union of these two countries for so long. It was the war of 1870, with the bitterness and desire for revenge left in its train, which has been one of the principal obstacles to the organization of a European Federation. The second Balkan War of 1912, with the hatred and bitterness which it caused, prevented the formation of a Balkan alliance. Without war the federation of the entire human race would have been accomplished long ago.

It is often asserted that war has produced the unity of the German Empire. Nothing could be further from the truth, which is that war prevented the unity of the German Empire for nearly nine centuries. As late as the fourteenth century Germany was divided into between five hundred and six hundred sovereignties which were almost continually at war with each other. In spite of the passionate longing of the German people to be united, the unity could not be accomplished even as late as 1860 because the kings of Hanover, Bavaria, and Württemberg would not give up their sovereignty, which means the right to declare war upon each other whenever they felt inclined to do so.   In Germany as elsewhere it was the philosophy of force that prevented unity. "No country had so little militarism in the Middle Ages as England," says Mr. Lacombe.[1]   Consequently it was the first nation to unify, while Germany's unity, on account of the dominance of the philosophy of force, was the slowest of all in forming.   When it is realized that national unity merely means that the people inhabiting a country have found another way of adjusting their differences, other than wholesale murder on the field of battle, it is at once apparent that war is always a process of dissociation, never of association.

The indirect result of war as a process of dissociation retards the progress of the human race much more than the direct result in the number of men actually killed and maimed.   This is because association is not an addition, but a multiplication of vital power.   Ten men working together under a system of division of labour produce, not ten times as much as ten men working alone, but one hundred times as much.   In the same way war is not a subtraction of vital power but a division.

Since even the philosophy of force recognizes that war is a social disease when it occurs within the limits of human society, and since the growth of communication and of interdependence has made the entire human race into a single social organism, all war must now be considered as a social disease.   Health is a state which makes for growth,

[1] *L'histoire considérée comme science*, p. 4.

for the intensification of life, and for happiness. Moreover, health is the natural condition because it corresponds with the maximum of vital intensity. If the intensity of life is not the natural state then it must be feebleness of life which is natural. This would mean that the natural state of a living being would be to possess the weakest possible amount of life, that is to say not to be a living being, but this is contradictory. Growth and life are therefore synonymous terms. The growth is at first physiological, then economic and intellectual. A person who becomes every day poorer and less intelligent is in a morbid state. Since mutual aid is the most effective process for intensifying life, the failure to employ this process results in a diminution of life and therefore in a state of social disease. Therefore, all hostilities between men, which have as an inevitable result a dissociation, is a diseased condition. It is precisely because it is a commencement of dissociation and contrary to nature that homicide is considered as immoral; for, as we shall see later,[1] morality, according to Darwin, is the sum of rules to which we should conform ourselves in order to attain the maximum of vital intensity.

Since the state of social health for the human species is in the association of all men, this is also the natural state. Otherwise we should have to say that the natural condition of a being is the condition of disease; i.e., that the maximum of vital

[1] See the chapter on "Darwin's Theory of Social Progress."

intensity consists in the condition of a minimum of vital intensity, which is a *reductio ad absurdum.* But if the association of the entire human race is the natural condition of our species we can realize how much Marshal von Moltke deceived himself when he said that war (*i.e.,* the diseased condition of our species) conforms to the order of things established by God. If this were true, God would have established an order of things which is anarchy, and therefore the disorder of things. In other words God would have established a disorder which is an order. The contradiction could not be more complete.

The philosophy of force fails entirely to realize that the condition of social disease is due to error. The reason why the association of all men is not yet complete is because of the wide-spread belief that men can increase their well-being more rapidly by despoiling their neighbours than by working themselves to adapt the physical environment, *i.e.,* to produce wealth.

The social disease of anarchy in human relations is the result of the belief in the effectiveness of exploitation and banditism. The idea that men can enrich themselves most quickly by despoiling their neighbours has profoundly affected the structure of all our national and international institutions. By far the largest part of the energies of all national governments are absorbed in the provisions for national defence. But there would be no need of national defence unless there were danger of aggression and there would be no danger of aggression unless the motives for aggression were present, or believed to be present, in the minds of possible enemies. Collective homicide is always a means to an end. The immense majority of the wars of history have had exploitation as a motive of the aggressors. The disappearance of the idea that men can enrich themselves more quickly by exploitation than by productive labour will mark the greatest intellectual revolution in the history of the human race, and will open for our species the way to an era of prosperity and happiness of which we cannot now form the faintest picture.

A fuller consideration of this error will be given in the chapter on "Justice and the Expansion of Life," but a few illustrations will be useful in showing the nature of the error involved. In the first place, it is untrue to say that *men* can enrich themselves most rapidly by exploitation. In order that Peter may rob Paul, it is necessary first that Paul shall have produced something. The vast majority of the human race are engaged in productive labour. The philosophy of force ignores these, for it ignores the physical universe and the real struggle for existence, which is the struggle against physical environment. The statement must be limited then to mean that not men but the *exploiters* can enrich themselves more rapidly by preying upon their fellow-men than by productive labour. This amounts already to a great limitation upon the number of those who find exploitation advantageous.

We must still further limit this number by the consideration that it is only the *fortunate* exploiters who find it advantageous. The highwaymen, thieves, and burglars who are unsuccessful in all their ventures, must soon die of starvation. Within the State direct exploitation has long been considered criminal, has been prosecuted, and has steadily become less lucrative. On the other hand, indirect exploitation, authorized by the State, has been practised upon an immense scale in modern society. It takes the various forms of monopolies, protective tariffs, subsidies, bounties, and privileges of all kinds. But even here qualifications are necessary, which greatly reduce the number of possible beneficiaries. The woollen manufacturer, for example, protected by Schedule K of the old tariff in the United States, was enabled to draw tribute from all American consumers of woollen goods, who were obliged to pay him a higher price than they would have had to pay for foreign goods. But he was not the only beneficiary. He was obliged, in turn, to pay tribute to all the manufacturers who were benefited by the other schedules of protective tariff. If a balance were drawn up, showing the gains and the losses due to the protective tariff, the number of those who would find their gains greater than their losses would be very few.

It is the international form of the same idea,

that banditism is the quickest way to acquire
wealth, which underlies political conquest and the
system of armed peace.   It is almost universally
believed that a nation can use its military power
to gain important advantages for its people.
Norman Angell in *The Great Illusion* has examined
the different ways in which it is supposed that
military power can insure economic advantages—
markets and foreign trade, indemnities, colonies,
etc.—and has demonstrated that the supposed advantages are in all the cases which he considered
illusions.   But this demonstration of the economic
futility of military force, when used for aggression,
will become effective enough to induce the governments to give up the system of international
banditism and anarchy, and enter into a system
of world organization under justice and law, only
when the realization of this truth is sufficiently
wide-spread.   This is because the actions of men
are governed, not by the truth, but by what they
believe to be the truth.   If what men believe is
error, their actions will be in accord with this error,
and will lead to a rupture of vital equilibrium and
the condition of the social disease.   The action
of nations in continuing the system of war is a
consequence of wrong ideas.   It is like the action
of a man who touches a wire charged with a high
tension current of electricity.   He *believes* that
the wire is not dangerous.   As the result of his
error he suffers severely.   His vital intensity is
decreased and the injury to the organism may

even result in death. It is because the nations *believe* that exploitation by means of military power, aggressively used, is an effective method of promoting national welfare that they refuse to give up their sovereignty,—*i.e.*, right to attack each other on any occasion whatever,—and to establish the federation of the entire human race.

The dissociation of mankind, therefore, is due to error. But error cannot be eternal. Truth once discovered makes its way irresistibly until it is victorious. After Copernicus had discovered that the earth revolved around the sun, not all the forces of reaction, of persecution, of superstition, or of an obscurantist theology could prevent the intellectual revolution which established this truth in the minds of men. The great war has demonstrated on a colossal scale that error means death, that military force cannot be successfully used for aggression in the modern world, that the system of international anarchy, based upon national banditism and exploitation, is disastrous to the people of the nations which live under that system. With the results of error so plainly visible, it is only a question of time when the truth will be recognized, that justice, not force and exploitation, is the great secret of the expansion of life. It is the realization of the connection between the errors in the minds of men, and the social disease and death which result from these errors, which lies at the foundation of the great prophecy of hope, "the truth shall make you free."

8

CHAPTER V

THE SPECIAL SOCIOLOGICAL ERRORS

ABOUT a century ago, in 1806, Cuvier said of geology, that it was "a tissue of hypotheses and conjectures, so vain and so contradictory to each other that it had become almost impossible to pronounce its name without exciting laughter." All sorts of wild explanations were put forward to explain observed facts. For example, to account for the shells and fossils found high up in the Alps, the hypothesis was advanced that they had been carried there by the Great Deluge; another hypothesis was that they were only "freaks of nature," bearing merely an accidental resemblance to animals and plants; while the celebrated Voltaire suggested that the shells and fossils must have been dropped there by the pilgrims, who used to cross the mountains in former centuries on their way to Rome. It was the pre-scientific period in geology, when a great mass of facts had been accumulated, but all the observations were still in a chaotic condition. No clear guiding principle had been found, around which the known facts could be grouped. The entire subject was in confusion and disorder. The most childish and incredible theories could be formulated and published without injuring the reputation of their author.

The same situation, to a large extent, holds in the science of sociology a century later. Many persons still deny to sociology the right to be considered as an exact science, and pour ridicule upon it. Outside of the American universities very little serious attention is given to the subject in the academic world. In the German universities, for example, which have led the world in the studies of the humanities, philosophy, and history, not a single course in sociology was given as late as 1914.

The reasons why sociology is discredited at the present time are largely the same reasons which discredited geology a century ago. Numerous observations have been collected, and numerous facts have been placed in evidence, but no Ariadne's thread has been discovered which leads out of the labyrinth, and all manner of hypotheses can be advanced without any necessity for bringing them to the touchstone of concrete facts. With the exception of a few noteworthy books, the subject of sociology is in a state of complete incoherence. Biological phenomena are confused with social facts. Men who call themselves specialists in the subject can still seriously identify the relations between France and Germany, for example, with those between a cat and a rat without doing great injury to their reputation and without exciting much ridicule. Some examples of the false reasoning, sophistries, and contradictions, still current in the subject, are given in the present chapter—enough to show the pre-scientific condition of the subject. And the state of sociology is reflected in all the other social sciences of which sociology should be the keystone. "We live in the stone age of political science," says Prof. Lester F. Ward. "In politics we are still savages."[1]

Sociology seems to confirm the law of three states formulated by the founder of the science, August Comte. It is still almost completely in the metaphysical period. It has not yet entered into the second state, the positive phase. It does not place itself in direct and immediate contact with the concrete facts. Vague theories, general propositions, affirmations which are naïve, in their lack of precision, still characterize many of the books on the subject.

As an example of the purely metaphysical reasoning which is still so common in the literature of the subject, and which takes no account of the most elementary concrete facts, the following phrase from August Comte himself is illuminating:

War constitutes at the beginning the most simple means of procuring subsistence.[2]

---

[1] *American Journal of Sociology*, March, 1905, p. 645.

[2] *Cours de philosophie positive*, 3rd edition, 1889, volume iv., p. 506.

This illustration is the more remarkable coming from one of the greatest philosophers of our time and one who has protested with such power against the metaphysical spirit. As soon as he penetrates into the domain of social phenomena, he falls into the most abstract reasoning. Comte failed to see the simple fact that in order that conquerors might be able to obtain food from their victims, it is necessary that the victims should first have produced a supply of food from the earth. War, then, is not the most *simple* means of procuring subsistence. On the contrary it is a very complex means, since it is a means of at least two degrees; involving first, the production of a food supply by the victims, and second, the series of acts necessary in order that the conqueror may seize that supply. When one tribe of Indians falls upon another tribe, conquers it, and seizes its corn, the effort required for this war of conquest is employed for purely destructive purposes and does not add a single ear of corn to the available supply. The corn comes from the earth and is produced by labour, and the massacre of the labourers who produce it does not increase their productiveness.

Comte, moreover, on account of a failure of reasoning which is one of the most widespread of our intellectual defects, thinks only of the conqueror. If the statement is laid down as representing a general law, how is it possible to affirm that war is the most simple means of procuring subsistence for the *victim?* War does not procure any subsistence for him. On the contrary it causes the victim to lose that which he had produced by his labour, and which the conqueror seizes from him. As soon as we bring it to the test of concrete facts, therefore, Comte's statement breaks down in two ways. For the conqueror, war is not the most simple method of procuring subsistence, but is a very complex means, involving first production by the vanquished and second robbery by the conqueror; and in the case of the vanquished it is not a means of procuring subsistence at all.

In the sciences of astronomy or physics an obligation is felt to observe the facts closely and to make direct observations, but when we pass into the social realm, this obligation is no longer felt. Theory is abstracted from all contact with concrete facts and the most superficial association of ideas is considered sufficient.

To the aboriginal Indians, looking across the river at the cornfields of a neighbouring tribe, and not sufficiently trained in the science of economics to envisage the complete process of production, war may *seem* the simplest means of procuring subsistence.

But a scientific sociology ought to be sufficiently advanced to recognize that the simplest means of procuring subsistence is by productive labour, and to take account of the primary processes of production as well as the secondary processes such as exchange and robbery; even if it does not go so far as to examine the inevitable social reactions which result from aggression—the resistance of the victim, the increasing reciprocal preparations for defence, and the increasing diversion of labour from productive to unproductive purposes. Where the processes of exchange have been established the amount of grain available, of course, will increase with the proportion of labour which can be used for productive purposes, or with the security of the country. But the effect of war is precisely to retard the work of productive agriculture, on account of the insecurity which it creates in the country. At no time, and in no place, neither at "the beginning" nor at the present time, has war facilitated the means of obtaining subsistence. Its effect has always been diametrically opposite.

The error of false comparison runs through much of the philosophy of force. Plants struggle for sunlight or moisture in a field, therefore, the advocates of this philosophy claim, struggle is a natural law, and the citizens of civilized states ought to massacre each other until the end of time. It would be difficult to find a "therefore" more arbitrary, on account of the enormous difference between plants in a field and the citizens in a civilized state. The true biological analogies have been pointed out in a preceding chapter, and the superficial comparison of the philosophy of force is mentioned again here only because it is an example of the class of errors in logic. Purely external analogies can be of no service in building the structure of a positive science. It is necessary to compare facts which are comparable.

The largest, and practically the most important group of errors consists of those due to one-sided reasoning, or what has been called the unilateral aberration. This error is caused by the failure to realize that in all matters connected with the relations between men the action of one party makes only one half of the operation, and that we must necessarily misunderstand the operation as a whole unless we think of the action of the two parties together: as that defence necessarily implies attack; that victory necessarily implies defeat, and that there can be no conqueror without a corresponding conquered.

The hypnotism of the defensive is one of the most common forms of one-sided reasoning. When an appeal is made for recruits they are always enlisted "to defend their country," but nothing is ever said about attacking the other man's country. In the same way it is the business of the soldier to sacrifice his life in the defence of his nation. Nothing is said about what must constitute his real work if he is successful, the killing of other men who are similarly engaged in defence. The official documents published by all the countries involved at the beginning of the great war furnish striking examples of the unilateral aberration in orthodox diplomacy. Every government demonstrates to its own satisfaction, and that of its own people, that it is fighting only in self-defence, but if no one attacked, there would, of course, be no need of defence.

A characteristic example of one-sided reasoning and the hypnotism of the defensive is given by de Molinari, who says:

It is war that has produced security.[1]

At first sight it is difficult to understand how anyone could attempt to sustain a proposition so false. The truth is, of course, the exact opposite. War always has established insecurity and destroyed security. Only the disappearance of war could really establish security. The error could only be made by one who places himself at the point of view of the defensive, and considers all wars under the hypnotism of this one-sided view. In another place de Molinari also affirms that war has established security by bringing an end to the attacks of barbarians. He evidently forgets that these attacks were the most important part of the war, and that without them security would have always been complete. In this case, as in all other analogous cases, insecurity comes from war, and security has commenced from the moment when wars have ceased.

The same one-sided reasoning which is so com-

[1] *Grandeur et décadence de la guerre*, Paris, 1898, p. iv.

mon in regard to active or dynamic war is also almost universal in regard to latent or potential wars, the condition of armed peace. In practically all the discussions of armament, the tendency is to consider the problem of two parties—war— in terms of one. For example: Winston Churchill, as First Lord of the British Admiralty, has laid down the following rule:

The way to secure peace is to be so strong that victory in the event of war is certain.

When this "axiom" is stated in terms of two nations, it amounts to saying that for two nations to keep the peace, each must be stronger than the other. This is, of course, a physical impossibility, and the great war was brought about, in large measure, by all the nations attempting to achieve this physical impossibility—each nation trying to secure peace by being stronger than all the others.

Another illustration of one-sided reasoning is found in the argument that "preparedness" is the cause of civilization. After the defeat of 1870 many of the French people claimed that if France had been better prepared for war this would not have taken place, and that the retardation of civilization which followed would not have been produced. Therefore, preparation for war is the cause of civilization. It is not necessary to consider here whether peace can be secured by being prepared for war according to the unilateral axiom of Winston Churchill (and of the Navy Leagues of all nations). It is merely necessary to note that we are still dealing with the hypnotism of the defensive. The true reasoning is as follows: If the Germans had not been prepared for war before 1870 it would not have taken place, hence civilization would have advanced with the greatest rapidity in Europe. Preparation for war is not the cause of civilization, but the chief obstacle which prevents its development.

Another form of one-sided reasoning runs as follows: War has made it possible to dominate barbarism; therefore, war has made civilization. Thus we are told that without war the white race could not have settled the North American Continent, which would still be overrun by wandering tribes of Indians. But the success of a method of justice and friendship used by William Penn in dealing with the Indians and settling Pennsylvania without war, demonstrates that this is not true, and indicates how it might have been possible to civilize the entire continent without the sacrifice of lives and treasure and the waste of time involved in the Indian Wars, which were caused chiefly by the injustice of the white settlers; or by their quarrels, in which they enlisted the aid of the Indians as in the case of the French and Indian Wars.

But sometimes it is the barbarians who have attacked the civilized people, as when the Turks overran Constantinople and eastern Europe in the fifteenth century. But the fact that the civilized people had to act on the defensive and employ force to meet that used in the attack by the barbarians, does not change the fact that war has not advanced civilization, if we look at war from the point of view of the whole operation instead of taking a one-sided view. Always war has retarded civilization, and even when the more civilized peoples have triumphed, which is far from being always the case, war has meant a loss of time, a circuitous route in the progress of civilization instead of a direct route. The development of the Balkan peoples has been retarded for several centuries on account of war, and their backward condition has retarded the progress of all the other peoples of Europe. The Asiatic invasion of the territory of Russia in the thirteenth century established despotism among the Russians, and this despotism has retarded their progress for six centuries. Whenever we examine the facts from the point of view of the whole effect instead of the unilateral aberration, we find that war has never advanced, but always retarded, civilization.

It is only through the error of one-sided reasoning, that moral benefits can be attributed to war. As usually interpreted, a righteous war is one in which *our* nation was victorious or fought for a just cause, but if our nation was right, the enemy must have been wrong, and since war is essentially a matter of two parties, no war can be more than fifty per cent. righteous.   Both parties to a dispute may be wrong, but they cannot both be right. If it is noble for a man to sacrifice himself for an ideal, to defend his country and his rights, and to lay down his life for a great cause, then it is equally base and ignoble to attack other men's lives and rights, to tyrannize over their consciences, to destroy their ideals by force.   But every aggressor must of necessity commit these misdeeds.   Since there can be no war without an aggressor, war must be counted not as the cause of the progress of civilization but as one of the chief causes of the degradation of the human race.

The test for one-sided reasoning is the rule of universality.   Let us apply this rule, for example, to the following statement by Ernest Renan.

. . . Fidelity to a monarch (something which democracy holds to be base and stupid) is that which gives strength and extends the possession of territory.[1]

Renan is thinking of the fidelity of the Prussians to King William I. which resulted in the gain of Alsace and Lorraine for Germany.   As usual, in one-sided reasoning, he is thinking only of the conqueror and leaves the conquered out of account, but if the fidelity to the King resulted in the gain of territory for Germany, it resulted equally in the loss of these provinces to France, for it is impossible that one State should annex a

[1] *La réforme intellectuelle et morale*, p. 293.

province without another State losing it, since space cannot be created. If we admit for the sake of argument that it is advantageous for the despoiler to despoil his own species, it is nevertheless contrary to all logic to affirm that it is also advantageous to the *despoiled;* but the despoiled should receive attention as well as the despoiler in a general statement. The conquered is just as much of a reality as the conqueror. If Renan had said: "Fidelity to a monarch extends the territory of the *conqueror*," he might have been correct, but when he says, "Fidelity to a monarch extends territory," the statement is untrue. In other words, in order that general reasoning should be logical it must not be one-sided. If we wish to know whether reasoning is correct, we must examine it from all sides. For example, if the general statement is made "it is in the interest of all nations to respect the right of their neighbours," this can be verified immediately by applying it to many nations. For example, if France had always scrupulously respected the rights of Germany and Germany the rights of France, the prosperity of both nations would now be much greater than it is. Therefore in conducting themselves in this manner, scrupulously respecting the rights of their neighbours, they would have been acting in conformity with their true interests.

After the errors due to one-sided reasoning come a series of confusions which indicate the shallowness of the discussion of the subject. For example, war is often confused with victory. Thus in advocating a war to defend "national honour" and "vital interests," the assumption is always present that the war will result in victory. If the war should result, not in victory, but in defeat, there is no guarantee, of course, that the "national honour" or "vital interests" will be secured. Austria was ready to go to war with Servia in 1913 because the "vital interests" of Austria demanded that Servia should not have a "little window on the sea" of the Adriatic. In 1914 Austria did actually declare war on Servia because her "national honour" demanded that the assassination of the Archduke should be punished. On both sides the assumption was made that war would result in victory. But with growing world-unity, the assumption that war and victory are synonymous is not always justified even when the opposed forces are apparently so unequal as those of Austria and Servia. In the modern world the possibility of international complications must always be taken into account. No one can prophesy at the beginning of a war what the end will be.

In this confusion of war with victory, we are dealing with the same confusion which was at the bottom of the duelling system as a method of defending individual honour and interest. This theory was exploded for the case of the individual duel, when Aaron Burr, who was in the wrong, killed Alexander Hamilton, almost universally considered to have had justice and right on his side, in the last great duel fought in the Anglo-Saxon world.

It is this confusion of war with victory which is at the bottom of our belief in war as a method of solving international problems. Thus the *revanche* party in France has maintained for more than forty-four years that "war is the only solution of the question of Alsace-Lorraine." If this were true, why did not the war of 1870 solve the question? And if the war of 1870 could not solve the problem of Alsace-Lorraine, how can war solve this or any other problem? Suppose the Germans to be completely defeated and Alsace-Lorraine back in the possession of the French, then the Germans would have lost a province, with great German cities like Strassburg cut off from the living body of Germany, and they would begin to arm themselves to get it back as they did after Louis XIV. took it from them in 1648. It is evident that the assumption that war and victory are synonymous is unjustifiable, and as we shall see more especially in the next chapter, force cannot solve complex social and international problems. All that is meant by solving a question by war is that the victory should be on the side of the one who is speaking. However, no one can be absolutely sure of the victory. If they were, there would be no war. The Prince of Monaco does not declare war upon France, no matter how greatly his national honour or vital interests are injured, because he knows perfectly well that he would be defeated. In order that two countries shall go to war, there must be a chance for victory on both sides. But this means that there must also be a chance for defeat on both sides, and that the confusion of war and victory, therefore, is necessarily an illogical one.

Another confusion which presents a formidable obstacle in the way of world federation is that which identifies unity with despotism. The spectre of another Roman Empire ruled by a Cæsar raised to the height of a demigod, and trampling on the rights of nationalities, still haunts the minds of many thinkers when the idea of unity of the world is suggested. Renan says:

The nations will not endure forever. They have commenced and they will finish. The confederation of Europe, in all probability, will replace them. But this is not the law of the century in which we live. At the present time the existence of the nations is good, even necessary. Their existence is the guarantee of the liberty which would be lost if the world had only one law and one master.[1]

The confusion to which this identification of unity with despotism gives rise is clear. The federation of the world means the abolition of war and therefore the end of international anarchy, but when federation and unity are identified with

[1] *Qu'est-ce qu'une nation?* Paris, 1882, p. 28.

9

despotism, then anarchy and war become synonymous with liberty.

It is difficult to see how this confusion of unity with despotism can persist so obstinately when so many examples of federation without despotism are presented by the modern world. In North America the forty-eight commonwealths of the United States have entered into a voluntary federation without loss of liberty and without coming under the rule of a despot. The cantons of the Swiss Republic furnish another example of unity with liberty. An illustration of a still looser federation, more valuable because it foreshadows the loose form in which the unity of the world will at first be brought about, is given by the self-governing nations of the British Empire. Between these nations, which are sovereign in all but name, the use of force has been definitely abandoned, yet there is not a trace of despotism in this unity. On the contrary the principle of home rule has been carried to its most extreme degree.

Another confusion, similar to that illustrated by the quotations from Renan, consists in identifying federation with centralization. Many who consider the federation of the seventy million people of the German Empire or the hundred million people of the United States of America a good thing, consider nevertheless that the federation of the fifteen hundred million people of the human race would be an evil. In considering the limits of association it is apparent that there is no basis for this view in the nature of the association itself. On the contrary the benefits of association are in proportion to its extent and the larger the area it includes the more advantageous it becomes. The objection is based on the confusion of federation with centralization. The history of the process of federation in America and the strength of the sentiment in favour of State rights even after this doctrine has largely outlived its usefulness, indicates that there is no need to fear that national rights are likely to be swamped in a process of world centralization. All the indications are that in the future as in the past the process of unity will lag far behind the needs of the nations. The centrifugal forces will more than outbalance the centripetal. The remedy for bad organization or too much centralization is not to be found in disorganization or anarchy. It is to be found in good organization with a wise balance between the central and local powers.

Along with the errors of one-sided reasoning and the confusion due to lack of penetrating thinking should be classed such sophisms as:

1. That belief is a proof of reality,
2. The fallacy of the transitory phase,
3. The sophism *post hoc ergo propter hoc.*

1. The philosophy of force holds that if a belief has been dominant in the world for a long

time it must have some reason for existence; it must correspond with some real need. "War always has been and always will be, therefore it is a biological and sociological necessity." The advocates of this doctrine quote approvingly Pope's line "Whatever is, is right." This sophism is a part of the general tendency to make thought parasitic upon action, to justify the conditions which we find in the world about us without submitting them to critical analysis. It is intimately related to the social fatalism which we shall study more closely later, but this philosophy fails to take account of the fact that social and political institutions are created by men and that man is subject to error. An error which has been dominant for thousands of years does not become for that reason the truth. Neither the duration nor the universality of an idea has anything to do with the truth. At the time when witches were burned, the belief in witchcraft was almost universal in the Western world. At one time Columbus stood alone in opposing the almost universal belief that the earth was flat, yet Columbus was right and the almost universal belief was wrong.

2. The sophism of the transitory state consists in the assertion that a thing which is wrong or evil in itself is a good thing because without it a certain other desirable condition could not have been realized. Thus Spencer asserts that war has been a good thing in the past because it forced men to co-operate, and because without co-opera-

tion, and therefore without war, there would have been no civilization. Prof. Lester F. Ward asserts that slavery has been the sole means by which man has been enabled to attain the industrial stage. Therefore war, which has rendered slavery possible, has been the cause of the civilization of our species, because it could not have been realized, naturally, without industry. In the same way others affirm, for example, that the human spirit would never have attained the phase of positive thought if it had not traversed the errors of animism. I am not here concerned with the truth or falsity of the assertion that without these transitory phases the desirable later stages could not have been reached. Even if we adopt completely false assumptions, as that civilization would have been impossible without war, the conclusion does not follow that war was a good thing. The correct conclusion is that the true good would have been civilization without war, industrial labour without slavery, the positive spirit in thought without animism. War, slavery, and animism have been only evils, if for no other reason than that they have represented a loss of time.

To many the discussion of these sophistries will seem useless and academic. Slavery and animism have been abolished, they will say, and it is not necessary to prove that war has not been a good thing in the past. All we have to demonstrate is that it has served its purpose and is not a good thing at the present time. The reply is, first, that if sociology is ever to become a real science, it must follow the truth wherever it may lead; and, second, that the correction of error in any department of human life is always worth while because every error, through its ramifications, distorts social theory in many places. Thus the reasoning in regard to slavery and animism and other transition phases of this nature are all used as buttresses of the apology for war and the philosophy of force. Moreover, in the case of war, the reasoning does not apply only to the past, as in the case of slavery and animism, which have disappeared, but it has an important bearing upon the present. It is worth while to demonstrate that war has *always* been an evil in order to prevent the formulation of doctrines of the following character: "Given the state of barbarism in which we live, we have not yet left the period in which war is a good thing." From the logical point of view, of course, such doctrines cannot stand the test of criticism. To say that because we have not yet arrived at the stage at which war is no longer waged, it is necessary that we should continue to wage war, leads directly to contradiction. The human race will only enter upon the period in which war will no longer be waged on the day when it is convinced that it is futile to wage war. There will never be a period therefore, during which we shall believe that war is useless, and in which we shall nevertheless believe ourselves obliged to wage war. This reasoning holds true, of course, only from the point of view of all the nations, but the interdependence of thought is so great in modern life that when the truth is realized in one part of the world, that war is economically, socially, and morally futile, the new ideas will rapidly spread through the other parts of the world and the greatest obstacle in the way of world federation will be removed. We have seen in Chapter I that the philosophy of force is an international philosophy. The history of all intellectual advance teaches us that the disintegration of this philosophy will also be an international process.

The sophistry *post hoc ergo propter hoc* is one of the crudest fallacies of the philosophy of force. Whenever a good thing takes place after a war it is immediately placed to the credit of this war. Thus it is often argued that since the Civil War in America was followed by a great burst of industrial activity, the building of the great transcontinental railroads, and other proofs of the vital energy of the people of the North, therefore all this creative activity was caused by the Civil War. But when evil effects follow the war, as in the economic stagnation of the South in the same period, the war is not held responsible. This sophism is hardly worthy of scientific consideration. In science a cause is something which is invariably followed by the same effect. All students of the social sciences know that the causes of social phenomena are almost infinitely complex. To reduce these effects to a single cause results in complete confusion. This subject has already been touched upon in considering the true nature of social struggles.[1] It is not the purpose at the present time to inquire into these complex causes or to examine the economic facts of the argument; we are concerned here simply with the fallacy from the point of view of logic. It is impossible to deny that some wars are followed, not by activity and prosperity, but by a relapse into barbarism and stagnation such as followed the victory of the Turks in the Balkans, and the Civil Wars of Mexico and Venezuela. War produces then sometimes civilization and sometimes barbarism. The same cause, according to the philosophy of force, produces diametrically opposite effects.

A final sophistry is due to the failure to distinguish between the statement of a fact and the pronouncement of a judgment. If it is said that war has been permanent during the entire historic period, then this is a simple statement of fact, but if it is said that war has been a benefit, this is to pronounce a judgment. The statement of fact may be perfectly true and the judgment absolutely false. If the statement is made as follows, this confusion does not arise and we are dealing with realities. "During the historical period

[1] See Chapter III. on the Biological Errors, pp. 88–95.

man has waged war almost constantly. At the same time he has passed from savagery to civilization." But if one proceeds to affirm that since these two facts are parallel and simultaneous, one is the cause of the other, the logical deduction cannot withstand the first test of criticism. The reasoning has no power behind it. If only parallelism and simultaneousness are given in explanation, we are quite as well justified in concluding that civilization has progressed in spite of war as on account of war. In order that certain effects may be attributed to a certain cause, simultaneousness alone does not suffice in science. The direct bond of causality must be established.

The doctrine that war is the cause of civilization corresponds to the cataclysmic theory in geology before that subject became a science. As long as the geologists believed in the theory of universal cataclysm and special creation, the subject was veiled in a haze of metaphysics and contradictory hypotheses. Geology became a positive science only when the theory of slow and actual causes was adopted. The influence of earthquakes and cataclysms in shaping the earth's crust is, of course, still recognized, but this influence is assigned a relatively unimportant place in comparison with the effect of such factors as erosion by wind and water, the slow and invisible folding of the earth's crust due to pressure and contraction, and the deposit of sediment by rivers. In the same way sociology will become a positive science when it adopts the theory of slow and actual causes, that is, when it rejects the cataclysmic theory. The methodical study and classification of social facts by means of statistics, the new social psychology which is arising, the systematic observation of the action of social forces in the every-day life about us, indicate that sociology is now passing from the metaphysical stage into the phase of a positive science.

It is not difficult to understand why the cataclysmic theory should have been adopted at first in sociology. The social sciences have gone to history for much of their data, and until recent years much of history has been a catalogue of battles, conveying the impression that the "fifteen decisive battles" of the world have been the cause of the progress of civilization. Wars have been the great dramatic events of history, impressing themselves upon the popular imagination like floods and earthquakes, while the daily events of productive labour and social contact, the gradual accumulation of inventions, the slow extension of the bounds of human knowledge by exploration and discovery have not made this same dramatic appeal. Monuments have been erected to commemorate great wars and battles, because of the fact that they were out of the ordinary, and historians, finding very little to bear witness to the true history of civilization, have been compelled to take these monuments as the chief data of the past. The same process can be observed in the modern newspaper, where the accidents, the murders, and other extraordinary events are featured, precisely because they are out of the ordinary and therefore news, while the daily life of the people, the unceasing labour and constructive efforts, the slow and invisible forces of social progress, are almost completely ignored.

The slightest consideration of the actual facts of social life suffices to show how untenable is the cataclysmic theory that the physical struggle between men is the sole cause of social progress. It would be difficult to deny, for example, that the invention of fire, of the wheel, of the sail, of the wagon, of the steam engine and the locomotive, of the telegraph and telephone, of the automobile, of all those common things which play so important a part in our daily life, such as bread, cooking, and clothing, have contributed immensely to the progress of the human race. However, none of these inventions, nor any of a thousand others, which constitute the instruments of production and of our economic life, have been made *for the purpose* of combating the members of our own species. (Curiously enough, not even gunpowder was invented for the purpose of war.) All these inventions were made solely to aid in the struggle against the physical universe. Many of the inventions have of course been used in war; militarism uses every instrument which it can adapt to its purposes. But none of them have been made for the purpose of war or with a view to their use in the struggle between men.

The favourite argument of "social Darwinism" is familiar to almost everyone. War has been the cause of civilization, because it has constituted a process of selection in the human species. The strongest, and therefore the best, have survived in the battle, while the weak and the inferior have been killed off, and thus the race has been perfected.

This infantile theory has been so thoroughly exploded by eminent biologists like David Starr Jordan,[1] who have examined the actual facts of the effects of war on the race, that it is unnecessary to lose time in slaying the slain here. War produces a selection, of course, but it is a *reverse* selection. The actual facts of the process of selection by which militarism improves the race may be sketched as follows: Carefully select the flower of the race from each country; reject all but the very finest of the young men, those who are perfect in mind and body, and line these up by the millions against machine-guns and automatic rifles, mow them down by the thousands with shrapnel and high explosive shells, coming from unseen artillery miles away, until the casualty lists run up into the millions,—and leave behind the product of the slums, the undersized, the physically and mentally imperfect, the infirm and the weak, to be fathers of the next generation.

---

[1] See *The Blood of the Nations, The Human Harvest* (a study of the decay of races through the survival of the unfit), *War and the Breed*, and *War's Aftermath* (a study of the effects of the American Civil War and of the Balkan Wars upon the race).

This is the process that is called "improving the race," "keeping the moral fibre of the nation from rotting" and "preserving the virile qualities" of the nation.

Darwin has called attention to the manner in which this reverse selection is produced by militarism even in times of peace:

> In every country in which a large standing army is kept up, the finest young men are taken by conscription or are enlisted. They are thus exposed to early death during war, are often tempted into vice, and are prevented from marrying during the prime of life. On the other hand, the shorter and feebler men, with poor constitutions, are left at home, and consequently have a much better chance of marrying and propagating their kind.[1]

On account of the curious social myopia which characterizes the philosophy of force, and prevents its advocates from seeing anything except the cataclysmic biological facts, the militarists fail to note that the real process of selection does not take place by a process of selective homicide between men, but by economic processes. In so far as they have equal opportunity[2] those individ-

---

[1] Darwin, *The Descent of Man*, chap. v., p. 151.

[2] Darwin has noted the evil effects of the inheritance of wealth upon the process of selection, and says that "primogeniture with entailed estates is a more direct evil," since "most eldest sons, though they may be weak in body or mind, marry, while the younger sons, however superior in these respects, do not generally marry."—*The Descent of Man*, p. 151.

uals who are most gifted are able to insure their economic welfare, while the less gifted are not. Positive selection takes place in human societies by natural death, and the mortality among the poorer classes is much higher than among the well-to-do. Of course this factor of natural mortality, which is affected by economic selection, is much more powerful than war, since it acts constantly, while the cataclysm of selective homicide acts only at rare intervals.

The more rapidly the death of the weak-minded and incapable takes place, the more rapid will be the positive selection, and other things being equal, the more society would be composed uniquely of the capable and would tend to become more perfect. But the higher the mortality, the more common it is and the less it attracts attention. As a result this natural mortality, which takes place every day and all about us, does not affect the social consciousness. In other words, it is one of the slow and invisible factors which those who are hypnotized by the catastrophic theory of social progress are unable to perceive.

Since they are compelled to abandon the untenable ground of individual selection by war, the militarists fall back upon the theory of collective selection. Thus Professor Karl Pearson states the doctrine of collective selection:

History shows me one way and one way only, in which a high state of civilization has been produced, namely the struggle of race with race, and the survival of the physically and mentally fitter race. If men want to know whether the lower races of man can evolve a higher type, I fear the only course is to leave them to fight it out among themselves.[1]

Again, the advocates of the cataclysmic theory fail to see not only the slow and invisible causes of social progress but also the real effects of war between races. Instead of exterminating the so-called "inferior" races, conquest by a race of superior civilization often gives them an added chance of survival. Thus the number of Indians in the United States, according to the census returns,[2] is now rapidly increasing. The taking over of the Philippines by the United States has given the Filipinos an added chance of survival, not on account of the dramatic events of war, but on account of those gradual and effective but invisible processes of education and sanitation, the persistent, undramatic work of missionaries and teachers, scientists and engineers.

The cessation of warfare between the peoples of India, the introduction of railways and modern distributing systems, with the consequent abolition of famine, the spread of education and a knowledge

[1] Quoted by J. A. Hobson in *Imperialism*, pp. 141, 142.

[2] The number of Indians in the United States increased from 248,253 in 1890 to 265,683 in 1910. This increase of 17,430 represents a gain of 7 per cent. during the last twenty year period. See *Indian Population in the United States and Alaska*, Government Printing Office, Washington, 1915, p. 10.

of hygiene and the sanitary methods of modern civilization, have greatly decreased the death-rate in India and made possible the survival of a much larger and increasing population. So if the people of India are inferior (as is demonstrated, according to the advocates of the philosophy of force, by the fact that they were defeated in the struggle with the white race), the result of this struggle has been greatly to increase the survival power of the so-called "inferior race" which "went down" in the physical struggle.

In the same way the introduction of modern hygiene and sanitary methods in Africa and in the tropics is giving other so-called "inferior races" an added chance to survive. The slow and invisible causes are so much more important than the cataclysmic, that they completely reverse the action of the latter, and produce precisely the opposite result from that which, in the philosophy of force, is assumed to be the outcome of the race struggle.

Renan expresses the same idea as Professor Pearson, in another form:

The struggle against nature does not suffice. By means of industry man succeeds in reducing it to an unimportant matter. Then comes the struggle of races.[1]

Renan falls a victim to the first of the biological errors of the philosophy of force in thus practically ignoring the existence of the universe. "The

[1] *La réforme intellectuelle et morale*, p. 111.

struggle against nature does not suffice," he says, when this struggle is precisely existence itself, when it takes place every second, every instant, without ceasing, not only for the whole human race, but for the entire realm of life itself. Moreover, in speaking of the "struggle of races," Renan is not considering realities. Race is a physiological term: if wars took place only between the white races and the negroes, or between the white and the yellow races, it might be possible to identify war with the struggle of the races. But this is not the case. War takes place very often between peoples who are closely allied by descent, as between the Anglo-Saxons and the Germans. This can hardly be stretched to "the struggle of races." In reality, what Renan means by "the struggle of races" is the struggle between nationalities, and here he is under the hypnotism of the cataclysmic theory, failing to see that the struggle between nationalities does not take place by means of collective homicide, but by the processes of intellectual assimilation. We must seek in psychic processes the true nature of the struggle between races, as exemplified in Austria-Hungary, in Alsace-Lorraine, or in Poland, where the Prussians have tried in vain for one hundred and fifty years to Germanize the Polish people by force. As we shall see there, the true struggle between races takes place in the domain of social microscopy, if we may use this expression, and if a social selection takes place, it operates by *social procedures,* processes which have nothing to do with the slaughter of the battle-field, to which the cataclysmic theory assigns all results.

Moreover, Renan and all the militarists fail to take account of another fact which, when its bearing is realized, ruins completely the significance of their comparisons between individual biological phenomena and collective social phenomena. In 1806, Prussia was defeated at the battle of Jena. According to the philosophy of force, this was because Prussia was "inferior," and France was "superior." Suppose we admit for the moment that this was the case. The selection now represents the survival of the fittest, the selection which perfects the human species. But what shall we say of the battle of Leipsic? At Leipsic, in 1813, all the values were reversed; it is now France which is the "inferior" nation, and according to Renan it would be defeat this time, and not victory, which resulted in the positive selection. Furthermore, a large number of the same generals and soldiers who took part in the battle of Jena also took part in the battle of Leipsic. Napoleon belonged, therefore, to a race which was superior to that of Blücher in 1806, but to an inferior race in 1813, in spite of the fact that they were the same persons and had not changed their nationality. As soon as we bring these assertions to the touchstone of concrete reality we see at once how untenable and even ridiculous are direct biological comparisons.

This brings us to another interesting phase of the cataclysmic theory—the aberration of the *ultima ratio*, which runs all through the philosophy of force. The Imperial German Chancellor has recently given it expression in a speech in the Reichstag. This is the way it is phrased by Professor Rössler:

"War is the great examiner of humanity: it will remain the *ultima ratio* for the judgment of peoples."[1]

This theory sounds very well, but what shall we say when war pronounces within very short intervals of time, judgments which are absolutely contradictory? At Jena, Prussia is condemned; seven years afterward, at Leipsic, it is France. Moreover, Professor Rössler would be the last to agree to submit to the verdict, if it is against his own country. And finally, from an objective point of view, it is impossible to maintain that in war it is the most perfect nations which have always triumphed. According to this doctrine, we should have to say that the Romans were superior to the Greeks, the Arabs to the Spanish, the Danes to the English, the Mongols to the Russians, the Abyssinians to the Italians, etc. According to this doctrine, then, the nations which have made the civilization of Europe would all find themselves in the ranks of the "inferior," in the class of those who ought to be destroyed for the advancement of the human race.

[1] Quoted by J. Lagorgette in *Le rôle de la guerre*, p. 305.

Another form of the doctrine of collective selection consists in the theory that a social selection favourable to the human species takes place in war, because it destroys the badly organized State, and therefore tends toward progress. Dr. Schallmayer has stated this doctrine as follows:

The consideration of the perpetual danger of being forced into a war and of being shown to be inferior, by making it appear disadvantageous to the egoistical sovereign or the party government to think solely of their particular interests, prevents them from neglecting the general interest, even when the internal incidence of social forces might permit them to do so. In all cases where this conduct is not maintained, the proof of an unsuccessful war makes an end, sooner or later, of the bad governments, and prevents them from perpetuating themselves and extending to other communities.[1]

The selection produced by war, according to Dr. Schallmayer (and Renan has expressed the same idea[2]), is not a selection of individuals, or even communities, but of institutions; and the improvement of States is brought about chiefly by the fear of war and of defeat.

The author of this doctrine forgets the fact that social phenomena are founded upon inter-psychic forces. He overlooks the fact that men think.

[1] *Menschensziele* Monthly Review, published at Leipsic by O. Wigand, edited by H. Molenaar. 1908, No. 12, p. 385.
[2] See *La réforme intellectuelle et morale*, p. 111.

It seems that it would be difficult to push the disregard of actual facts further than this.

The perfection or imperfection of the State is the result of the corresponding perfection or imperfection of its institutions, and in their turn the institutions are the results of ideas. A society of men who believe that slavery is beneficial, or that inequality of the citizens before the law is the best basis of the social order, will be an imperfect society. Another society, composed of men who understand the injury done by slavery and the advantage of equality before the law, will be a more perfect society. But how can war serve to make the organization of society more perfect? Suppose that war occurs between a country without slaves and a country which maintains slavery, are we justified in assuming that the former will necessarily be victorious, that it will make conquests, and that thus the area of liberty will be extended and the area in which there is slavery will be contracted? And even if this unjustifiable assumption is made, the essential consideration is neglected that the first society did not suppress slavery as the result of selective homicide, but as a consequence of the direct observation of social facts. In order that a war may put to the test a slave-holding country and a free country, it is necessary that these two kinds of countries should exist before the war, which means that the reform must have preceded the combat, and this is in fact the process which we observe everywhere. It was

not as a result of the Reign of Terror that the
constitutionalists in France established the Rights
of Man. In so far as violence was employed, an
epoch of reaction, instead of the hoped-for new era,
was inaugurated; whereas in so far as the French
Revolution was successful, it was an intellectual
revolution resulting from the spread of the ideas
of Voltaire, Rousseau, and the other great French
philosophers of the eighteenth century.

In order to study the realities, let us consider
the two cases which may result from war. Either
a territorial conquest is made, as in the case of
the War of 1870, when Germany annexed Alsace-
Lorraine, or no territorial annexation takes place,
as in the War of 1866, when Prussia did not annex
any part of the Austrian territory. Collective
selection might be a reality in the first case, if the
conquering state, having superior institutions,
introduced them immediately into the new possessions. But this is far from being always the case.
The victorious state very often has institutions not
only inferior to those enjoyed by the conquered
territory before the war, but the institutions
introduced into the conquered territory may be
inferior to those established in the remainder of
the victorious state, as illustrated by the military
government of Alsace-Lorraine, symbolized by
the Zabern incident, or the Russian government
of Finland or Poland. Where does the pretended
positive selection take place in such a case? It
might be said, on the contrary, that if war consti-

tutes a collective selection (which is not true) the political effects are much more likely to be regressive than progressive.   War has as a result despotism; and despotism leads to a limitation and enfeeblement of the social life, not alone among the conquered, but also among the conquerors, because it is impossible to oppress a subjugated people without oppressing at the same time those who subjugate them.   It is absurd, then, to maintain that war has ever been able to produce, from this point of view, the progress of civilization.

Renan repeats the same argument in another form.   If the fear of being defeated were not always present, he says, "it is difficult to say to what degree of abasement the human species might descend."[1]   And on the same page, he continues:

When a population has produced everything which it is able to produce with its resources, it would begin to slow up if the fear of its neighbour did not spur it on; because the object of humanity is not enjoyment; to acquire and to create is the work of force and of youth: to enjoy is the part of decrepitude.   The fear of conquest is thus, in human affairs, a necessary spur.[2]

It is easy to show that security never produces the "abasement of the human species," as Renan affirms, but that, on the contrary, it is precisely the fear of conquest which produces this abase-

[1] See *supra*, p. 12.
[2] *La réforme intellectuelle et morale*, p. 111.

ment. Since the Treaty of Paris in 1783, for example, the United States of America has had no fear of being conquered by its neighbours. During these years, however, it would seem that some progress has been made. The population has increased from four millions to more than one hundred millions; in agriculture, in industry, commerce, technical invention, and in science, America may make some claim to be considered with the other nations in the front rank of progress. There are even countries in Europe, like Norway, Sweden, Denmark, and Switzerland, which have not been under the fear of being conquered during the past half-century or more on account of the political situation caused by the rivalry of the Great Powers; but nevertheless these countries have made great progress. The rural economy of Denmark, for example, is a model for the world, and much superior to that of its bellicose neighbour, Prussia.

The enormous cost of the British navy was borne because of the fear of German aggression. The huge armaments of Germany were voted because of the fear of conquest by France and Russia. And not only did the fear inspired by these armaments lead to an international reign of terror, and, as we have seen, logically and inevitably to war, but, even in times of peace, the "organized insanity" of the international armament competition, as Lloyd-George has called it, has constituted a very serious danger to the future of the European races. In England, for example, the problem of unemployment has been urgent and almost continually present. At times the number of unemployed has run up into the millions. If it had been possible for Great Britain to cut down its expenditures for national defence, this would have released capital for productive purposes and given employment to these millions of men.[1]

Moreover, myriads of the population of Great Britain live constantly below the bread-line, never having enough to eat, physically weakened, unable to resist the attacks of disease. The statistics of the recruiting officers represent a tragic national drama of physical degeneration of millions of the men of Great Britain, due to insufficient nourishment, living in the slums, etc. If it had not been necessary to divert so large a proportion of the British national income to the unproductive purposes of armament, more would have been available for employment in productive enterprises, for paying a living wage, which would in turn have increased the productive power of individual labourers; more could have been devoted to social reforms, such as the abolition of slums under a rational system of city-planning. By what species of argument can the philosophy of force maintain that the state of misery in which these millions are compelled to live contributes to the progress

---

[1] Bastiat has estimated that when one man is released from military or naval services the equivalent capital released at the same time is sufficient to give employment to two men.

of the British people? It is clear that if they had been well-nourished, they would have been strong and vigorous, able to resist disease, instead of an easy prey to epidemics. It is misery which degrades the human race and enfeebles it. It is precisely this "fear of being defeated" which is the cause of misery and of the degeneration of the race.

Russia is another example of the effects of the "fear of being defeated." The fear of the armaments of Germany and Austria has compelled the Russians to maintain an immense standing army. This has required an immense revenue, and to produce the revenue, the traffic in vodka was extended until it undermined the physical and mental productiveness of the race by more than thirty per cent., according to the estimates of the Russian government officials. Education, social reform, even in a country in which eighty-five per cent. of the people cannot read or write, had to be neglected because of the "fear of being defeated," which Renan praises so highly, but which is in reality the cause of the abasement of the human species.

Many other illustrations could be given, but they may all be summed up in a number. It is well known that the Great Powers can devote only one-third of their national revenue to the productive works of progress and civilization. The other two-thirds are swallowed up in the extraordinary expenditures caused by this "fear of being defeated." Education must be neglected, works of social reform and hygiene must be postponed, and the finest flower of civilization must be prevented from blossoming in each nation because the international reign of terror cuts off the economic strength of the nations at the roots. With more abundant resources, the race could be better nourished, better educated, higher in all respects in the biological scale. As soon as we examine the actual facts, we see how superficial are the views represented in the quotations from Renan and Schallmayer. And as sociology becomes more truly a science, it will become more and more necessary to take account of these invisible facts of the daily life about us, and to abandon the obsolete doctrines of the catastrophic aberration.

We see, then, that the forces of social progress are tremendously complex. To assign all this progress to a single battle, or even to a series of battles, means that we must voluntarily close our eyes to the most common phenomena of social life; it means that we must place ourselves on metaphysical heights, so far removed from the world of actualities that it is no longer possible to discern fact and reality. To attribute all progress to one factor, war, and to neglect all others, is to fall into a more colossal aberration than has been the misfortune of scientists in any other department of human knowledge.

Somewhat related to the cataclysmic theory of social progress, is a group of errors which have been called the anthropological romances. Following the example of Hobbes, a most tragic picture of the primitive condition of the human species has been drawn by the philosophy of force. According to this picture, murder was a permanent institution among our ancestors and was committed under the slightest pretext. Cannibalism was practised upon a large scale. At the beginning, man was a pugnacious and bloodthirsty animal, in comparison with whom the anthropomorphic apes were almost virtue personified. The following quotation will serve as an illustration of the picture of the primitive life of man as portrayed by the philosophy of force:

Without foresight or prudence, primitive man was far from being of that nature which has heretofore been attributed to him—following the principle of the greatest happiness, or of the least effort. He had no acquaintance with labour or with provision for the future, nor with exchange, nor society, nor morality. To these defects he added a ferocity and aggressiveness, a lust for violence, which led him to commit the most useless cruelties, and to appeal to arms to settle the slightest quarrel. These traits necessarily brought wars in their train, and what wars they were![1]

These romances have been called anthropological because they have been developed mainly by the anthropologists of Hobbesean tendencies. But they have since been adopted by the sociologists,

[1] J. Lagorgette, Le rôle de la guerre, p. 53.

and now form an integral part of the philosophy of force. They are called romances because they are based entirely upon *a priori* reasoning, without the slightest basis of evidence to justify them. The errors are characterized by a confident affirmation of the conditions and events which must have taken place some two hundred thousand years ago, although no written record has come down to us from this prehistoric period, no witness was present when they are alleged to have occurred, and the sociologists who make the affirmations so confidently offer not the slightest scientific evidence. Lacking all support of scientific foundation, these deductions are nevertheless put forward as statements of fact, without so much as a qualifying "it seems to me" or "in my opinion."

Among the most common of the anthropological romances are the romance of primitive slavery, and the romance of the pretended fundamental hostility between the tribes and hordes of primitive men. Of these, we have already had an illustration of the slavery romance, which has been developed in great detail by Professor Lester F. Ward.[1] For convenience, the end of the quotation is reproduced here:

The first step in the whole process is the conquest of one race by another. . . . The greater part of the conquered race is enslaved, and the institution of

[1] See *supra*, p. 11.

slavery begins here. The slaves are compelled to work, and labor in the economic sense begins here. The enslavement of the producers and compelling them to work was the only way in which mankind could have been taught to labor, and therefore the whole industrial system of society begins here.[1]

Since Professor Ward was not present at the moment when, "the conquered race having been reduced to slavery," "labor, in the economic sense, began," he must have deduced, *a posteriori* what seemed to him the most probable course of events. We are not dealing, then, with positive science, but with mental speculations. But as soon as we begin to apply the test of logical analysis to these mental speculations, it becomes evident that slavery could not have been a very ancient institution, and therefore that it could not have been a primitive institution. We find that slavery must have come much later than the establishment of industrial labour. Slavery, there-

[1] *American Journal of Sociology*, March, 1905, p. 594. A number of illustrations have been taken from the writings of Professor Lester F. Ward, especially because of the position of leadership which his intellectual power and magnetic personality secured for him among American sociologists of the last generation. Fortunately, the work of Professor Franklin H. Giddings, who may be considered the leader of modern American sociology, is free from the distortion of the philosophy of force. In his *The Principles of Sociology*, Professor Giddings frankly takes Adam Smith's *Theory of Moral Sentiments* as the starting point for sociology and follows Darwin, in finding in the social instincts—sympathy and the consciousness of kind—the chief cause of social progress.

fore, has not been able to produce the civilization of man; rather it is civilization which has made slavery. During tens of thousands of years man must have survived without slavery, and in this long period he raised himself to so great a height above the other animals that we may say he became civilized.

The proof that slavery could not have been a primitive institution is found in the fact that the establishment of slavery can only take place in a relatively advanced state of society. It presupposes the existence of the State, *i.e.*, an organized group with definite boundaries in which the bond uniting the citizens is territorial, and in which the division of labour has already been carried very far. In fact, slavery requires a powerful public force which can carry out its will by imposing fear, without which the slaves would not consent to submit to the sufferings of servitude. The slave always has the tendency to leave his master and flee. In order to prevent him from doing so, it is necessary to have him under surveillance, more or less vigilantly organized; and this surveillance necessarily presupposes territorial limits clearly marked, because it could not be extended to the confines of the universe. But the organization of States on the basis of territory is a very recent fact in history. While the human species has existed for possibly five hundred thousand years, the most ancient organized State was formed at most, ten thousand years ago. At this comparatively recent epoch, there were not more than two or three States on the entire globe. Humanity was therefore without slavery for probably forty-nine fiftieths of its existence. In the light of these facts, it is impossible to suppose that slavery was a primitive institution, without which civilization would never have been possible.

Moreover, it is easy to demonstrate that not only the division of labour, but even labour in an economic sense, has preceded slavery, and has not followed it. The anthropomorphic apes, which lived in troupes, did not have any slaves. We can easily understand why. Among other reasons, it would not have been useful to them, since the division of labour was still completely embryonic at that time. A consideration of the elementary facts of the case demonstrates that the division of labour was developed in human society before slavery. Without the division of labour, the master would have been bound as much as the slave, since it would have been necessary for him to remain with the slave at all times, directing his actions. Thus it would have required two men to do the work of one. We find the beginning of a division of labour, even among the animals who live in troupes (the setting of sentries, the obedience to leaders, etc.). At first the division of labour takes place among the sexes; the men go hunting, the women remain behind and prepare the food and clothing. The prehistoric remains show us that labour commenced

with the most simple operations, such as the
gathering of fruits, and developed with the creation of instruments and tools, which, beginning
with the palæolithic stone hatchet have advanced
to the highly complex and perfected machinery of
our own time. We can hardly imagine the first
man who fashioned a flint hatchet saying to himself, as the anthropological romance would have
us believe he said: "Now the period of labour
in the economic sense has commenced; I will go
and reduce my neighbour to slavery." For one
thing, he did not have the means of reducing his
neighbour to slavery, because his neighbour was
an individual who possessed just as much force
as he himself. Man did not commence by slavery
for the same reason that man, in common with
the other animals, did not commence by being a
cannibal,—because his own kind was for him
the most dangerous prey. The first savage has
therefore followed the line of least resistance.
He must have submitted to the universal law which
determines the direction of force. He must have
manufactured his hatchet himself, and, after this
first hatchet, have come in the same manner the
innumerable other tools which have been fashioned
by our ancestors from the Palæolithic Age to the
sixtieth century before our era, when the great
States of the valleys of the Nile and the Euphra-
tes were organized. By this epoch, the division
of labour had made considerable progress, and
when the workshops were in operation, it was

11

possible to imagine the advantage of slave labour. Then the leaders of expeditions of conquest would find it advantageous to bring back, not only the wealth of the conquered countries, but even the inhabitants of those countries. For it was the development of the division of labour alone which made it possible to give them work to do immediately, so that they would not constitute, for a single instant, useless mouths to be fed. But this highly developed division of labour presupposes the establishment of labour in an economic sense, and therefore of a comparatively high degree of civilization. Civilization, then, has not been the result of war and slavery, but war and slavery have been the result of civilization.

The anthropological romance of the pretended fundamental hostility of the primitive hordes of humanity, which has been quite popular since the time of Hobbes, is illustrated by the following quotation from Ratzenhofer:

Man, being a social animal, felt himself united to his original group by the sympathy of blood relationship. But when he came into contact with a man from another horde, the two individuals, conscious of belonging to two different communities, fell into a frenzied condition of fear and terror. Either they killed each other, or they severed all common relationship by flight. In the same way two hordes which came into relationship fell into a condition of fear and fury, as a result of the enmity of blood. Either they cast themselves upon each other in a struggle of extermination, or else they fled from each other in order to avoid all contact.[1]

And in a more recent work, Ratzenhofer adds:

Peaceful relations between the societies were for a long time impossible. Those groups which belonged to different races and to different civilizations avoided all contact as being injurious. When societies had neighbouring habitations, their relationships easily became very acute. The mutual political relations resembled a game of chess in which the object was for the ones that were best informed to seize quickly the opportune moment to fall upon the neighbour and subjugate him.[2]

It is necessary to repeat that this anthropological romance, like that of primitive slavery, is made out of the whole cloth of pure mental speculation. No witness was present two hundred thousand years ago to describe the conduct of the human tribes, and when we examine such evidence as we have, and apply logic and common sense to the problem, Ratzenhofer's imaginary process seems to be very far from the probabilities.

In general, we have three means of obtaining information concerning primitive man. One is the body of biological and geological facts, from which we may infer the nature of primitive man and the conditions under which he lived. A

[1] *Wesen und Zweck der Politik*, Leipsic, Brockhaus, 1903, p. 9.
[2] *Sociologische Erkentniss*, p. 288.

second is an increasing mass of archæological materials, which reveal many things about the life of the first men who left traces of their existence; and the third is a general parallelism between some features of primitive society and some features of the lowest societies of existing savages, which may be considered as in a condition of arrested development.

If we examine the biological facts first, it would seem that the further we go into the past, the more man should resemble the animals. Therefore, he ought to conduct himself as the animals do. How does it come, then, that when two bands of wolves meet each other, they do not "cast themselves upon each other in a struggle of extermination"? And this in spite of the fact that the wolves are carnivorous animals, so that if one band conquered the other, the conquerors might eat the conquered, which would be an advantage. But for frugivorous animals, of what use would be a struggle of extermination? We observe that bands of monkeys, for example, do not engage in any struggle of extermination when they come into contact. Even Ratzenhofer contradicts himself by admitting this:

> The animal species nearest to man, or the anthropoid monkeys, are not combative; they avoid relations with hostile animals, and only become dangerous when they are attacked or over-excited.[1]

[1] *Sociologische Erkentniss*, p. 133.

Why should the primitive hordes engage in a struggle of extermination at every meeting? No animal acts without having some object, and the more closely man resembles an animal, the more he ought to act in accord with this rule. Ratzenhofer tells us the reason for this hostility of the primitive hordes. He says that, "belonging to different *races* and different *civilizations*, they must resent all contact as injurious." The expression, "different *civilizations*," is worth noting, as belonging to primitive time, when there was no civilization, but a state of nature like that among the anthropomorphic monkeys. It is difficult to see how the differences of civilization at this epoch could have resulted in these terrible struggles, when these differences did not exist. At the period when differences in civilization appeared, primitive times had been past by thousands and thousands of years. Nor is the difference of races any better reason for these terrible struggles. When the chimpanzees and the makis meet in the tropical forest, they do not throw themselves on each other in a struggle of extermination, even though there is a greater difference between the makis and the chimpanzees than between the most widely separated of the human races.

Moreover, Ratzenhofer, with the characteristic superficiality of the philosophy of force, fails to see that contact between widely different bands and races would have been impossible in primitive times. He confuses conditions in modern times, when we have perfected means of communication, so that different races, such as Europeans and Patagonians, come into contact, with primitive periods, when there were no means of locomotion except by foot. It would have been impossible in primitive times to go from Europe to Patagonia. Primitive man might, indeed, have made a voyage on foot from what is now Canada, to what is now La Plata, but a voyage of this character would have required an exceedingly long period of time. On account of the difficulties of communication, long voyages were very difficult for primitive man, and the contacts must have taken place only between tribes more or less neighbouring. But if they were neighbours, they would have been subject to the same conditions of the habitat, and would not have been very different in development.

The data from archæological materials also demonstrate that Ratzenhofer is wrong in asserting that peaceful relations were impossible among primitive men. Even in neolithic times, a considerable commerce and exchange existed, and we find objects of Asiatic origin in Europe at this period, while the Phœnicians practised numerous exchanges with the populations of western Europe at a period when they still lived in a condition of small tribal groups, related only by bonds of common descent. Finally, the theory of actual causes, which teaches us to look for a parallelism between primitive society and the lowest societies in existing savages, renders a verdict against the primitive hostility romance. Thus, M. Lagorgette says:

> The experience of a great number of travellers shows that almost all the non-civilized races exhibit a very kindly attitude on the first visit, and that the later hostile dispositions are reprisals for the evils which they have suffered from the civilized races.[1]

Even Ratzenhofer confirms this evidence.[2]   He emphasizes the fact that the first Europeans landing in America in the fifteenth century were received in a most friendly fashion by the aborigines.   But if there is no combat, no struggle of extermination, on first contact between races so different as the Spanish and the Redskins of America, still less ought there to have been any between primitive tribes who resembled each other so much more closely.   To affirm that peaceful contacts are possible now, but that they were not possible two hundred thousand years ago, is to run counter to the evidence of actual social processes.   We have seen that geology became a positive science, solely when it adopted the theory of actual causes.   Surely it is high time for sociology to abandon the categorical affirmations of the anthropological romances and begin to assume the character of a serious science, dealing not with

---

[1] *Le rôle de la guerre*, p. 210.
[2] See his *Sociologische Erkentniss*, p. 134.

fantastic imaginary conditions, but with the realities of the life about us.

Another special error of the sociological order is the pretended antiquity of war. All through the philosophy of force, we find primitive humanity represented in the form of small hordes constantly pillaging and massacring each other. Since we do not possess any documents concerning this epoch, this representation belongs also in the category of the anthropological romances. This romance is invented on account of the necessity for defending a thesis. In showing that war has existed from primitive times, and that nevertheless humanity has become civilized, the purpose is to demonstrate that war has made civilization.

We have seen that primitive man did not wage war, because, in common with all the other animals, he had a hereditary instinct which prevented him from attacking his own kind.[1] As Darwin says, "the instincts of the lower animals are never so perverted" as to lead them regularly to unnatural acts, such as destroying their own species; and he shows that these instincts must have been supreme in the antiquity of the human race:

If we look back to an extremely remote epoch, before man had arrived at the dignity of manhood, he would have been guided more by instinct and less

[1] See *supra*, p. 68.

by reason than are the lowest savages at the present time.[1]

At the very earliest, then, war could not have taken place until a comparatively high degree of intelligence had been developed, which enabled man to overcome this strong hereditary instinct. When men massacre each other, it is said that they act like animals. This is a profound error; it is when men do *not* massacre each other that they act like animals. This fallacy is a part of the error which confuses struggle with combat between members of the same species. Lions struggle every day with antelopes, but they do not fight with other lions. Man struggles every day as the lion does, that is to say against the animals and the plants. Every head of cattle killed in a slaughter house is a part of this struggle. But if man had acted as animals do with regard to his own species, the federation of the human race

[1] *The Descent of Man*, p. 62. It is interesting to find Darwin quoting on the same page and with apparent approval the following comment on this passage by a writer in the *Spectator:*
"Mr. Darwin finds himself compelled to reintroduce a new doctrine of the fall of man. He shows that the instincts of the higher animals are far nobler than the habits of savage races of men, and he finds himself, therefore, compelled to reintroduce —in a form of the substantial orthodoxy of which he appears to be quite unconscious—and to introduce as a scientific hypothesis the doctrine that man's gain of *knowledge* was the cause of a temporary but long enduring moral deterioration. . . . What does the Jewish tradition of the moral degeneration of man through his snatching at a knowledge forbidden him by his highest instinct assert beyond this?"

would have been an accomplished fact many centuries ago.

In the second place, it is easy to demonstrate that war has not preceded production, as the philosophy of force holds, but that production must have preceded war. This is because war requires the storing up of capital, which must have been the result of a preceding productive labour. Even in the most primitive times, a savage who went to rob his neighbour must have provided himself with enough food so that he would not die of starvation, and so that he would have sufficient strength to insure some chance of victory. Moreover, he would only be able to steal things which were light and easily transportable, so that he would still be under the necessity of obtaining bulky articles by productive labour. It is somewhat ludicrous to imagine the conqueror removing the houses, the workshops, and the crops of wheat, for the sake of saving himself the trouble of productive labour by which he could have procured these things directly.

But it may be objected, suppose he forces the vanquished to perform this labour. This would be very well; but it would be necessary for the conqueror to subject the territory of the vanquished to his direct domination, which would demand a high degree of governmental organization, possible only to a fairly advanced degree of civilization. Nor is it possible to assume that the conqueror could require his slaves to perform this labour, for as we have seen, the institution of slavery could not be established until a State with territorial limits had been created, which also demands a very advanced state of civilization.

Moreover, it is easy to demonstrate, not only that humanity has not commenced with war, but also that systematic war, war in the state of a permanent institution, as it exists in our time, is a comparatively recent fact. This is not because of the innate goodness of earlier men. The apes are not better than men, but they are not organized systematically and perpetually for war. This is because such an organization demands high mental faculties which they do not possess. As long as man was not highly developed he could not organize systematic war for the same reason. Mr. V. de Lapouge gives the evidence thus:

We do not find war, nor even individual murder existing among the highly developed monkeys. Contrary to the opinions of certain palæontologists, the instinct of crime appears to be developed in a measure as our species has disengaged itself from the rest of the animal kingdom. Murder, and war which is assassination by wholesale, are human acts and not the atavistic legacies of far distant ancestors. It is with the progress of civilization that the art of killing has been developed, that war has ceased to have personal motives, and has become an anonymous massacre of men indifferent to each other.[1]

[1] *Les sélections sociales*, p. 209.

Mr. Lagorgette also makes a very penetrating remark:

Animals are almost entirely ignorant of fratricidal struggle. On account of lack of intelligence, they do not recognize the apparent usefulness which it would have for them to destroy their own kind, and as a result they do not attack them.[1]

From the first sporadic acts of robbery and exploitation to the condition of permanent war which exists in our time, there is an immense distance. The successive scale of banditism which lies between is something like this: clandestine theft, robbery by force, raids, permanent tribute, and finally, territorial conquest, *i.e.*, complete exploitation of the vanquished by taxes levied for the conqueror. Thousands of years must have been necessary for humanity to mount the successive degrees of this disastrous scale. The period of sporadic raids must have lasted for many centuries, because the human race, during a long period, could not conceive of a more systematic form of pillage. Of all forms of exploitation, political conquest is necessarily the most recent, since it presupposes an intellectual and political development of high order. However, it is the desire for political conquest which has given birth to standing armies, and it is the creation of standing armies which has produced the state of systematic

[1] *Le rôle de la guerre*, p. 35.

war, of the hostility of nations erected into a principle of public law, which exists in our day.

Permanent and organized war has commenced successively in different regions of the earth, in accordance with the measure in which they have been civilized. In Egypt, in Chaldea, in Assyria, there existed military empires from the thirtieth century before our era. But it is also necessary to note that even in our day, there are peoples which have not yet arrived at the stage of organized war, precisely because they have remained in an inferior state of social development.

The process employed by the philosophy of force to demonstrate that war has existed from the origin of humanity is very simple. The name *primitive* is given to some period of history chosen in the most arbitrary fashion, *e.g.*, Egypt in the fortieth century before our era. Since war has existed from this epoch, the deduction is made, that it has existed from the origin of humanity. But this process is as anti-scientific as it is simple. The fortieth century before our era is an epoch relatively recent in comparison with the age of our species, which has probably existed, according to specialists in geology, for at least five hundred thousand years. The Egyptian civilization under Mena was very far advanced; it had already a written language, and its civilization was the result of a very long evolution. Nothing could be more deceptive than to call this period primitive. But it would be still more naïve to believe that the institutions which were common then had fallen from the skies. If systematic warfare existed in Egypt at the time of Mena, it must have been preceded by a series of facts dating back to the animal period of the quaternary time. For Egypt also, then, before Mena there must have been a primitive period in which systematic war did not exist.

But what is more recent still than war, is the prestige of war. The idea that it is beneficial, and has been the cause of the progress of the human race, is a philosophic speculation. However, philosophic speculations are relatively very recent facts in human history, extending probably, not beyond the seventh century before our era. The period of the glorification of war extends from about the time of Heraclitus of Ephesus, who has been called the father of militarism, and who died about 480 B.C. In our age, therefore, when Marshal von Moltke tells us that war is an element of order established by God, he formulates a very modern idea, considering the general antiquity of the human race, but an idea which has already wrought more evil to the peoples of Christendom than any other error of the human mind.

CHAPTER VI

THE DECLINING ECONOMIC, SOCIAL, AND MORAL
EFFECTIVENESS OF FORCE

IN what precedes, we have been concerned with
the biological and sociological errors of the
philosophy of force, and of the doctrine that war is
the cause of human progress. But war—the use
of force—is never an end in itself; it is always a
means for obtaining some other desired end. In
order to understand how far force can be effective
for securing those ends, economic, social, and moral,
for which men strive, it is necessary to examine the
instrument itself more critically, and to clear up
certain confusions in regard to the nature of force
when used in human relations.

The fundamental confusion, which is especially
common in militaristic writings, leads to curious
reasoning in a circle. In recent years, an interesting shifting of the ground of the militaristic
defence of war has taken place. When the advocates of the philosophy of force are confronted with
the moral arguments against war, they usually
take refuge in the thesis that the causes of war
are economic and material. But when they are

overwhelmed with the proofs of the economic futility of war, they fall back upon the claim that the
causes of war are ideal and moral, not economic and
material. Thus Admiral Mahan, whose intellectual
power has placed him in the front rank of the defenders of militarism, says in one of his latest works:

The armaments of the European States now are
not so much for protection against conquest as to
secure to themselves the utmost possible share of the
unexploited or imperfectly exploited regions of the
world—the outlying markets or storehouses of raw
material, which, under national control, shall minister
to national emoluments.[1]

This naked statement of the materialistic purpose of armament for aggression and exploitation
is in striking contrast with Admiral Mahan's
definition of the purpose of armament in an article
written shortly afterwards,[2] on "The Folly of The
Hague." Here he holds up armament as the
beneficent power which protects the quiet and
the weak, and allows them to sleep securely. His
new point of view is:

Armament is the organization and consecration of
force as a factor in the maintenance of justice, order,
and peace. It is the highest expression of that ele-

[1] Mahan, *Armaments and Arbitration, or The Place of Force in
the International Relations of States*, 1912, p. 113.
[2] *The Semi-Monthly Magazine Section*, Sunday, October 28,
1913. Published for a syndicate of American newspapers by the
Abbott & Briggs Company, New York.

ment in civilization—force—which has created and now upholds society, giving efficacy to the pronouncements of law, whether by the legislature or in the courts. Organized force, alone, enables the quiet and the weak to go about their business and to sleep securely, safe from the assaults of violence without or within.

It is clear that Admiral Mahan would not contradict himself so flatly as in these two passages, if he did not labour under a fundamental confusion, which runs through all his writing and through that of practically all militarists, as to the real nature of physical force.

Three kinds of physical force must be distinguished in order to reason clearly upon the subject and to avoid the self-contradiction to which Admiral Mahan falls a victim when he thus includes all three under the one term armament. These three kinds of physical force are:

1. Force used for attack—aggression.
2. Force used to neutralize attack—defence.
3. Force used to prevent attack—police force.[1]

It is clearly the last of these—police force—that Admiral Mahan means when he speaks of

[1] A convenient classification would be obtained if the first two kinds of force—aggression and defence—should be characterized as violence, while the third form—police force—acting always under the direction of law, and in the service of society as a whole, should alone be characterized as force.

armament as the consecration of force for the maintenance of justice, order, and peace. But this is just what armament is not. Its activities are confined almost entirely to defence and attack. We do not speak of a mining town, with no central authority for maintaining order, and with every inhabitant—gamblers, thieves, and good citizens alike, armed to the teeth and shooting at sight, as having a very high degree of justice, order, and peace, although there is armament enough and to spare. This is the present condition of anarchy in international relations, with no strong central authority to enforce order, and armament confined to the functions of national attack and defence.

It is easy to show that the whole problem of the use of force in human relations centres about the first kind of physical force—aggression. Aggression is the form in which physical force first makes its appearance in human relations, and it calls forth in turn defensive force and police force. If there were no danger of aggression, of course there would be no necessity for defence. Incidentally, it is worth noting that from this point of view, all effort which tends to remove the motives for aggression is to be considered as a work of defence. And when the futility of using physical force for aggression becomes apparent to a community which is sufficiently intelligent to organize a co-operative effort, a division of labour results and the function of defence is delegated to a police force, charged with the duty of preventing aggression and maintaining order. And in proportion as the motives for aggression disappear, even the police force can be reduced to a minimum.

The process may be clearly followed in the history of the western mining towns of America, where at first every man has to depend upon his own six-shooter for defence against the ever-present danger of attack. When a strong public opinion arises, which makes such acts of aggression as horse-stealing, or "shooting up the town," immoral acts, the citizens, impelled by their common need for defence, co-operate in forming a vigilance committee, or a Law and Order League. Later, it is found advantageous to delegate this defensive function to a sheriff, and the work of establishing courts of justice, and a regular police force rapidly proceeds. It is in the motives for aggression, then, that we find the centre of gravity of the problem of force in human relations. In proportion as men believe that military force can be used effectively for purposes of aggression, to advance their national welfare, the danger of attack will be always present, and, what is more important, they will be unwilling to co-operate in any form of federation or international police force, because this would imply the giving up of part of that "sovereignty," which means the right of attacking one's neighbour whenever it may seem that aggression would be advantageous.

In fact, it is easy to show from militaristic writings that the belief in the effectiveness of aggressive physical force, provided only that this belief is held by a sufficient number of influential men in the nation concerned, renders inevitable the employment of such force; in other words, that this belief logically makes war inevitable. For if force can be used aggressively to advance national welfare, armed conflict will be the logical result of the selfishness of nations, and therefore to them, a law of nature. Defence will therefore be necessary sooner or later. Since, according to the militarist philosophy, attack is the best means of defence, it then becomes a matter of duty for the ruler of the nation which is compelled to defend itself to choose the most favourable moment for attack. The logical chain is thus complete from a belief in the effectiveness of aggressive physical force to the inevitability of war. This chain of reasoning has been concisely stated, in its practical application, by a German advocate of the philosophy of force.

No one will thus dispute the assumption that, under certain circumstances, it is the moral and political duty of the State to employ war as a political means. So long as all human progress and all natural development are based on the law of conflict, it is necessary to engage in such conflict under the most favourable conditions possible.

When a State is confronted by the material impossibility of supporting any longer the warlike preparations which the power of its enemies has forced upon it, when it is clear that the rival States must gradually acquire from natural reasons a lead that cannot be won back, when there are indications of an offensive alliance of stronger enemies who only wait the favourable moment to strike—the moral duty of the State towards its citizens is to begin the struggle while the prospects of success and the political circumstances are still tolerably favourable. When, on the other hand, the hostile States are weakened or hampered by affairs at home and abroad, but its own warlike strength shows elements of superiority, it is imperative to use the favourable circumstances to promote its own political aims. The danger of a war may be faced the more readily if there is good prospect that great results may be obtained with comparatively small sacrifices.[1]

Substantially the same ideas are held by the war parties in each of the Great Powers engaged in the war. Thus Lord Roberts, in his famous Manchester speech, reported in the *Manchester Guardian*, October 31, 1912, has advocated that England adopt the same policy:

Germany strikes when Germany's hour has struck; that is the time-honoured policy of her Foreign Office. That was the policy relentlessly pursued by Bismarck and Moltke in 1866 and 1870. It has been her policy to the present hour. And, gentlemen, it is an excel-

[1] Bernhardi, *Germany and the Next War*, in the chapter entitled, "The Duty to Make War," pp. 52–53.

lent policy. It is, or should be, the policy of every nation prepared to play a great part in history.

In America President Roosevelt has repeatedly emphasized the fact that the belief in the effectiveness of force to advance a nation's moral or material interests may make war an imperative national duty. In his message to Congress December 4, 1906, President Roosevelt said:

It must ever be kept in mind that war is not merely justifiable, but imperative upon honourable men and upon an honourable nation when peace is only to be obtained by the sacrifice of conscientious conviction or of national welfare.[1]

The relation between the belief in the effectiveness of military force used for aggression and the inevitability of war has been clearly stated by a distinguished Belgian author, Dr. Charles Sarolea, whose work *The Anglo-German Problem*, has won the highest praise from the King of the Belgians and others in close touch with political conditions in Europe. Dr. Sarolea summarizes the relation as follows:

Both the English Imperialist and the German Imperialist believe that the greatness of a country does not depend mainly on the virtues of the people, or on the resources of the home country, but largely on the capacity of the home country to acquire and to retain large tracts of territory all over the world. Both the English Imperialist and the German Im-

[1] Quoted by Bernhardi, *Germany and the Next War*, p. 52.

perialist have learned the doctrine of Admiral Mahan, that the greatness and prosperity of a country depends mainly on sea-power. Both believe that efficiency and success in war is one of the main conditions of national prosperity.

Now as long as the two nations do not rise to a saner political ideal, as long as both English and German people are agreed in accepting the current political philosophy, as long as both nations shall consider military power not merely as a necessary and temporary evil to submit to, but as a permanent and noble ideal to strive after, the German argument remains unanswerable. War is indeed predestined, and no diplomatists sitting around a great table in the Wilhelmstrasse or the Ballplatz or the Quai d'Orsay will be able to ward off the inevitable. It is only, therefore, in so far as both nations will move away from the old political philosophy, that an understanding between Germany and England will become possible. . . . We must repeat for the last time the *Leitmotiv* of this book: If, as the result of some internal difficulty or external contingency, those military and Imperialist motives be allowed to gather strength, then indeed the political pessimist is right— war is inevitable. . . . It is the ideas and ideals that must be fundamentally changed: "*Instauratio facienda ab imis fundamentis.*" And those ideals once changed, all motives for a war between England and Germany would vanish as by magic. But alas! ideas or ideals do not change by magic or prestige—they can only change by the slow operation of intellectual conversion. Arguments alone can do it.[1]

[1] Sarolea, *The Anglo-German Problem*, 1912, pp. 362–65.

The problem of aggression, therefore, constitutes the key to the whole problem of the place of force in human relations, since defence and even police force are necessary only because of the danger of aggression. From this consideration it follows that the crux of the philosophy of force centres about the question of the effectiveness or futility of the instrument of force for accomplishing certain objects which men desire; and the hope for a rationally organized world, in which war will not be "inevitable," depends upon the possibility of changing the widely accepted belief in the advantages of aggression. To understand the decreasing effectiveness of force, which has now proceeded so far, as Norman Angell has demonstrated in *The Great Illusion*, that it has become futile in our modern interdependent world, it is necessary to survey briefly the different forms in which struggle is successively carried on between human associations.[1]

The most imperative need of man, as of all other animals, is food. The means by which men have sought to procure nourishment are: searching for and gathering food from nature, hunting, fishing, the domestication of animals, and agriculture. When all other means have failed, men have over-

---

[1] See J. Novikov, *Les luttes entre sociétés humaines et leurs phases successives* (Paris, Alcan, 2d edition, 1904), for a more detailed account of the successive forms of struggle than is given here. Novikov devotes several chapters to the nature and processes of each of the successive forms of struggle, illustrating his analysis with a wealth of historical material.

come their hereditary instinct, and have killed their own kind in order to devour them. They have thus waged purely physiological or alimentary wars, like those waged by animals of one species against those of another species. But human food is the most difficult to procure, since it is necessary for a cannibal to attack a prey as strong and intelligent as the hunter. In accordance with the law of force, that it tends to follow the line of least resistance, the cannibal finds it better to search for a prey which possesses inferior mental faculties, and therefore can oppose less resistance. Cannibalism has been abandoned as soon as it has been possible to procure nourishment in any other manner.

As we have seen in a preceding chapter, the physiological struggle has two forms, absorption and elimination. After the phase of cannibalism, which is a process of absorption, the physiological struggle has gone on by a process of elimination. Men made war, not for the purpose of devouring each other, but to assure themselves of subsistence —a hunting ground, the bank of a river rich in fish, trees producing nuts and fruits. In this case, the death of the vanquished ceases to be an object, and becomes a means. If the more feeble abandons the prize which is coveted, he can preserve his existence.

Once assured of being able to secure a permanent supply of nourishment, this ceases to be the principal pre-occupation of man. The next most urgent need which becomes an object of his attention is the desire for well-being, or in other words, wealth. The most rapid way to procure wealth, *i. e.*, all those objects necessary to supply the needs of man, is to produce the desired objects himself; but this is not the only means. He can either rob some other individual of these objects, or force some other individual to make them for him. Since the victim will not give up his wealth of his own free will, without any corresponding remuneration, and since no one wishes to work without any reward, the aggressor must employ force, and economic wars break out between men. These assume two aspects clearly distinguished: at first, raiding expeditions, with the object of seizing such wealth as is movable; later, expeditions having as an object to make the victor the master of the immovable objects, cleared spaces in the forest, rich lands, dwellings, etc. At the same time that the goods are taken possession of, the men are seized also. The vanquished becomes a beast of burden; he is forced to work for the conqueror. In the phase in which the pillaging expeditions are made, the vanquished, seized as booty, was transported to the territory of the conqueror. In the phase of the conquering expeditions, the vanquished remains in his own country, but is reduced to servitude.

The economic wars replace the alimentary wars, then, at a certain stage of social evolution. Naturally, the economic wars result in numerous victims. Nevertheless, in this phase, as in the second phase of the physiological wars, the death of the vanquished is not an end, but a means. Moreover, when the feebler becomes the slave of the stronger, it is a greater advantage to the conqueror to have the slave live, since he benefits from his labour.

At a more advanced stage of civilization, men perceive that one of the most lucrative functions is that of government. By imposing taxes, the conqueror can obtain the wealth of the producers in a much more complete manner and much more easily than by seizing his property directly. When this observation is made, it is found much more advantageous to take possession of the government of a conquered territory than to seize the movable and immovable wealth directly. The earlier methods of slavery, pillage, and confiscation of land are renounced, and the conquerors are content to avail themselves of the benefits of the government. Thus the economic wars are transformed into political wars, and become what are now known as conquests.

At a still later stage of social development men make a new observation, namely, that the way other people think has a very great influence upon their destiny. A certain set of ideas, certain religious theories, or political and social doctrines, appear to be more beneficial than others. In order to enjoy the prosperity which these psychic possessions which are judged to be useful could procure for them, men are led to wish to inculcate these ideas into their fellow-men by persuasion, or, if this means does not succeed, by force. From this motive arises a series of wars in which the objective is purely of the mental order. In the wars of religion, for example, the object was not to confiscate territory or to seize wealth, but simply to change certain ideas. Thus Philip II. of Spain waged the devastating wars against Holland because he wished to force the Dutch to remain Catholic. The Dutch people resisted because they did not wish to remain Catholic. The Spanish were not seeking, then, to seize the wealth of Holland. If they desired to take possession of the Dutch Government, it was not for the sake of the profit which it would have given them, but in order to have the power to stamp out heresy.

We see, then, how the wars between human associations change their object insensibly as they pass from the lowest phase of the war for food, to the highest phase, in which they become exceedingly complicated, of a struggle to make other men adopt our mental possessions. The successive phases of the struggle between human associations may be summarized as follows:

1. The physiological struggle;
2. The economic struggle;
3. The political struggle;
4. The intellectual struggle.

The order in which the different forms of struggle

have appeared is also the order in which they are most effective. Since the intellectual forces are the most powerful, the struggle for existence has resulted in the survival and dominance of the most intelligent. The economic processes produce a more rapid adaptation of the physical environment than the physiological or alimentary processes; the political processes result in a more rapid adaptation than the economic processes; and finally the intellectual processes result in a more rapid adaptation than the political processes. The effectiveness of an instrument is in proportion to the rapidity with which it enables us to accomplish our object, *i. e.*, the adaptation of the universe, so that the abandonment of the lower for the higher forms of struggle is equivalent to the abandonment of slower for more rapid and effective processes.

The explanation of the declining economic, social, and moral effectiveness of force is found to a large extent in this progress of civilization, which has changed the struggle between human associations from its lowest phase, the physiological struggle, to its highest, the intellectual struggle. Physical force becomes increasingly ineffective as we rise in this scale until, when we reach the stage of intellectual struggle, we find that physical force is an absolutely futile instrument with which to try to change intellectual convictions.

The causes for the futility of force are to be found largely in two factors: (1) the resistance of the individual who is attacked, and (2) the increasing complexity and interdependence of modern society.

The effect of resistance in rendering force futile has been analysed by Norman Angell in the following summary:

For one to impose his will upon the other by force implies resistance; thus two energies are cancelled and end in sterility or waste. For even when one triumphs, there are still two slaves: the vanquished slave to the victor, the victor to the need of maintaining supremacy and being ready to use force against the vanquished. This creates a form of relationship as wasteful in economics as it is disastrous in morals. It explains the failure of all those policies based on coercion or aggression—privilege and oppression within the State, conquest and the struggle for power between States. But if the two agree to combine forces in the common fight against Nature for life and sustenance, both are liberated and they have found in that partnership the true economy: still better, they have found in it the true basis of human society and its spiritual possibilities. For there can be no union without some measure of faith in the agreement on which it is based, some notion of right. It indicates the true policy whether national or international—agreement for united action against the common enemy, whether found in Nature or in the passions and fallacies of men.[1]

The effects of the increasing complexity and interdependence of society in rendering force futile

[1] *War and Peace.* (Published at 29 Charing Cross, London.) March, 1915.

may be illustrated by a mechanical analogy. For a simple mechanical operation, such as felling a tree, or breaking the shell of a cocoanut, where a direct application of force is the only thing required, the stone hatchet of primitive man was a very effective instrument. But if something goes wrong in the mechanism of a watch, the problem of adjusting it is removed to the plane of other forces, on account of the complexity of the mechanism. The watch may require machine oil, or a screw-driver operating under a microscopic eyepiece, or an electric current to demagnetize it. The increasing complexity of the mechanism has rendered the stone hatchet ineffective. It may be used to smash the watch, but it cannot adjust what is wrong and make it go. In the same way, physical force, which may have a certain amount of effectiveness in a simple, elementary form of society, loses that effectiveness as society grows more complex and interdependent. As the struggle passes from the physiological phase to the economic, political, and intellectual phases, the instrument of physical force, which can only be used for purposes of destruction, becomes irrelevant to the objects which men seek to attain.

Economically, the irrelevance arises chiefly from the fact of interdependence, and from the further fact that physical force is not an economic force. It can destroy, but it cannot produce, and as a result of the growing interdependence caused by association, this destruction reacts upon the one who employs the violence. If two tribes live on opposite sides of a river or swamp, with no contact or vital circulation between them, it is a matter of indifference to one of the tribes if the other is destroyed by a flood or an earthquake. But suppose the river is bridged or the swamp is drained, so that the two tribes come into contact, and a vital circulation is formed, a division of labour begins to take place. One tribe has, let us suppose, a better soil or a more favourable climate, and devotes itself chiefly to agriculture. The other tribe may possess mines of coal and iron; it may specialize upon manufactures, exchanging its products with members of the first tribe for food. After interdependence is established in this way, as the result of the division of labour, the fate of each tribe is no longer a matter of indifference to the other. If the one which specializes in agriculture is wiped out by a flood or an earthquake, the members of the other tribe may starve to death; and if the manufacturing society is exterminated, the agricultural society will suffer for want of clothing, shelter, tools. It will be forced to return to the condition which preceded the establishment of the division of labour. Its civilization will be degraded, and many of the members of the tribe will die off. For either of the tribes to exterminate the other after interdependence has been established, would be an act of suicide. For one tribe to attack the other with the object of advancing its own economic welfare, would be about as sensible and as relevant to the object desired as for the heart to attack the lungs, or for the right hand to cut off the left.

Where force is not used for purposes of total destruction, but is used to cause only a partial death or mutilation of the economic rights of others, its apparent effectiveness is only temporary, because the injustice which it produces results in unrest, maladjustment, cumulative opposition and resentment, a combination of opposing forces, and final overthrow. In other words, the result of the attempt to use physical force to secure economic advantage produces automatically enough force on the opposing side to neutralize the physical force of aggression. This neutralization of physical force results either in an unstable equilibrium or in a deadlock, and a decision can only be reached by removing the struggle to the higher planes of economic, political, and intellectual forces.

In studying the political irrelevance of physical force we come upon one of the doctrines most confidently affirmed by the philosophy of force —that the State has been formed by violence. This doctrine has been illustrated by quotations from the English sociologist Herbert Spencer (p. 8), the German sociologist Ratzenhofer (p. 10), and the American sociologist Ward (p. 11). According to these scientists, the State has been created by violence, and they affirm confidently that any other theory of the formation of the State is in flat contradiction to the teachings of sociology, and will only prepare the way for disastrous political experiences.

We have already considered this fallacy in our study of the general sociological errors of the philosophy of force, in which we have seen that war is always a process of dissociation, never of association. In order to understand more clearly the error which is involved, it is worth while to consider briefly the true nature of the State.

Even the philosophy of force cannot deny that the State is an association. What is meant by an association? It is a group of individuals, between whom an agreement, either tacit or formal, has been made not to injure each other. What is meant by injury? It means not to kill or rob each other, or, in other words, not to wage war.

The State, according to the philosophy of force, is formed by conquest. But in order that a conquest may be made, necessarily two associations must previously exist, the one which attacks (which Professor Ward calls the spermatozoid), and the one which defends itself (which he compares to the ovule). Since these two primitive associations are formed by alliance (*i. e.*, the absence of war between the individuals which compose them), it is therefore the union of men which has formed the first State, and not war between human associations. Certain States in

modern times, like Turkey, are of course the result
of conquest and banditism; but nevertheless, it is
a profound error to believe, as Hobbes has argued,
that the essence of the nature of the State consists
in·its being an enterprise for conquest and exploitation.

Although Spencer and other sociologists recognize that the foundation of the State is co-operation and not violence, they maintain, as we have
seen in Chapter I., that without wars, banditism,
and conquest the State would never have been
produced.   This arises also from a misconception
of the true nature of the State.   Without banditism, the State would have been created by social
organization, by the voluntary action of the
citizens.   This is the process which we see going
on under our eyes; and it is only the anthropological romances, and the failure to study the slow
and invisible causes of the evolution of society
which prevent us from realizing that the processes
we observe in the daily life about us have always
been the forces of social progress.   We can observe
the process of the amalgamation of societies
proceeding through millions of relations, all
consisting of variations of the elementary facts of
the transportation of people, of products, and of
ideas.   It is known that commercial relations
have been established since the highest antiquity,
between the most diverse regions; e. g., metal
instruments originating in Asia have been found
in the prehistoric remains in Europe, and it is

known that the Phœnicians carried on commerce long before the beginning of written history. Moreover, the witness of contemporary events shows us that the State is never founded upon force. States are being organized under our eyes, by a process in which force does not play the slightest rôle. During the nineteenth century, the American colonists and pioneers emigrated to the western part of the continent, and founded numerous States. After taking up and clearing the land they cultivated it and began to exchange products. As a result of this activity, thousands of needs for organization were born, which led the colonists to establish numerous institutions of political machinery. War did not play the slightest rôle at any time in all this process of organizing the Territories and States of the far West. But the facts which we observe in our own time are of the same kind as have occurred at all epochs.

The human race did not appear in each region of the earth as the result of a miraculous creation. The testimony of science is that man has radiated from a single centre of dispersion. There was then a long period in which the earth, with the exception of a relatively small region, was uninhabited by our species, and the outlying parts have been successively colonized by our ancestors. The process which took place in the western part of America during the nineteenth century, took place everywhere on the earth at a more ancient epoch. Men have come into a certain region, and have commenced to adapt the soil to their needs; in other words, to produce wealth. As a result they have been forced to establish immediately some kind of organization, because without organization, community life would have been impossible. War has not played any more of a rôle in this ancient process of organization than in the modern process.

The State is the region within a certain perimeter, within which association dominates over dissociation, or in other words, where juridical relations, established between the citizens, exclude anarchistic relations. The frontiers of a State are marked exactly by the line at which war ceases. Within this line, citizens are not authorized to combat each other by means of homicide and robbery. Beyond this line, the people are authorized to combat with these means. It is as a result of this characteristic that the States are "sovereign." According to our present ideas, a State is not sovereign, and is therefore not a State in the complete meaning of the term, if its foreign policy is not completely independent, if it has not absolute liberty to wage war upon its neighbours whenever it seems desirable to do so. The fundamental difference between the relations of the citizens within the State and the relations of the States within humanity, consists in this: the first are juridical; the second anarchistic. Between citizens, war is an accident: the normal condition is the complete absence of tension. Between sovereign States, juridical relations are a happy accident: there is perpetual tension, and latent, if not actual war.

The philosophy of force affirms that the State could not have been created without the employment of force, and that any one who denies this doctrine is convicted of absolute ignorance of sociology. But force signifies war, and war signifies anarchistic relations. To say that the State could only have been produced by war, is to say that the State could only have been produced by anarchistic relations. In the last analysis, then, this amounts to saying that juridical relations can only be created by anarchistic relations, or in other words, that a thing can only be created by its contrary. It is difficult to imagine a more complete contradiction.

Why does Germany constitute a State at the present time? Because Prussia, Saxony, Bavaria, Württemberg, have ceased to be sovereign States, *i. e.*, free to declare war upon each other at any time they choose. If Bavaria should invade Württemberg, a federal decision made by all of Germany would oblige the Bavarians to return to their own territory. The relations between the German States are now of a juridical order. But if tomorrow Prussia, Saxony, Hesse, and Bavaria were to become again sovereign States, *i. e.*, to pass from juridical relations to a state of war, either active or potential, immediately the State of Germany would cease to exist.

We may follow the process even further. Suppose that the administrative districts of Bavaria, such as Franconia, Suabia, and the Palatinate, should proclaim themselves sovereign, and commence to wage war. There would no longer be a Bavarian State. Or suppose that in Franconia the cities of Bayreuth, Bamberg, and Hof divided up into sovereign unities; the Franconian State would cease to exist. In the same way, we may follow the process down to the ancient six hundred German sovereignties, principalities, free cities, etc., or even down to the Bezirks and villages. If war is established between the small units, the State formed by the superior unit is destroyed. Finally, going to the lowest limit, if even in a village each house became a unit free to declare war, the existence of the State would be suppressed completely and absolutely, since it is impossible to give the name of State to the inhabitants of a single house.

Suppose now that we follow the process in the inverse direction. What was it that prevented for so long a time, the creation of the State called Greece? It was because Sparta, Corinth, Thebes, and Athens were not willing to renounce the right to wage war on each other. At the present time, these cities would consider it insane to wage war on each other; they desire to remain in juridical relations, and not in anarchistic relations. As a consequence, the State of Greece does exist. It is war, then, which prevented the formation of the Hellenic State during so many centuries.

The philosophy of force, seeing that certain modern nations have been formed as a result of coercive wars, has concluded in a superficial fashion that war has formed all states. But how is it possible to fail to see that in order to force two social unities to amalgamate into a single one, it is necessary that at least one of these unities should desire to maintain a state of war, or in other terms, anarchistic relations? If the two units consent to form an alliance (to establish juridical relations), the employment of force would become completely superfluous. If, in 1861, the North was obliged to employ force, this was solely because the South, in firing on Fort Sumter, showed that it was determined to employ force against the North. When the force of attack was neutralized by the force of defence, the way was reopened for the real binding forces of common interests, economic, social and moral, to re-establish the Union. In the same way, it was the common interests of the German people, economic, social and moral, expressed in their passionate longing to be united through long generations, and illustrated by the national uprising of 1813 and the Frankfort Parliament of 1848, which finally made it possible to break down the resistance of the six hundred kings, princes, electors, etc., who did not wish to give up their sovereignty, *i. e.*, the right to declare war on each other whenever they so desired.

War has not been the cause of the formation of the German State; war was the cause which prevented the German State from being formed for so many centuries.[1]

The same causes which have operated in the past operate at present. What is the obstacle to the creation of a United States of Europe? The fact that Germany, France, Russia, and England are not willing to renounce the right to make war upon each other. It is war which prevents at the present time the formation of a Pan-European State, just as it prevented for so long the formation of a Pan-Hellenic State. We can see, then, how far wrong Spencer and the other sociologists of the philosophy of force are, in affirming that war has made the great societies. The truth is just the contrary. War has prevented them from being made.

According to Professor Ward, conquest is a fertilization which results in an increase of life, since it causes human societies to pass from an unorganized phase to the organized phase. Precisely the opposite is the truth. All conquest is a diminution of life, a time of arrested development, an obstacle preventing the passage from an imperfect organization to a more perfect organization. Here again, we find physical force ineffective to achieve the desired political result.

When a conqueror occupies a country, his

[1] See *supra*, pp. 104-7, for a consideration of war as a dissociation.

conduct may vary between the limits of a complete extermination of the vanquished and an absolute respect for their rights. Evidently, if the vanquished are massacred to the last man, Professor Ward would not affirm that an intensification of life had taken place. Those who are killed most certainly do not experience any intensification of their life, and for the conquerors, none the less, the massacre of the vanquished is not an intensification of life, for the simple reason that they lose those individuals who might have been their associates, and vital intensity is in direct proportion to the number of the associates. Conquest cannot therefore intensify life, if there is a total or partial extermination of the vanquished. On the other hand, it seems difficult to deny that the sum of vital power of the new organism which issues from the conquest will be exactly in inverse proportion to the injustice exercised by the conqueror. In other words, the conquest will be the more beneficial the less the rights of the conquered are violated, which amounts to saying that life would have been most exuberant if there had been no conquest at all.

If after the conquest, oppression and despotism are quickly effaced, civilization and social vigour reappear. If, however, after the conquest, the vanquished is subjected to a régime less just than that which he enjoyed at the time of his independence, barbarism is an inevitable consequence. Hundreds of examples of this case might be cited.

The régime established by the Turks in the European provinces of their Empire was frightful. Greece became a desert under the Turkish rule. At the epoch of its splendour, Attica alone had 400,000 inhabitants, while all Greece in 1830 did not have 600,000. The city of Athens, from being the abode of an Aristotle and a Praxiteles, had fallen to the rank of a miserable village which did not have a single school or a single stone-cutter. How would Professor Ward fit into his universal law this admirable example of social fertilization and of vital exuberance?

The example is often cited of how a civilized society takes possession, by fire and sword, of a country previously occupied by savages. If, following this conquest, the country becomes civilized, it is said that it is force which has produced this beneficent result. This is only an illusion which arises from a superficial observation of the facts. It is not simply as a result of conquest that certain populations can pass from a wandering and anarchistic life to a sedentary and juridical life; it is organization alone which can produce this result. The Philippines have not been civilized by force; the civilization is the result of education, the introduction of modern methods of hygiene and agriculture. It is because a collection of individuals previously disorganized become organized that they make progress, and not in any degree as a result of collective homicide. In so far as force has played any rôle in the progress of the Philippines, it has only been as a police force, which neutralized the military force of aggression of the various warring tribes, and thus left the field free for the real forces—economic, political, and intellectual—of social progress. Nor is it true to say that organization cannot be accomplished without collective homicide. There are many other means of bringing about the process of education and organization, as illustrated in the work of the Jesuits in South America, and of the missionaries in other parts of the world. On the other hand, homicide may be practised during many years without leading to any organization.

In general, there are two kinds of political union which result from conquest, the one real, and the other artificial. Real union can only be obtained by justice and the action of social forces. Physical force produces only artificial unions, which tend to break up at every instant. They result in an enfeeblement of life, both for the conquerors and for the conquered, as long as they last. Examples of these artificial unions are the union of Germany and Alsace-Lorraine, of Russia and Poland, of Austria and the Trentino, of Hungary and Transylvania. Far from being force which creates the State, it may be said that the strength of a State is in inverse proportion to the amount of force which was used at its foundation.

One of the occasions on which force is supposed to have been politically effective was in the abolition of slavery in the United States. But this theory fails to account for the fact that slavery has also been abolished in all other parts of the world, *e. g.*, in the colonies of the British Empire, without war. If we ask why slavery has been abolished in all other parts of the world, we find that it was the result of the conviction that slavery was economically and morally wrong. It was the same force which was effective in the United States. In the North this conviction was reached early. Even at the beginning of the war, a strong party in the South held the conviction that slavery was economically and morally wrong. The discussion went on during all the four years of the Civil War, and General Lee is reported to have said, just before his surrender, that at least it was fortunate that the South had become convinced that slavery should be abolished.

Another proof that it was intellectual conviction and not physical force that abolished slavery is found by comparing the results obtained in the emancipation and the enfranchisement of the negro. Both were supposed to have been accomplished by physical force. In so far as force could accomplish the result it was done, and both freedom and suffrage were guaranteed to the negro by an amendment to the United States Constitution. The negro retained his freedom, but he did not retain his right of suffrage. Why? Because the South was convinced that slavery was economically and morally wrong, but it was not convinced that the vote should be given to uneducated negroes.   In the political domain, as well as in the economic realm, physical force is irrelevant and ineffective; the victory is obtained only through struggle in the higher plane, and by intellectual forces.

The political futility of force is recognized in all enlightened communities where the party in power, although actually in command of the military forces of the country, refrains from using this physical force to try to keep itself in power when defeated at the polls.   In socially unenlightened communities, such as Venezuela or Mexico, in so far as the belief in the political effectiveness of physical force obtained, its real futility was demonstrated by the unceasing revolutions, and the degradation of civilization, which carried down with it those who attempted to advance their welfare or obtain political objects by an irrelevant instrument.   Society and political progress are only possible when the irrelevance of physical force to obtain political objects is realized by the members of a community.

The most striking illustration of the realization of the irrelevance of physical force in intellectual struggles is found in the cessation of the wars of religion.   Lecky has traced with a master's hand the process by which religious persecutions declined and the wars of religion disappeared as the result of the intellectual discussions and the rising spirit of rationalism which undermined and

disintegrated their motives.[1]   The disappearance
of the religious wars was not so remarkable, however, as the disappearance of the motives for
these wars, the fact that men lost all desire to
impose their intellectual convictions by physical
force upon others.   The story of this change in
ideas is one of surpassing interest in the history of
human evolution.   From the time when the first
heretics questioned the dogmas almost universally
held in the Roman Catholic Church, through the
discussions and the debates of Castellio, Socinus,
Zwingli, and the other leaders who compelled
Calvin and the Geneva theologians to defend
their position by arguments instead of by cannons
and thus removed the struggle to the realm of
intellect, to the victory of rationalism over persecution and force as a means of establishing
truth, the story of the rise of tolerance constitutes one of the most dramatic illustrations in history of the futility of physical force in the realm
of intellectual struggle, and of the abandonment

[1] See W. E. H. Lecky, *History of the Rise and Influence of the Spirit of Rationalism in Europe*, New York, 1871, especially chapter v.:
"The Peace of Westphalia is justly regarded as closing the era
of religious wars. . . . Among all the possible dangers which
cloud the horizon, none appears more improbable than a coalition
formed upon the principle of a common belief, and designed to
extend the sphere of its influence. . . . Wars that were once
regarded as simple duties became absolutely impossible. . . .
That which had long been the centre around which all other
interests revolved, receded and disappeared, and a profound
change in the actions of mankind indicated a profound change
in their belief."—Vol. ii., pp. 110-11.

of the use of this force as soon as its futility was recognized.

It is the cataclysmic theory of history which prevents us from realizing the superior effectiveness of intellectual forces over physical forces, since intellectual processes must be classed among the real and invisible causes of progress. If after the Great War the democratic forces in Germany gain a victory over the Junkers and get possession of the German Government, the superficial methods of the cataclysmic theory will doubtless lead to a widespread belief that this political revolution and the resulting progress were caused by the war and constitute a justification for much of its suffering and destruction. The steady growth of the German Social Democracy during the past generation; the fact that it has gained one per cent. of the total German vote on the average every year for the past twenty years; that in 1912 the Social Democrats had secured 34% of the total Germany vote, and that the continuance of this irresistible progress must inevitably have given them the control of the Government within a few years, will probably be entirely lost sight of. Yet the victory of democracy will nevertheless be due primarily to these intellectual forces, and to the work of education, propaganda, organization, and agitation which the Social Democrats have carried on, year after year, and which the cruder methods of the Junkers, with their reliance upon the political power and the military force which they control, had been utterly unable to resist.

In the same way if the disintegration of the Hapsburg Empire should follow the war the cataclysmic theory will hold this to be the result of the war, while the real causes: the steady growth of the consciousness of nationality, the spread of education, the influence of a cheap popular press, the renaissance in the Slavic literature among the racial elements of Austria, the fact that for many years organization has been going on which upon an agreed signal—the death of the Emperor, Franz Joseph—had planned a simultaneous uprising against the military force by which the heterogeneous elements of the Austro-Hungarian Empire alone were held together,—all these slow and invisible causes, in which the true explanation of the inevitable decentralization of the Hapsburg military empire must be found, will be almost certainly disregarded in favour of the simple and superficial explanation of the cataclysmic theory. It is significant that in recent years the Junkers of Germany and the military ruling class of Austria-Hungary had begun to recognize the relative futility of physical force and had been compelled themselves to take up the more effective, intellectual weapons, organizing counter-propaganda and educational campaigns, removing some of the more flagrant injustices which served their opponents as effective arguments, and making many concessions to the spirit of liberty and nationality,

14

concessions in flat contradiction with the policy dictated by their own philosophy of the effectiveness of force.

The declining effectiveness of force is not only a consequence of the progress of civilization. It is also a cause. As the rôle of physical force becomes less important, due to the realization of its ineffectiveness, more of the energies of men are set free for the higher forms of struggle, economic, political, and intellectual. This increased activity in the higher forms of struggle again makes physical forces less effective, so that we have a cumulative result with the law of acceleration entering into play. The material advance in civilization also, due to increasing co-operation and the division of labour, places new and increasingly powerful instruments at the disposal of intellectual forces—instruments of education, the popular press, postal and telegraphic systems, rapid means of transportation; and these new and powerful instruments greatly increase the effectiveness and rapidity of operation of the intellectual forces. Social evolution is essentially a progressive modification of conflict by association and interdependence, and in the course of this modification conflict itself is transformed from a physical into an intellectual struggle.

The result of this process of the declining effectiveness of force is that in our modern interdependent civilization physical force used for aggression has become futile to advance those ends, economic, social, and moral, for which men live and strive.

Why, then, it may be asked, does force still play so large a rôle in human relations?

The reason is because unfortunately it is not facts which determine the actions of men, but their *belief* in regard to these facts. It is not enough that physical force, used for aggression, should be futile; it is necessary that men should realize its futility.

The question whether the system of international anarchy can be replaced by a system of international justice and law depends upon the question whether an intellectual revolution can be accomplished, replacing error by truth in the minds of men.

Have we any basis to hope for such an intellectual revolution? What are the forces making for such a revolution, and what are the obstacles in the way of its accomplishment? These are the questions we shall study in the next chapter, and upon the answer which history shall give to this fundamental question, depends the hope of the redemption of human society.

CHAPTER VII

THE INTELLECTUAL REVOLUTION

ONE of the chief characteristics of the philosophy of force is its crudely fatalistic theory of society and political institutions. Running all through the literature of its philosophy is the assumption that it is no use trying to correct false ideas in the minds of men, because their "fighting instincts" render war "inevitable"; because "history repeats itself"; or, because "you cannot change human nature." It is everywhere taken for granted that man's conduct is not influenced by his ideas, since he is not guided by reason or "logic." We find the belief almost universal in this philosophy that war is not, like law or constitutional government or any other human institution, the result of human effort and opinion, good and bad, but is imposed by outside forces which men cannot control.

This social fatalism throws an interesting light upon the general lack of knowledge of the most elementary fact of social science—that ideas are the source of institutions. Obsessed by the idea of struggle, the advocates of the philosophy of force ignore entirely the most wide-spread and effective form of this struggle—the intellectual struggle—to which must be traced ultimately all social progress. And the most effective reply to this social fatalism is found in the activities of those who profess this belief, but who nevertheless devote much of their energies to the intellectual struggle, to propagating their ideas, and advocating their philosophy of social fatalism.

What is implied in the argument that war cannot be abolished because "you cannot change human nature"?

When analysed, it means that man is at bottom a selfish animal, that as long as he can use force effectively to advance his welfare, he may be relied upon to do so, that nations, since they are made up of men having this fundamentally selfish characteristic, may be relied upon to act in the same selfish manner, and that war will be the inevitable result of the clash of these competing selfish national interests.

In other words, social fatalism and the argument for war based on "unchanging human nature" rest on the belief in the effectiveness of force.

But suppose it could be demonstrated to the people of the nation that nothing can be gained by aggression, would it be necessary to change human nature to induce this nation to give up aggression?

The disappearance of piracy offers an interesting analogy. In this case also it was argued that piracy would never disappear because you cannot change human nature. But when public opinion became sufficiently enlightened to realize the damage caused to commerce by the insecurity of the high seas, it created such effective police measures that piracy as an institution became an increasingly unprofitable and dangerous occupation, and finally completely disappeared, the "unchanging human nature" to the contrary notwithstanding. In other words, when force became obviously ineffective for achieving the end which the pirates desired, it was abandoned.

Another analogy is given by the disappearance of the religious wars.[1] When men realized the futility of physical force for changing intellectual convictions and religious beliefs, the religious wars ceased. No change in human nature was necessary and the "fighting instincts" remained as vigorous as ever. All that occurred was a change in certain ideas in the minds of men, in regard to the effectiveness or futility of physical force in intellectual struggles.

But force has now become futile, as we have seen in the preceding chapter, to advance any of those interests, economic, social, or moral, for which men live and strive.

What will any of the nations—Germany, England, France, Russia, Austria-Hungary, Italy, Turkey—gain from the Great War to compensate them for the loss in life and treasure, the burden of

[1] See *supra*, pp. 206–208.

huge war debts and of pensions for millions of widows and orphans, the legacy of bitterness and hatred, the increased militarization of the minds of the people, and the destruction of millions of the flower of the race?

It is obvious that no adequate compensation for sacrifices of such magnitude can be found in material gain, conquest of territory, war indemnities, or capture of a rival's trade.

Only an intellectual revolution, a turning away from the false philosophy of force which has produced such disastrous fruits, can render an adequate compensation for the devotion and self-sacrifice with which millions of men have given their lives for what they believed to be a great ideal. Only a reconstruction of society upon the sounder foundations of a philosophy of co-operation and justice can make it possible to say that these sacrifices have not been made in vain.

What are the indications that we may hope for such an intellectual revolution, which will prepare the way for the organization of a new Europe and a new world?

The war alone cannot be expected to produce such an intellectual revolution. Mankind is, of course, much more impressed by cataclysmic events, by the unusual and dramatic on a vast scale than by the ordinary occurrences of everyday life, and the treaty of peace which ends the war may be expected to mark the beginning of a new epoch in human history. But the military events will not determine what the character of this new epoch will be. In fact, in so far as it is affected only by the surface events of the war, it may be said that the human race is as likely to draw the wrong conclusions as the right ones.

The condition after the war is likely to resemble that which followed the Thirty Years' War. Two main currents of thought may be traced to the events of that period. On the one hand, Hobbes, looking out upon the world as he saw it, drew his picture of "the war of each against all" as the natural state of man and applied the philosophy of force to the theory of the State. On the other hand, the futility of force was widely recognized, and the same events which led Hobbes to write his *Leviathan* impelled Grotius to write his *De Jure Belli ac Pacis*, which laid the foundations of the science of international law, and marks the beginning, at least, of the conception of a society of nations living under a reign of justice.

In the same way, it is possible that the end of the Great War may mark the beginning of two powerful currents of intellectual forces which will struggle for the mastery during the next generation. On the one hand, we may have an immense strengthening of militarism. If an unjust treaty of peace should be made by short-sighted statesmen and diplomats, Europe would be left an armed camp. The resulting peace would be only a temporary truce, and the nations would concentrate all their resources for the renewal of the struggle as soon as they could recuperate their losses. The philosophy of force and the spirit of militarism have been immensely strengthened by the censorship of the press and the concentration on the work of destruction in all the belligerent countries, and this definite militarization of the minds of the people, if the war is continued long enough, will greatly strengthen the forces of reaction.   The process which is going on may be judged from the folowing statement in the London *Morning Post*[1] less than three months after the beginning of the war:

The absurd talk about this war being a war against militarism has now subsided. . . . There has been in the recent past a horrid disease of internationalism. . . . Militarism, said to be so bad a thing in itself, has become the sole business of the nation. . . . Democracy may still exist, but it is no longer in evidence. . . .

If this is an indication of the condition in England,—the most democratic of all the countries engaged in the war,—the effect of the process of militarization and of the suppression of the freedom of the press and of speech in the other countries can readily be imagined.   Nor can it be assumed that the effects of this condition will be only temporary, and that after the war everything will be restored as if by magic.   A process of militarization of public opinion cannot be carried on day

[1] Leading article, October 20, 1914.

by day through a period of months and even years, without profoundly affecting the social philosophy of the nations engaged in such a gigantic struggle. And the intellectual interdependence of nations has become so great that the effect of this increase of militarism will be felt in all the neutral countries as well. The world cannot exist half-democratic and half-militaristic. Not even tariff walls or a policy of isolation can prevent the invasion of ideas, and if the philosophy of force becomes more firmly established in Europe as the result of the war, it will inevitably spread to America and the other continents.

The effect of the war upon the psychological forces of inertia and indifference will, of course, be important. The introduction into the human minds of a new idea, especially if it is opposed to a philosophy of life which is widely disseminated, necessitates an intellectual readjustment which is nearly always an uncomfortable if not a painful process, and which therefore meets with a resistance more or less violent. Writing as long ago as 1894, Novikov pointed out the influence of this factor of inertia as follows:

We no longer share the delusions of our coarse ancestors. We know war does not enrich the victors, we know we cannot work on man's conscience by material means, we know that in order to combat an opinion we must set up another opinion in opposition to it. We know all that, but, alas! the ancient ideas imbedded in our brains for long generations are not easily uprooted. The inefficacy of war for settling economic, political, and spiritual questions is evident; but we persist in our time-worn ways, and continue from tradition to use that method.

In reality the civilized peoples today conduct wars simply because their savage ancestors did so of old. There is no other reason. It is a case of pure atavism, a survival, a routine. From sheer spiritual laziness they will not abandon their accustomed habits. Then because the idea of carrying on war without any motive is revolting to them, they erect theory on theory, system on system to justify it.[1]

Here again the influence of the Great War may be counted upon to aid in the task of overcoming the inertia and indifference which have been among the chief obstacles to a change of ideas in the past. A wide-spread demand for the democratic control of the foreign policies of the nations, witnesses to the disappearance of the old idea that international relations do not intimately concern the welfare of the people, and had best be left to the diplomatists and the "experts" in the philosophy of force. Never have the conditions been so favourable for a thorough discussion and a fundamental re-examination of the philosophy upon which rests not only international relations, but as we shall see in the next chapter, the entire structure of society.

The changes which are going on in the minds

[1] J. Novikov, *War and Its Alleged Benefits*, pp. 76–77.

of men as a consequence of the Great War are much more important than those which will be made on the map of Europe, and the results of the struggle in the intellectual realm are fraught with greater issues for the future of humanity than the results of any military campaign.

In spite of the unfavourable factors of militarization and inertia, there are many indications that the time is ripe for the intellectual revolution which must precede a reconstruction of human society on sounder foundations. The fallacy that war is an effective method for advancing national welfare, so widely spread as the result of a superficial reading of the historical events of 1870, has been completely exposed. Moreover, in the presence of the incontestable facts of the Great War, such as casualty lists running up into the millions, we shall probably have less of the glorification of war. The doctrine that collective homicide is the cause of human progress will not be in such high favour in the future, especially with the democracies of the nations which will have to bear the burdens of the war. A significant change can be noticed in the public opinion of the nations of Europe, as reflected in the official documents issued at the beginning of the war, in which there is a general repudiation of all aggressive design and each nation insists that it is fighting only a defensive war for its national existence.

This almost universal repudiation of aggressive design, which indicates the rise of a new international morality, based on a more enlightened public opinion, has a two-fold significance. In the first place it probably indicates an intuitive and growing popular conviction of the futility of force, used aggressively. In the second place, even where it has not gone so far as to remove all danger of aggression in the future, it indicates that the motives for aggression are becoming sufficiently attenuated so as to make possible the formation of a League of Peace. Such a league is the only means which can satisfy the common need for which the leading statesmen of all the nations say they are fighting,—a sense of security against the danger of aggression from any one of their number.

Since the effect of such a League of Peace would be to raise the struggle between nations from the purely destructive form—the physiological struggle —to its higher economic, political, and intellectual forms, it would thus open the way for an unprecedented advance for the whole human race. Instead of a blood-stained and brutalized Europe staggering up from this conflict to begin another forty-four years of insane armament competition leading to a still more calamitous breakdown of civilization, we may have at least the beginnings of a world federation—a reconstructed world society definitely turning away from the old path of force which has proved so disastrous, and finding instead a new path of progress, with co-operation and justice as the touchstones of

political and social action. For the significance
of a League of Peace lies in the fact that it gives
official recognition to the realization on the part
of the nations that force, used for aggression, has
become futile to advance the welfare, economic,
social or moral, of their people.

The realization of the economic futility of force
is likely to have its most practical effect in modifying the foreign policies of nations. The Franco-
Prussian War of 1870 with the huge indemnity
extorted by the victors from the vanquished,
undoubtedly led to the belief by superficial
observers that war could be made to pay, but this
motive is probably not now important as a direct
cause of war. Men will not fight until the moral
stuff of mankind is damaged. But the strife and
friction caused by false ideas of the effectiveness of
force to promote national welfare are undoubtedly
contributing causes to the atmosphere of suspicion,
fear, and distrust, which are the foundations of
international anarchy and the armed peace.

The recognition of the futility of force for promoting national advantage may also be expected
to contribute to the movement for the freedom
of the seas, including the establishment of the
immunity of private property at sea and the
substitution of international control of the high-
ways of the nations for control by the greatest
naval power. And with this movement toward
greater freedom of trade and international co-

operation will come a weakening of the old mercantilist conception of the nations as rival trade units, while a recognition of the community of economic interests of the family of nations will lead to a gradual undermining of the fallacy that the prosperity of one State can only be obtained at the cost of the disadvantage of another State.

The realization of the economic futility of force is important because economic facts are the foundations of social well-being and, as we shall see in a later chapter, the welfare of society constitutes the rational and scientific standard of morality.[1] The realization of the social futility of force will lead inevitably to a recognition of the true nature of social struggles, which always take place by means of psychic processes. In recent years there has been a marked tendency towards an increasing recognition of the futility of physical force to achieve social results. Illustrations of this tendency are found in the partial abandonment, after repeated failure, of Prussian and Russian methods of denationalizing the Polish people, in the grant of a constitution to Alsace and Lorraine, and in the granting of Home Rule to South Africa. The passing of the Home Rule bill for Ireland is especially significant because it marks the turning away from the old methods of force tried in vain for more than three hundred years.

[1] See Chapter XI., "The Relation of Morality and Self-Interest."

The appeal to force by a minority in order to maintain itself in power is likely to become less and less frequent as the futility of force to withstand a united public opinion becomes more apparent. With the cessation of reliance upon force by minorities to thwart the will of majorities, the occasion for the use of force by these majorities will become increasingly rare and the political revolutions, which embody the results of intellectual revolutions, will take place without bloodshed and violence. Since 1906, especially, the Russian revolutionists have learned that they must rely upon intellectual processes for ultimate victory, and they have been tirelessly at work in the intervening years. In so far as the Russian Revolution of 1906 relied upon violence, like the French Revolution, it became affected by the instrument which it used. It led to a cumulative development of violence, and this in turn led to a reign of terror, to a recoil of all the saner elements who recognized the indispensable need of law and order, to reaction, to the "man on horseback," and the inevitable failure to establish that new heaven and new earth for which men were willing to give their lives with such complete abandonment and self-sacrifice.

The realization of the futility of force to advance the moral ideals of mankind will constitute the most important effect of the intellectual revolution. Men will not fight until they are appealed to on some moral issue,—on the ground of some high ideal of justice, or of altruistic motives. In the Great War the support of the German people was gained only by the appeal to their devotion to the existence of the Fatherland and the altruistic motive of protecting its ally, Austria-Hungary. In the same way the appeal to the Russian people emphasized the need of their little Servian brother. To the French people the liberation of Alsace and Lorraine from the Prussian conqueror was the motive. The British people enlisted to free Belgium; and the Italian people were carried into the war by a passion for "unredeemed Italy," the *Italia irredenta*. The war was proclaimed as a great moral crusade to crush militarism or navalism, to overthrow Prussianism or Russianism, and to free Europe from its reign of terror. Under the influence of these moral ideals, in every country all consideration was abandoned for the great ecodomic interests of national welfare, the sacrifice of life and treasure, the immense burden of suffering and misery for the present generation and their posterity.

But soon after its beginning a marked degeneration of purpose became evident.[1] As the forces of reaction were strengthened by the war, the demand for retaliation replaced that for the sanctity

[1] A remarkable collection of the evidence of this degeneration of moral purpose during the first twelve months of war has been published in *War and Peace*, vol. iii., numbers 22–26, August-November, 1915. See also Norman Angell, *America and the New World-State*, Part II., for a discussion of the moral reactions of force.

of international law; a lust for annexation and conquest began to dominate the militaristic press;
and the repudiation of the higher motives announced at the beginning of the war has gone on
increasingly. It seems even possible that a war
entered upon on the part of the Allies to destroy
Prussian militarism may result in enthroning militarism in all Europe for a decade or a generation.
The demonstration upon so large a scale that wars
entered upon with high ideals must fail to attain
those ideals because they fail to recognize the
nature of the instrument which they use and
the process by which moral progress is made,
may result in profound changes in the ideas and
actions of men, just as the demonstration on a
large scale of the failure of physical force to
suppress heresy led to the rise of tolerance and the
abandonment of physical force in the realm of
intellectual conviction.

When the futility of force becomes widely recognized and the true nature of social struggle is
known, we may expect an enormous increase of
activity in the intellectual realm—the most
fruitful field of struggle. We may expect the
creation of a new science of social engineering,
seeking to improve institutions by modifying
ideas, and using all the marvellous instruments
of the press and the telegraph, the church and
all educational institutions, the moving-picture
and the phonograph, now almost entirely under

the control of blind social forces. The irresistible growth of democracy in all parts of the world will be tremendously stimulated. We may expect whole libraries of books to be written upon methods of propaganda and the organization of campaigns for changing and enlightening public opinion, just as they are now written upon military strategy and tactics. Monuments and tablets of honour will be erected to the great educators, statesmen, authors, and men of genius, just as they are now erected to the great leaders of armies and navies whose work has been chiefly destructive, but whom we believe to be the leaders and saviours of civilization, because of the dominance of the doctrine that war has been the cause of human progress.

The chief advantages which will flow from such an intellectual revolution, however, will occur through the establishment of a sounder and truer social philosophy as the foundation for a reconstructed civilization. Our detailed analysis has shown that the whole philosophy of force is false and constitutes one of the most colossal and disastrous errors that has ever darkened the soul and mind of man. For a large part of the human race, even though it does not make this careful analysis, the great outstanding fact of the war itself will furnish a sufficient demonstration that the path of force is a wrong one and military power is a futile instrument to advance the welfare of any nation or even to protect a nation from the loss of the flower of its manhood and the destruction of its national wealth. On the part of the growing democratic forces of the nations at least we shall witness a definite turning away from a philosophy which has proven itself false by leading so directly and so inevitably to such a breakdown of civilization.

But if the old path of force is wrong, how are we to escape from it, where shall we find the main highway of true progress, from which the human race has wandered so far astray?

As between nations, at least, the new path is known. It consists in world organization—the establishment of a system of international justice to replace the disastrous international anarchy of the past. Can this special solution be generalized for the entire social order? Can any guiding principle be found for the whole problem of the place of force in human relations?

At least it is a gain to have found, even though it has been at such a terrible cost of life and treasure, that the path which has been followed in the past is a wrong one. The recognition of error is the first step towards truth. And at least we can go so far as to say that we will take as a touchstone of social and political action in the future this question, "*Will this action, if adopted, lead towards a diminution of physical force in human relationships?*"

Since force is socially, morally, and economically

futile to advance human progress, we are logically compelled to ask ourselves the next question, "What condition leads towards a minimum of this element of physical force in human relationships?" We can find the solution of this problem most easily, if we turn it around and ask, "What condition leads towards a maximum of force in human relationships?" The reply to this question is *Injustice*. We find a direct relationship between the amount of injustice of a given social order and the amount of force necessary to maintain that order, whether we consider national injustice, as where a dominant race like that of the governing minority in Austria attempts to suppress the national aspirations of 80% of the Hapsburg Empire by military force; or political injustice, as where an autocratic minority as in Russia and Prussia relies upon the control of military power to maintain its position; or economic injustice, as in Colorado, where machine-guns and mine guards, state militia and federal troops, were necessary to bolster up a wrong industrial system.

Conversely the more nearly a social structure approaches the condition of justice the less will be the amount of force required to maintain the balance in this society. If then we desire to escape from the wrong path of force, which leads only to destruction, we have only to turn back to the true path of social progress, the path of justice. With the establishment of justice, social, political, international, the necessity for force automatically disappears.   The two elements, force and justice, are inversely proportional in any social structure.

In returning to the true path of social progress, the path of justice, we are returning to the social teachings of Darwin.   Darwin's whole theory of social progress is based on the moral law, the foundation of which he states as the principle of reciprocity: "As ye would that men should do to you, do ye to them likewise."[1]   The task of reconstruction, then, depends primarily upon an intellectual revolution.   We must not only overthrow the false philosophy of force, but we must enthrone in its place the true philosophy of social, political, and international justice.

It is, of course, apparent that however great the favouring conditions, such an intellectual revolution cannot accomplish itself, but must be the result of hard intellectual work, of the contributions of many minds who come to the task from all the fields of human interest.   The reconstruction of social theories upon the sounder foundations of co-operation, justice, and the moral law can only take place by the same process of conscious intellectual effort by which the anti-social, antiscientific, and anti-democratic philosophy of force which we have been studying was established. Nietzsche has outlined for us the systematic intellectual process by which the false philosophy of force, which has played such havoc with the social structure of mankind, was established:

[1] Darwin, *The Descent of Man*, chap. iv., p. 142.

We who hold a different belief—we, who regard the democratic movement, not only as a degenerating form of political organization, but as equivalent to a degenerating, a waning type of man, as involving his mediocrizing and depreciation: where have *we* to fix our hopes? In *new philosophers*—there is no other alternative: in minds strong and original enough to initiate opposite estimates of value.[1]

The task of reconstruction in social philosophy is distinct from that which Nietzsche outlines, in that it does not consist in setting up a false standard of value and then building a theory to correspond. The new social philosophy must begin with a thorough examination of the structure of society; science must be its guiding star, and its watchword, "The truth shall make you free." Its greatest hope lies in the fact that it runs with, not counter to, the great world currents of democracy and the fundamental social instincts of the human race.

This intellectual revolution, this replacing of the idea of force by the idea of justice as the guiding principle of social and political action, is fraught with an untold wealth of promise for the advancement of the human race. Thus far we have failed to reap the fruits of that unparalleled advance in the physical world, in the mastery of the laws of nature and the increased productivity of labour, which have been the dominant characteristics of the past century. No addition has

[1] Nietzsche, *Beyond Good and Evil*, "The Natural History of Morals," p. 22.

been made to the sum total of human happiness.
Paradoxical as may seem such a consequence of
this enormous increase in the productivity of each
individual workman, the amount of poverty, disease, and suffering, the slums of the cities, and the
burden of fear and of care in the life of the common
man have been greatly increased since the coming
of the industrial revolution.

Mr. A. R. Wallace, the co-discoverer with
Darwin of the theory of evolution, has reached the
conclusion that the human race has degenerated
morally during the past century.[1] May it not be
that this failure to make social, intellectual, and
moral progress corresponding to the progress
which we have made in the physical world is due
to the fact that we have relied upon this false
principle of physical force as an effective measure
in human relations?   This is the conclusion which
at least one noted historian[2] has reached. He
states his conclusion as follows:

The slow moral progress of European civilization
during the last two or three centuries, compared with
its wonderful intellectual and material progress, may
with little hesitation be attributed in large part to the
unfavourable influence of its war ethics upon its every-
day moral code.   The war code is applied to politics,
to ordinary business, and to the relations of the industrial classes. . . . So long as nations act under the

[1] Wallace, *Social Environment and Moral Progress*, 1913.
Chapter xvii., p. 169.
[2] Philip Van Ness Myers, *History as Past Ethics*, pp. 379–380.

illusion that they may without moral wrong employ violence to obtain justice, just so long will there be individuals who with good conscience will seek justice through violence.

The change in ideas and the establishment of a true theory of human relationship which must precede social reconstruction may be compared with three other intellectual revolutions which have profoundly affected the minds of men and led to marvellous advances in the realms of physical science, philosophy, and astronomy.

In the physical sciences we had an intellectual revolution at the time of the Reformation and Renaissance, when men turned away from the principle of intellectual force—authority—as a method of discovering truth and found instead the method of experiment and direct observation. In that marvellous change in the minds of men when they abandoned the barren path of the deductive method and struck out upon the new highroad of the inductive method we find the cause of that marvellous advance in our knowledge of the physical universe and of our conquest of the forces of nature which has been the glory of the nineteenth century.

In the same way in the intellectual revolution which is now taking place, in which men are turning away from the old barren path of destructive violence and finding instead the highroad of social, political, and international justice, we are entering upon an era of advance which may enable us at last to reach the social and spiritual heights corresponding to the progress which has been made in the mastery of the material universe.

In philosophy we had an intellectual revolution in the time of Immanuel Kant, when men turned away from the external universe as the essential truth and found instead the mind and the spirit of man as the eternal reality. Kant's critical study of the laws of the mind, and of the senses by which we perceive the manifestations of nature, led to a marvellous extension of the power of man to understand the universe, and is the threshold from which modern philosophy starts on its quest for the Holy Grail of Truth.

In the same way in the social revolution, by turning away from the struggle of physical force in the external world and concentrating our energies instead upon the struggle for truth and justice in the intellectual realm, we shall be opening the way for a reconstruction of our social institutions upon rational lines, and in conformity with the true principles of human relationships which emerge as the result of this intellectual struggle.

In astronomy the intellectual revolution which marked the change from the old Ptolemaic system, in which the earth was considered as the centre of the planetary system, to the true or Copernican system in which the sun became the centre, illustrates most clearly the nature of the present intellectual revolution, in which men are turning away from false theories as to the nature and structure of human society and are finding instead the true principles of co-operation and justice upon which all human relationships are naturally based. Under the false Ptolemaic system, with the earth as the centre, an extraordinarily complex system of cycles and epicycles, of crystal spheres and celestial orbits, had to be built up to explain the revolution of the planets and the sun around the earth, while every new fact which was discovered increased the complexity of the system. As soon as the sun came to be considered as the central body, however, the solar system became extraordinarily simple, with the planets revolving in majestic ellipses around a common focus at the sun, while every new fact that was discovered fitted into its proper place and made the system more perfect and more complete. Thus the way was opened for Kepler's discovery of the three great laws of planetary motion; this in turn led the way to Newton's discovery of the law of gravitation and so the foundations were laid for all the marvellous developments of the modern physical sciences.

In the same manner a false social philosophy, out of accord with the great fundamental facts of human society, has led to an infinite complication and distortion of the whole social structure, while a new and true social philosophy, based upon direct observation of the facts of social life and upon their scientific study and systematization, will lead to an equally marvellous advance in the social and spiritual life of mankind. If the path of error in social philosophy has led to untold misery and suffering for the human race, we may expect that the path of truth will lead to a redeemed human society and a sum of human happiness— a life more abundant—such as "eye hath not seen, ear hath not heard, neither hath entered into the heart of man" in all the Golden Ages of the past.

In this great task of replacing error by truth in the social philosophy of mankind we shall need the aid of all the sciences of the humanities,— sociology, economics, history, political science, philosophy, and ethics. As sociology[1] approaches more nearly to the standard of a real science, we must look to it more and more for the annunciation of great general principles which shall guide social and political action.

To economics we must look for an exposure of the fallacies which underlie the belief in the antagonism and the economic rivalry of nations; for the spread of an understanding of the true facts of international relations and of a practical realization of the economic solidarity of the entire human race.

In the science of history we shall receive most aid from the new school which is turning away

[1] Besides the epoch-making works of Novikov, those of Müller-Lyer, in Germany, and of Professor Giddings, in America, are among the most valuable contributions in modern sociology.

from the philosophy of force, the study of military and political events as the chief factor in evolution, and is tracing instead the true History of Civilization. This new school of history is beginning to find a clear guiding principle in Kant's theory of universal history as the growth of a world community, reconciling the freedom of individuals and of individual nations with the accomplishment of a common aim for mankind as a whole.[1]

In political science, especially, an unprecedented advance may be expected to result from replacing the false principle of force by the true principle of justice as the foundation of States.

From the practical application of philosophy, logic,[2] and ethics to social problems in the light of Darwin's theory of the moral law as the basis of all social progress, we may expect an indispensable strengthening of the intellectual foundations upon which must rest democracy, and the morality and rational religion of the future.

When we understand how the distortion of the false philosophy of force has spread all through the social structure,[3] we shall realize that all social

[1] See F. S. Marvin, *The Living Past: a Sketch of Western Progress*, Oxford University Press, 1913, and Philip Van Ness Myers, *History as Past Ethics*. Ginn and Company, 1913.

[2] See John M. Robertson, *Letters on Reasoning*, Watts & Co., London, 1905, for illustrations of how non-academic logic may contribute to social progress, and for a summary of the work by Jevons and others which has been done already in this field.

[3] See Chapter VIII., "Force and the Social Structure," for a number of illustrations of this distortion.

workers have at bottom the same task,—the establishment of a true philosophy of social, political, and international justice, as the basis for the reconstruction and redemption of human society. The peace movement, with its goal of world federation, is the unifying thesis of all social reform, and from a realization of this fact and the resulting co-operation of all forces making for social progress may be expected an unparalleled accession of power and rapidity of advance. Social workers have been justly compared by Mr. Hobhouse to a number of guerrilla bands, striving at cross purposes, and even warring against each other, but with the coming of the intellectual revolution they will be transformed into an army of social reform, irresistible in the strength of its unity and of its demand for righteousness and justice as the universal principle of the expansion of life.

The reconstruction of ideas must precede the reconstruction of society, however, and it is to this intellectual revolution and the indispensable clarification of thought that we must first direct our attention. Thus far we have been engaged in a detailed examination of the errors of the philosophy of force,—biological sociological, political, economic, and moral. Following this work of destruction, the clearing of the ground of the ruins of the old structure in order to make way for the new, we shall proceed, after a survey of the extent to which the philosophy of force has distorted the whole structure of modern society, to a study of Darwin's true theory of social progress, as the basis for the establishment of the new and liberating philosophy of justice.

PART II

MUTUAL AID AS A FACTOR OF SOCIAL PROGRESS

CHAPTER VIII

FORCE AND THE SOCIAL STRUCTURE

THE philosophy of force, which is writ large in the conduct of nations, runs all through the social structure and distorts all our ideas of human relationships. We have noted already in Chapter II., the manner in which "social Darwinism" has supplied an apparently scientific foundation for anti-social theories ranging from extreme individualism and the policy of laissez-faire to the most ruthless forms of modern Imperialism. Wherever we examine closely the institutions of the society in which we live we can trace the effects of the tool—force—which man has used and misused in the course of his evolution. In what follows we shall try to find how far the introduction of force, and of the philosophy which goes with it, has reacted upon the society which has used it.

The organization of the States for war profoundly influences the political life of the nation and results in certain definite social phenomena, affecting even the personal conduct and ethics of each individual citizen. Herbert Spencer[1] has traced

[1] *Principles of Sociology*, vol. ii., part v., chapters xvii and xviii.

the effect of this distortion through the philosophy of force, in two remarkable chapters on the militant type of society and the industrial type of society—types which are found to a greater or less degree in every nation.

The fundamental principle of the militant type of society, according to Spencer, is compulsory co-operation. He describes some of its characteristics thus:

Under the militant type the individual is owned by the State. While preservation of the society is the primary end, preservation of each member is a secondary end—an end cared for chiefly as subserving the primary end. . . . Chronic militancy tends to develop a despotism. Labour is carried on under coercion; and supervision spreads everywhere.

Under the system of compulsory co-operation a social structure is developed which strongly resists change. The principle of inheritance, becoming established in respect of the classes in which militancy originates, tends eventually to fix also their special functions . . . tends to fix the position of each in rank, in occupation, and in locality. . . . Organizations other than those forming parts of the state-organization are wholly or partially repressed. The public combination occupying all fields excludes private combinations. . . . Obviously, indeed, such combinations based on the principle of voluntary co-operation, are incongruous with social arrangements on the principle of compulsory co-operation. Hence the militant type is characterized by the absence, or comparative rarity, of bodies of citizens associated for commercial purposes, for propagating special religious views, for achieving philanthropic ends, etc.[1]

Spencer thus shows in a striking manner how the questions of liberty and democratic government are bound up with the problem of war and the philosophy of force. The modern names for what Spencer calls the militant and the industrial types of society are militarism and democracy. The terms are diametrically opposed. Democracy is based on government by consent and the principle of voluntary co-operation, in which authority proceeds from below. "Government of the people, by the people, for the people," is Lincoln's definition. Militarism is based on the principle of government by force, on the principle of compulsory co-operation in which authority proceeds from above. It is no accident that the most autocratic governments are found in those countries where militarism has most undisputed sway. Both are logical results of the belief that society is founded upon force and that authority proceeds from above downward. The principle of both is government of the people, by the rulers, for the State.

The profound distrust with which the democratic forces in the European countries have looked upon the influence of the army and navy officers in the councils of the autocratic Powers may be considered to have been amply justified by the course of events leading up to the outbreak of the

[1] *Principles of Sociology*, vol. ii., chap. xvii., pp. 572–576.

war. Even in times of peace the recent history of the clashes between the military and civil authorities in the Dreyfus affair in France, the Zabern incident in Germany, and in the Ulster crisis in England illustrates the difficulty which the civil authorities find in trying to subject military power to democratic control. In America the fundamental opposition between democracy and militarism has been emphasized by President Wilson in his message to Congress, December 8, 1914, in which he said:

Allow me to speak with great plainness and directness upon this great matter, and to avow my convictions with deep earnestness. I have tried to know what America is, what her people think, what they are, what they most cherish and hold dear. I hope that some of their finer passions are in my own heart —some of the great conceptions and desires which gave birth to this government and which have made the voice of this people a voice of peace and hope and liberty among the peoples of the world, and thus speaking my own thoughts, I shall, at least in part, speak theirs, however plainly and inadequately, upon this vital matter. . . .

From the first we have had a clear and a settled policy with regard to military establishment. We never have had, and while we retain our present principles and ideals, we never shall have, a large standing army.

Not all military officers are militarists, and there are, of course, many militarists outside the military profession. Militarism is essentially a state of mind,—a social philosophy; and the chief democratic objection to large standing armies and military training is that it tends to multiply those who hold this militaristic social philosophy.

If military force could be confined to the functions of defence and police force, its increase would not be regarded with the distrust which it arouses at the present time in democratic nations. But until a League of Peace is formed, no country can have any guarantee that a military force created for defence will not be used for aggression. In fact, as we have seen in Chapter VI., it is a logical part of the militaristic philosophy of force that since war is a law of Nature, and therefore inevitable, attack at the most favourable opportunity is not only the best method of defence, but an imperative national duty.

The dangers of a military caste have been emphasized by Lord Bryce, the recent British Ambassador to America, who points out that during the hundred years of peace in the English-speaking world a number of disputes which might have led to war did not do so because in America

fortunately . . . the country was free from that pernicious influence of a professional military caste which works such frightful evil in Europe, being indeed driven to desire opportunities for practising the work for which the profession exists.[1]

[1] *The British Empire and the United States*, by W. A. Dunning, with an introduction by the Right Hon. Viscount Bryce, New York, 1914, pp. xxix–xxx.

Bismarck is still more definite in pointing out this danger. In his autobiography he gives a vivid account of this constant pressure of the thousands of officers of the Prussian army towards war. He explains the difficulty which he had in resisting this powerful militaristic pressure in the crisis of 1867, in 1875, and how he made use of this pressure to overcome the resistance of the King and the peace forces of Germany in order to plunge the country into war with Austria in 1866 and with France in 1870. Nevertheless, he adds, it constitutes a grave danger for the nation:

It is natural that in the staff of the army not only younger active officers, but likewise experienced strategists, should feel the need of turning to account the efficiency of the troops led by them, and their own capacity to lead, and of making them prominent in history. It would be a matter of regret if this effect of the military spirit did not exist in the army; the task of keeping its results within such limits as the nations' need of peace can justly claim is the duty of the political, not the military, heads of the State.

That at the time of the Luxemburg question, during the crisis of 1875 . . . and even down to the most recent times, the staff and its leaders have allowed themselves to be led astray and to endanger peace, lies in the very spirit of the institution. . . .[1]

The connection between the ideas in the minds of men and their social and political institutions

[1] Bismarck, *His Reflections and Reminiscences*, vol. ii., chapter xxii., p. 102.

has suggested a definition of the militarist as one who believes that society is founded on force, and that the basis of civilization is the soldier; while the civilist believes that society is founded upon co-operation and justice, and that the basis of civilization is the citizen.

In autocratic countries the conservative parties are invariably militaristic, since they must rely upon military force to maintain their positions against the rising democratic and socialistic movements which threaten to undermine their privileges. This has been especially true in Germany and Russia, where the ruling classes have relied upon a large standing army as their chief defénce against what they regard as the disintegrating forces of the social order. On the other hand an absolute government is necessary for a militant state if the army is to be kept at the highest pitch of efficiency and preparation for war. *Give us a King or Give us Peace* is the title of a book by Guesde, a member of the French Ministry during the war, which demonstrates the fundamental opposition between a republican form of government and a warlike national policy.

The philosophy of force has separated the idea of the State from the conception of the highest welfare of the people, and has erected the State into a new kind of national god to which human sacrifices must be made. The abstract ideal of the State is a necessary element of the philosophy of force, because the sacrifice of the community for

the sake of the community would be too obviously
a contradiction in terms.   Thus, von Treitschke,
who has been the chief exponent in Germany of
Bodin's doctrine of the supreme authority of the
State, says:

War is elevating, because the individual disappears
before the great conception of the State. . . . The
highest moral duty of the State is to increase its
power.   The individual must sacrifice himself for the
higher community of which he is a member; but the
State is itself the highest conception in the wider
community of man, and therefore the duty of self-
annihilation does not enter into the case.   The
Christian duty of sacrifice for something higher does
not exist for the State, for there is nothing higher than
it in the world's history; consequently it cannot
sacrifice itself to something higher.   When a State
sees its downfall staring it in the face, we applaud
if it succumbs sword in hand.   A sacrifice made to
an alien nation is not only immoral, but contradicts
the idea of self-preservation, which is the highest
ideal of a State.[1]

In England, Spencer Wilkinson, Chichele Professor of Military History in Oxford University,
starts from the same principle to prove that the
abandonment of force as between nations is
permanently impossible.   He writes[2]:

. . . The employment of force for the maintenance
of rights is the foundation of all civilized human life,

[1] Treitschke, *Politik*, vol. i., §3.
[2] *Britain at Bay*, Constable & Co., London.

for it is the fundamental function of the State, and apart from the State there is no civilization, no life worth living. The mark of the State is sovereignty or the identification of force and right, and the measure of the protection is furnished by the completeness of this identification.

The fine flower of nationality, which has been defined by writers like Renan[1] and J. S. Mill[2] as a unity of ideals based upon common sympathies and the consciousness of common experiences, has been distorted and debased by the philosophy of force into a spurious Colonialism on the one hand and Imperialism on the other. In tracing the causes of the success of the distorted "social Darwinism" we have seen how it has served as the scientific defence for Imperialism, and how the idea of "the struggle for existence" and the "survival of the fittest" has been magnified to the immense scale of the life struggle between rival empires. J. A. Hobson, who has given the subject the most scientific study, has traced the distortion of nationalism by the philosophy of force as follows:

Nationalism is a plain highway to internationalism, and if it manifests diversions we may well suspect a perversion of its nature and its purpose. Such a perversion is Imperialism, in which nations, trespassing beyond the limits of facile assimilation, transform the wholesome stimulative rivalry of

[1] *Qu'est-ce qu'une nation?*
[2] *Representative Government,* chapter xvi.

various national types into the cut-throat struggle of competing empires.

Not only does aggressive Imperialism defeat the movement towards internationalism by fostering animosities between competing empires: its attack upon the liberties and the existence of weaker or lower races stimulates in them a corresponding excess of national self-consciousness. A nationalism that bristles with resentment and is all astrain with the passion of self-defence is only less perverted from its natural genius than the nationalism which glows with the animus of greed and self-aggrandizement at the expense of others. . . .

The new policy has exercised the most notable and formidable influence upon the conscious state-craft of the nations which indulge in it. While producing for popular consumption doctrines of national destiny, and imperial missions of civilization, contradictory in their true import, but subsidiary to one another as supports of popular Imperialism, it has evolved a calculating, greedy type of Machiavellianism entitled "real-politik" in Germany, where it was made, which has remodelled the whole art of diplomacy and has erected national aggrandizement without pity or scruple as the conscious motive force of foreign policy. Earth hunger and the scramble for markets are responsible for the openly avowed repudiation of treaty obligations which Germany, Russia, and England have not scrupled to defend. The sliding scale of diplomatic language, hinterland, sphere of interests, sphere of influence, paramountcy, suzerainty, protectorate, veiled or open, leading up to acts of forcible seizure or annexation which sometimes continue to be hidden under "lease," "rectification of frontier," "concession," and the like, is the invention and expression of this cynical spirit of Imperialism. While Germany and Russia have perhaps been more open in their professed adoption of the material gain of their country as the sole criterion of public conduct, other nations have not been slow to accept the standard. Though the conduct of nations in dealing with one another has commonly been determined at all times by selfish and short-sighted considerations, the conscious, deliberate adoption of this standard at an age when the intercourse of nations and their interdependence for all essentials of human life grow ever closer, is a retrograde step fraught with grave perils to the cause of civilization.[1]

The most serious effect of Imperialism is its demoralizing influence upon the ethics and social philosophy of the nations which embark upon an Imperialistic career.[2] This is especially true of democratic nations. The effect of the subjugation of the Philippines upon the democracy of America can be clearly traced in the strengthening of the forces of reaction and militarism.[3] The improvements which have resulted from the American occupation are frequently cited by those

[1] *Imperialism: A Study*, p. 8.

[2] J. M. Robertson in *The Evolution of States* (Putnam, 1913) traces clearly the effect of Imperialism in lowering the standard of ethics and weakening the total strength of society in Rome (pp. 21–25), in Greece (pp. 50–52), and in the Florentine Republic (p. 249).

[3] See Norman Angell, *America and the World-State*, chap. ii., part ii. (Putnam 1915), "A Retrospect of American Patriotism," for illustrations of the effect of the subjugation of the Philippines in strengthening militarism in America.

who believe in the value of conquest as reasons why the United States should "clean up" Mexico and neighbouring territory subject to periodic revolution. Among the imperialists in America the belief is widely held that "might makes right," and it is significant that the democratic and conservative political forces have taken up positions for and against Philippine independence. In the same way the Tories in England bitterly opposed the policy of the Liberals in "unconquering" British colonies and their action in acknowledging the futility of force by granting Home Rule to South Africa and Ireland. For generations the belief in the philosophy of force made necessary by the domination of Ireland has distorted the political theories and the social structure of England, and the same effect, though not as yet in so critical a measure, follows from the forcible domination of Egypt and India. In Germany, France, Russia, and Japan the forces of militarism and Imperialism are indissolubly joined together.

The classic diplomacy of the nations is based upon the philosophy of force, with its assumption of the essential rivalry between nations rather than the harmony of their interests. The orthodox diplomacy of the European nations especially is intimately connected with the ideas of autocracy, and is usually the last branch of the government to be subjected to democratic control. The diplomatic service of most countries is still the preserve of the aristocratic classes and the character of international diplomacy is greatly influenced by this fact. Since it is assumed that the interests of nations are mutually antagonistic and that the advantage of the one can be secured only at the cost of another, the use of force and the threat of force are the chief instruments of the diplomat's power. "In diplomacy force is always a factor," says Admiral Mahan[1]; and Major Stewart L. Murray in his book,[2] to which Lord Roberts has written a laudatory preface, has explained the relation between diplomacy and force as follows:

The policies of the various States must, therefore, be regarded as in a perpetual state of conflict, more or less concealed, and requiring perpetual give-and-take adjustments by negotiation. These perpetual negotiations are conducted by the diplomatic services of each country, which are thus occupied in ceaseless efforts to preserve peace. But if a special conflict of policies cannot be settled by negotiation, if one nation refuses in this matter to compromise, then, unless one nation gives way through fear, because it is not strong enough or is not ready enough, there remains nothing except to resort to force, to war. Every negotiation, therefore, implies in itself that the pen is held in one hand and the sword in the other. . . .

The foreign commercial policies of nearly all nations are based upon the idea of mutual antag-

[1] "The Place of Force in International Relations," *North American Review*, January, 1912, p. 34.

[2] *The Future Peace of the Anglo-Saxons*, London, Watts & Co., p. 19.

onism instead of interdependence, and find their sanctions in the philosophy of force. Mr. Henry C. Emery, Professor of Economics at Yale University has traced the influence of the Darwinian theory upon the modern commercial policies of nations in a lecture published by the War Department for distribution in connection with the educational work of the army, in which he said:

The full significance of the Darwinian theory of the formation of species through natural selection based on a struggle for existence, was not at first appreciated so far as its bearing on the history of human societies was concerned. When, however, national antagonisms once more came to make themselves consciously felt it was found now that our conceptions regarding the problem of race struggle took on an entirely new aspect. Here was a scientific theory ready at hand to give a profound philosophic basis to a nationalistic conception of history, both past and future, which the writers of the middle of the nineteenth century supposed they had disposed of forever. . . . History has been largely rewritten in the light of this new philosophy, and more and more has the economic element come to be emphasized as the determining factor in the history of national struggles. . . .

I have referred to the early period of mercantilism, when every weapon of a nation was utilized to advance its own interests at the expense of rivals. . . . The last twenty-five years has seen the development of a neomercantilism, which, although more enlightened in detail than the commercial policy of the seventeenth and eighteenth centuries, still takes as its starting point the rivalry between nations rather than the harmony of their interests, and uses, or stands prepared to use, the weapons of that earlier period. . . . These weapons were various, including protective tariffs, prohibition and bounties on exports and imports as the occasion might demand, commercial treaties, the arts of diplomacy, and finally war.[1]

Militarism is directly related to protectionism in several ways. A nation which carries on frequent wars with other nations must seek to be self-sufficing and to produce itself all the commodities needful for carrying on its national life. This is the chief argument used against reducing the duties on agricultural products in Germany, an essentially industrial nation, where the duties on foodstuffs add greatly to the cost of living and hold back the economic development of the nation. On the other hand the increasing cost of modern armaments exerts a constant pressure towards indirect taxation and tends to maintain customs duties which will yield a high revenue where these already exist, or to compel their establishment by free trade countries. The protectionist measures taken by England to meet the increased financial burden due to the war illustrate this process. Thus the entire economic life is strained and warped on account of the philosophy of force. Henry George has clearly stated the relation of force to international trade as follows:

[1] *Some Economic Aspects of War*, 1914, Washington Government Printing Office, p. 7.

17

Trade does not require force; free trade consists simply in letting people buy and sell as they want to buy and sell. It is protection that requires force, for it consists in preventing people from doing what they want to do. Protective tariffs are as much applications of force as are blockading squadrons, and their object is the same—to prevent trade.[1]

More recently, Eduard Bernstein has pointed out the connection of the current economic theories with the philosophy of force. Discussing the reasons for the ineffectiveness of the modern economic interdependence of nations to prevent war, in the June, 1915, number of *Die Friedenswarte*, he says:

Anyone who reads the literature of the militarist Imperialism of the day will constantly discover its intimate connection with protectionist theories; and its strong influence on European thought is increased by the fact that there remains only a small minority of political thinkers familiar with the true doctrine of Free Trade and able to appreciate its far-reaching effects on international relations. Those who do not adopt the theory of protection, adopt an eclecticism in economics which lacks all theoretical foundation, and is, therefore, defenceless against the arguments of the imperialists. That is how it has come about that in the age of the most fully developed world commerce, a world war is raging, and the peoples engaged in it are roused to a degree of hatred and bitterness un-

[1] Henry George, *Protection or Free Trade?* chapter vi.

known in times when no sort of close contact between them existed. This explains why the mighty development of commercial, literary, and personal intercourse did not fulfil the expectation that it would prove a power for peace.[1]

The belief that society is based upon force is widespread among the members of the legal profession, who come in contact chiefly with abnormal social phenomena and with the mechanism by which society deals with those who refuse to co-operate. The Roman Law, in which authority is derived from above, is especially favourable to the development of the militaristic philosophy. But law is fundamentally a question of determining under what conditions the force of a state shall be exercised (conditions which are defined by Magna Charta, *habeas corpus*, Bill of Rights, etc.), and the greatest minds in the legal profession have always recognized that the ultimate sanction and the power which directs these conditions for the use of force is public opinion.[2] The development of popular government is the story of the modification of the conditions under which force is used. For a democracy in which authority is derived from below, and which can rest securely only upon foundations of justice, nothing is more important than a clear understanding of the relative rôles

[1] Quoted in *War and Peace*, July, 1915.
[2] David Jayne Hill's *World Organization as Affected by the Nature of the Modern State*, is an illuminating study of force as a factor in political relations.

of ideas and force—of the intellectual and the physiological struggle—in civilization.

The essential function of business as a co-operative link between an existing demand and a possible source of supply, and its basis in mutual confidence and the observance of contract is often overshadowed in the minds of business men by the more obvious elements of competition. The English author of a recent book states the philosophy of force for the business world as follows:

You cannot abolish war from a competitive system of civilization: competition is the root-basis of the system of civilization and competition is war. When a business man crushes a trade rival from the market by cut prices, there is exactly the same process at work as when a business nation crushes a trade rival by physical force. The means vary but the end in view and the ethical principles in question are identical. In both cases the weaker goes to the wall; in both cases it is woe to the vanquished.[1]

Monopoly in business reproduces the principle of compulsory co-operation of the philosophy of force. Admiral Mahan[2] has stated the analogy between industrial and political organization thus:

The force of concentrated capital is as real and material as the force of an organized army, and it has the same advantage over a multitude of unorganized

[1] Rifleman, *The Struggle for Bread*, p. 209.
[2] "The Place of Force in International Relations," *North American Review*, January, 1912.

competitors that an army has over a mob. At times, well within memory, the contest has narrowed down to a conflict almost personal, at times quite personal, between concentrated financial powers, ending at times in a disabling reverse or a disastrous overthrow to one or the other. As the disadvantage of such contests has become apparent to the greater competitors, there has succeeded a disposition to co-operation, corresponding to alliance between political entities for their mutual benefit.

In recent years the philosophy of force has become the dominant philosophy in the relations between capital and labour.[1] Revolutionary syndicalism, *sabotage* and "direct action," dynamite methods of trade-unionism and machine-gun methods of mine owners, epidemics of strikes and lockouts, are all manifestations of the belief in the effectiveness of force to solve industrial problems on the basis of compulsory co-operation.

Socialism, with its splendid ideals of the co-operative commonwealth and the rational organization of society, has suffered severely from the distortion due to the philosophy of force, especially in its early period. Its chief error consists in the failure to see (1) that the basis of human society, now as from the beginning, is that mutual aid and solidarity of the human race which it

[1] See *Violence and the Labour Movement*, by Robert Hunter (Macmillan, 1914), for a survey of anarchism and syndicalism in relation to labour, and for a study of the place of force in modern industrial relations. See also, John Graham Brooks, *American Syndicalism: The I. W. W.* (Macmillan, New York, 1913).

is seeking to establish and (2) that the present "class struggle" is only a distortion of the social structure from its true character, which has come about as the result of false ideas in regard to the advantages to be gained from the exploitation of man by man.

Originating in a highly militarized nation and revolting against militarism, Socialism has nevertheless been profoundly influenced by the militaristic type of society. Probably very few Socialists at the present time believe in the efficacy of force as an instrument for social progress, but in the popular mind at least, the emphasis of Socialism on the class struggle and its early advocacy of violent methods have greatly hindered the spread of the social truth which formed its strength. "The Communists disdain to conceal their views and aims" wrote Marx and Engels in the *Communist Manifesto* in 1848. "They openly declare that their ends can be obtained only by the forcible overthrow of all existing social conditions." This standpoint, though long since passed in the development of modern Socialism, still represents the movement in the minds of its opponents and keeps many from examining into its social philosophy. On the other hand, much of the opposition to Socialism is based on the individualistic theory of "social Darwinism" that the organization of society on co-operative principles would do away with competition and struggle and would thus lead to social stagnation and disaster.

The fine spirit of international brotherhood of Socialism has been largely nullified by the belief in the efficacy of military force to achieve social and political results. Thus Hyndman and other leaders of the British Socialist Party have supported the great war which began in 1914 in order to "crush German militarism," while the German Social Democrats have supported the same war for the purpose of "crushing the Russian autocracy."

The rise of woman, one of the most remarkable spiritual, intellectual, political and economic movements in the history of the world, is intimately connected with the question of the place of force in civilization. In so far as it succeeds, it results from a diminution in the rôle of physical force in human society. It is possible to arrange the European nations in the order of the position which is accorded to woman and this order corresponds closely with the decline in the rôle of physical force, and the stage of civilization which has been attained. Beginning with Turkey where women have almost no rights and where the whole history has been a catalog of battles, we can trace this parallelism as we ascend to, say, the Scandinavian countries, Denmark, Norway, Sweden, and Finland, where women have almost complete political and economic equality with men, where the rôle of physical force reaches a minimum, and where, by tests of low percentage of illiteracy, low infant mortality, absence of tuberculosis and alcoholism, general well-being and high standards of art, literature, music, and science, we reach the most perfect forms of social organization and the highest types of modern civilization.

In countries which, like Germany, are in a transition state from autocratic government to democracy, the forces of reaction—the militarists, imperialists, Pan-Germans, and conservatives of all kinds—are found bitterly opposing the enfranchisement of woman, while all the liberal political forces—Social Democrats, Progressive Peoples' Party, etc.—include woman suffrage as an essential part of their democratic programs.

The same division is found in England where women are allowed to vote in municipal affairs and county affairs, but are debarred from participation in national and imperial policies because, as the imperialists claim, women cannot understand imperial affairs. In reality this means that the imperialists fear that the social intuitions of women would revolt at the applications of the philosophy of force to imperial ambitions, and this fear is probably justified. In this connection it is instructive to note the general sense of moral shock with which the distortion of the woman's movement by the philosophy of force, as revealed in the relatively harmless and unimportant outbreak of militancy upon the part of the English suffragettes, was received all over the civilized world. When rightly understood, this sense of moral shock is a striking testimony to the universal faith of mankind in the fundamental incompatibility of the true social instincts of woman and the false methods of force and violence which have so often dominated the action of men.

The essential opposition between militarism[1] and the rise of woman has been summed up by Grace Isabel Colbron, in *The Public*, as follows:

It is this spirit of militarism, the glorification of brute force, and this alone, that has kept woman in political, legal, and economic bondage throughout the ages; and there is still enough of it remaining in our enlightened twentieth century to make the idea of woman's participation in public office and public life a thing to be scoffed at by the majority, ridiculed and opposed.

It was not any manifestation of superiority of the masculine mind that first threw the chains of political serfhood around one-half of humanity; it was merely the fact that in the dark ages of the world's history, brute force, that is, militarism in one or another form, reigned supreme. Where brute force was lord, woman with her differently constituted muscular development was considered an inferior being simply because she did not bear arms.

The philosophy of force has been drawn into the service of race prejudice and has been considered as the justification for innumerable racial

[1] See also *Militarism v. Feminism; an Enquiry and a Policy Demonstrating that Militarism Involves the Subjection of Women*, published by George Allen & Unwin, Ltd., Ruskin House, London.

wars, feuds, and lynchings. It is the basis for those theories of punishment, now happily obsolete except in the martial law of some nations, that rely upon the frequent use of the death penalty and methods of terrorism to enforce obedience to laws. The belief in the effectiveness of force still holds back the reform of the penal system, keeping it upon the old basis of revenge and punishment, instead of bringing it into accord with the modern ideas of reformation. The use of force in corporal punishment in the educational systems of many countries is due to the same mistaken notion of its effectiveness, this time as an intellectual discipline.

The greatest distortion of all, however, is to be found in the ethics of individual conduct. Among large sections of the intellectual classes, and especially among the aristocratic circles in the European universities, the ethics of Christianity have been replaced by the philosophy of force as a practical moral code. It is only when transferred to the domain of the personal life, that we realize fully the blasphemous character of the philosophy of force; but after all Nietzsche has simply carried out the philosophy of force to its logical conclusion as a standard of individual morality. Thus he says in the *Antichrist:*

Ye have heard how in old times it was said, Blessed are the meek, for they shall inherit the earth. But I say unto you, Blessed are the valiant, for they shall make the earth their throne.

And ye have heard them say, Blessed are the poor in spirit. But I say unto you, Blessed are the great in soul, for they shall enter into Valhalla.

And ye have heard men say, Blessed are the peace-makers. But I say unto you, Blessed are the war-makers, for they shall be called, if not the children of Jehovah, the children of Odin, who is greater than Jehovah.

Whatever else we may say of Nietzsche, we must at least admit that he is intellectually honest in carrying out the principle of struggle to its logical conclusions. As Professor Figgis says:

Nietzsche deserves the gratitude of all friends of humanity for the service he has done, in showing that the whole sphere of private life cannot in the long run be different from the ideals accepted in public affairs.[1]

And Prof. Philip van Ness Myers who also recognizes his contribution to a truer social philosophy adds:

It is the inconsistencies and hypocrisies involved in the double standard of national and individual conduct that is one ground of Nietzsche's bitter attack on the ethics of Christendom. Rightly understood, Nietzsche's work is a *reductio ad absurdum*—a classic satire on the philosophy of force.[2]

[1] *Studies of Political Thought from Gerson to Grotius*, 1907, p. 96.
[2] *History as Past Ethics*, Ginn & Company, 1913, p. 380.

CHAPTER IX

DARWIN'S THEORY OF SOCIAL PROGRESS

THE central principle of Darwin's theory of
human progress, is found in mutual aid and
the moral law.[1] A greater contrast can hardly be
imagined than that between the true Darwinian
theory of social progress, as given in his own writings, and the doctrines of the philosophy of force
which we have examined in the preceding chapters,
and which are widely believed to find their scientific foundations in Darwin's works.

The philosophy of force finds the cause of the
advance of civilization in the elements of fear,
collective homicide, and the struggle of one part
of mankind against the other—in the law which is
claimed to run through human society as well as
the animal world, of "Nature red in tooth and
claw." The belief in this distorted social Darwinism is so universal that it comes to many persons
with a sense of shock as well as with a sense of
refreshment of the spirit, to rediscover Darwin's

[1] Darwin's theory of social progress is contained in chapters
iii., iv., v., and xxi. of *The Descent of Man.*

true message and to learn that he finds the cause of the advance of civilization in the social habits of man, in co-operation and mutual aid for the struggle against the physical universe, and in the moral law. This rediscovery of Darwin's social message, if it becomes an integral part of the intellectual revolution, will profoundly modify social theories and political institutions in the future, for, whereas the "social Darwinists" in the past have founded their philosophy upon the forces which make for social disintegration and injustice, Darwin bases his philosophy of social progress upon the forces that make for social organization and justice.

It is interesting to note, before beginning the examination of Darwin's social theories, that both Alfred Russel Wallace, the co-discoverer of the theory of evolution, and Huxley, who is usually considered its greatest exponent, agree with Darwin that the chief cause of social progress and human evolution is to be found in ethical factors. We have already noted Huxley's sharp division between social evolution and natural evolution in Chapter II., and his theory of social progress is summarized in the following quotation from his Romanes lecture[1]:

Social progress means a checking of the cosmic process at every step and the substitution for it of another, which may be called the ethical process; the end of which is not the survival of those who may happen to be the fittest in respect of the whole of the

[1] *Evolution and Ethics*, pp. 81–83, 203.

conditions which obtain, but of those who are ethically best.

As I have already urged, the practice of that which is ethically best—what we call goodness or virtue—involves a course of conduct which, in all respects, is opposed to that which leads to success in the cosmic struggle for existence. In place of ruthless self-assertion it demands self-restraint; in place of thrusting aside, or treading down all competitors, it requires that the individual shall not merely respect, but shall help his fellows; its influence is directed, not so much to the survival of the fittest as to the fitting of as many as possible to survive. It repudiates the gladiatorial theory of existence. It demands that each man who enters into the enjoyment of the advantages of a polity shall be mindful of his debt to those who have laboriously constructed it; and shall take heed that no act of his weakens the fabric in which he has been permitted to live. Laws and moral precepts are directed to the end of curbing the cosmic process and reminding the individual of his duty to the community, to the protection and influence of which he owes, if not existence itself, at least the life of something better than a brutal savage.

Let us understand, once for all, that the ethical progress of society depends, not on imitating the cosmic process, still less in running away from it, but in combating it.

The theory of Wallace is substantially the same as that of Huxley. It is noteworthy that both Wallace and Huxley emphasize the break between the cosmic process and human society, so that their theory of social progress, instead of being an integral part of the theory of evolution, marks a distinct development. Both attempt in some manner to bridge the gap between the "ethical" man and the "natural" man, and the attempt of both is unsatisfactory. In order to find some method by which the "natural" man may evolve his "unnatural" world of ethics, Dr. Wallace seems to feel the need of some *deus ex machina* and, abandoning his scientific basis of evolution, is driven to suppose some "influx" from "the unseen universe of spirits" to solve the difficulty. Huxley attempts to solve the problem in a simpler way. The self-restraint of the moral world arises from factors which are organic in the natural man. The difficulty of this solution is that it contradicts the clear-cut antithesis between the natural man and social man which is so vividly emphasized in Huxley's writings, and this constitutes the weakness of Huxley's whole position.

The superiority of Darwin's genius is shown in the fact that he does not abandon his scientific basis like Wallace, nor does he fall into the error of self-contradiction like Huxley. Darwin's theory of social progress is an integral part of his theory of evolution. There is no discontinuity in the universal sweep of his great cosmic principle from its lowly beginnings in the realm of nature to its highest development in the moral law, to which he traces the progress of human society towards perfection.

Darwin rejects, as entirely lacking any foundation in scientific evidence, the anthropological romance of the pre-social "natural" man, living in a state of continual warfare of each against all, which was created by Hobbes and seems to have been adopted without modification by Huxley. In a letter to John Morley written by Darwin in 1871, he says:

I do not think there is any evidence that man ever existed as a non-social animal.[1]

On the contrary, all the scientific evidence which we possess goes to show that not only primitive man but even the members of the animal kingdom who constituted the immediate ancestors of man were social beings. Darwin sums up the evidence thus:

Judging from the habits of savages and of the greater number of the Quadrumana, primeval men, and even their ape-like progenitors, probably lived in society.[2]

Darwin even goes so far as to suggest that man has probably sprung from some comparatively small and weak species like the chimpanzee instead of from one as powerful as the gorilla. He points out what an immense advantage it must have been to man to have descended from such a comparatively weak creature, since it would have

[1] *More Letters of Charles Darwin*, vol. i., p. 327.
[2] *The Descent of Man*, p. 78.

necessitated development of social qualities which led him to give and receive aid from his fellow-men:

> An animal possessing great size, strength, and ferocity, and which, like the gorilla, could defend itself from all enemies, would not perhaps have become social; and this would most effectually have checked the acquirement of the higher mental qualities such as sympathy and the love of his fellows.[1]

He proceeds to trace the manner in which the social instincts and mutual aid operate as survival factors, leading to that development of the mental faculties which replaces the modification of bodily structure as the most effective form of adaptation to changed conditions. He constantly expresses the importance of mutual aid among even primitive men, of whom he says:

> Even at a remote period he practised some division of labour.[2]
>
> Each man did not manufacture his own flint tools or rude pottery, but certain individuals appear to have devoted themselves to such work, no doubt receiving in exchange the produce of the chase.[3]

Kropotkin, whose survey of savage life in all parts of the globe corroborates Darwin's conclusion, sums up the evidence thus:

[1] *The Descent of Man*, p. 79.   [2] *Idem*, p. 143.
[3] *Idem*, p. 65.

Wherever we go we find the same sociable manners, the same spirit of solidarity. And when we endeavour to penetrate into the darkness of past ages, we find the same tribal life, the same associations of men, however primitive, for mutual support. Therefore Darwin was quite right when he saw in man's social qualities the chief factor for his further evolution, and Darwin's vulgarizers are entirely wrong when they maintain the contrary.[1]

The moral sense, according to Darwin's theory, is the most important factor in social evolution, because it is the basis of all human society. The moral sense alone makes co-operative effort and the division of labour possible. Mutual aid is the chief factor of social progress, and indeed of all human evolution, since man's dominant position in the world depends almost entirely upon the fact that he is a member of society. Darwin traces the cause of this dominance as follows:

Man in the rudest state in which he now exists is the most dominant animal that has ever appeared on this earth. He has spread more widely than any other highly organized form, and all others have yielded before him. He manifestly owes this immense superiority to his intellectual faculties, to his social habits, which lead him to aid and defend his fellows, and to his corporeal structure. . . . The intellectual powers and social habits of man are of paramount importance to him. . . .[2]

[1] *Mutual Aid a Factor of Evolution*, p. 110.
[2] *The Descent of Man*, pp. 63–64.

The intellectual powers, and especially articulate language, on which his wonderful advancement has mainly depended, have been developed as the result of his social habits. The advantages of his corporeal structure, especially his erect position and his hands, have been valuable only as they have been directed by the intellect, so that man's dominant position in the world, in the last analysis, is due to his social habits. The moral law, which is based on these social habits, and is the cementing force which holds society together, thus becomes, in the true Darwinian theory, the central and most important factor of social evolution.

As soon as we enter the social domain then, the struggle against the physical environment changes its form. Short-sighted selfishness tends to defeat its own end because of the strife which it engenders, which makes co-operation and indeed all society impossible. If any of the advantages of association are lost the society falls to a lower plane of evolution and the individual who is a part of this society falls with it. As Darwin says:

Selfish and contentious people will not cohere, and without coherence nothing can be effected.[1]

Indeed, an enlightened selfishness would now lead a member of society to do many things which from a short-sighted point of view would appear to be against his own interest. Darwin describes how selfishness itself may lead to an increase of

[1] *The Descent of Man*, p. 145.

sympathy, which is so important an element among the social instincts.

With mankind, selfishness, experience, and imitation probably add . . . to the power of sympathy; for we are led by the hope of receiving good in return to perform acts of sympathetic kindness to others; and sympathy is much strengthened by habit. In however complex a manner this feeling may have originated, as it is one of high importance to all those animals which aid and defend one another, it will have been increased through natural selection; for those communities which included the greatest number of the most sympathetic members would flourish best, and rear the greatest number of offspring.[1]

When we enter the realm of social evolution, therefore, the struggle to adapt the physical universe takes on a new aspect. It becomes a struggle of societies against the physical environment, instead of individuals, and here mutual aid rises to the rank of first importance. Darwin describes the process by which the small strength and speed of man, his want of natural weapons, etc., are more than counterbalanced, firstly, by his intellectual powers, the development of which he traces chiefly to the social habits of man; and

secondly, by his social qualities, which lead him to give and receive aid from his fellowmen. No country in the world abounds in a greater degree with

[1] *The Descent of Man*, p. 122.

dangerous beasts than Southern Africa; no country presents more physical hardships than the Arctic regions; yet one of the puniest of races, that of the Bushman, maintains itself in Southern Africa, as do the dwarfed Esquimaux in the Arctic regions.[1]

The struggle between societies replaced the struggle between individuals at a very early stage, and the advantage gained by the individual came to him indirectly through the benefit to the whole community:

Judging from the habits of savages and of the greater number of the Quadrumana, primeval men, and even their ape-like progenitors, probably lived in society. With strictly social animals, natural selection sometimes acts on the individual, through the preservation of variations which are beneficial to the community. A community which includes a large number of well-endowed individuals increases in number, and is victorious over other less favoured ones, even although each separate member gains no advantage over the others of the same community . . . In regard to certain mental powers the case . . . is wholly different: for these faculties have been chiefly, or even exclusively, gained for the benefit of the community, and the individuals thereof have at the same time gained an advantage indirectly.[2]

In Darwin's theory, however, it is not, as in the case of the philosophy of force, collective homicide, which plays the chief rôle in this struggle. As

[1] *The Descent of Man*, pp. 79–80.   [2] *Idem*, p. 78.

early as 1864, seven years before he published *The Descent of Man*, Darwin wrote to A. R. Wallace that

the struggle between the races of man depended entirely upon intellectual and moral qualities.[1]

And in *The Descent of Man* he repeatedly emphasizes the importance of morality as a group survival factor:

It must not be forgotten that although a high standard of morality gives but a slight or no advantage to each individual man and his children over the other men of the same tribe, yet that an increase in the number of well-endowed men and an advancement in the standard of morality will certainly give an immense advantage to one tribe over another. A tribe including many members who, from possessing in a high degree the spirit of patriotism, fidelity, obedience, courage, and sympathy, were always ready to aid one another, and to sacrifice themselves for the common good, would be victorious over most other tribes; and this would be natural selection. At all times throughout the world tribes have supplanted other tribes; and as morality is one important element in their success, the standard of morality and the number of well-endowed men will thus everywhere tend to rise and increase.[2]

Although wars of extermination may play a rôle among savage tribes too ignorant to realize the

[1] *Life and Letters of Charles Darwin*, p. 271.
[2] *The Descent of Man*, p. 148.

advantages of abandoning destructive competition in favour of co-operation and alliance, this factor can play only an unimportant rôle among civilized people:

> With highly civilized nations continued progress depends in a subordinate degree on natural selection; for such nations do not supplant and exterminate one another as do savage tribes.[1]

The true causes of progress, though very difficult to determine, are to be found in intellectual and moral qualities, according to Darwin:

> It is very difficult to say why one civilized nation rises, becomes more powerful, and spreads more widely, than another; or why the same nation progresses more quickly at one time than at another. We can only say that it depends on an increase in the actual number of the population, on the number of the men endowed with high intellectual and moral faculties, as well as on their standard of excellence.[2]

It is these same intellectual and moral qualities which constitute the survival factors in the struggle between civilized and barbarous nations:

> At the present day civilized nations are everywhere supplanting barbarous nations, excepting where the climate opposes a deadly barrier; and they succeed mainly, though not exclusively, through their arts, which are the products of the intellect.[3]

[1] *The Descent of Man*, p. 158–59.   [2] *Idem*, p. 156.
[3] *Idem*, p. 144.

Darwin recognizes war as one of the factors in the disappearance of the less civilized races, just as a geologist recognizes earthquakes as one of the causes of the folding of the earth's crust, but he assigns to it a subordinate rôle and reveals his truly scientific spirit, by enumerating it only among a dozen other slow and invisible causes:

Extinction follows chiefly from the competition of tribe with tribe and race with race. Various checks are always in action, serving to keep down the numbers of each savage tribe—such as periodical famines, nomadic habits, and the consequent deaths of infants, prolonged suckling, wars, accidents, sickness, licentiousness, the stealing of women, infanticide, and especially lessened fertility. If any one of these checks increases in power even slightly, the tribe thus affected tends to decrease; and when of two adjoining tribes one becomes less numerous than the other, the contest is soon settled by war, slaughter, cannibalism, slavery, and absorption. Even when a weaker tribe is not thus abruptly swept away, if it once begins to decrease, it generally goes on decreasing until it becomes extinct.[1]

He describes also the slow and invisible causes of the disappearance of the barbarian races before the civilized races:

[1] *The Descent of Man*, p. 198.
The true cause of the extinction of races, according to Darwin, is to be found in these slow and unrecognized factors. Collective homicide plays but an incidental rôle, serving at most to hasten an otherwise inevitable process.

When civilized nations come into contact with barbarians the struggle is short, except where a deadly climate gives its aid to the native race. Of the causes which lead to the victory of civilized nations, some are plain and simple, others complex and obscure. We can see that the cultivation of the land will be fatal in many ways to savages, for they cannot, or will not, change their habits. New diseases and vices have in some cases proved highly destructive; and it appears that a new disease often causes much death, until those who are most susceptible to its destructive influence are gradually weeded out; and so it may be with the evil effects from spirituous liquors, as well as with the unconquerably strong taste for them shown by so many savages. It further appears, mysterious as is the fact, that the first meeting of distinct and separated people generates disease. Mr. Sproat, who in Vancouver Island closely attended to the subject of extinction, believed that changed habits of life, consequent on the advent of Europeans, induces much ill-health. He lays, also, great stress on the apparently trifling cause that the natives become "bewildered and dull by the new life around them; they lose the motives for exertion, and get no new ones in their place."[1]

After surveying the whole field of the causes, Darwin returns to the factor of a lessened fertility of women which follows changed conditions among barbarous peoples not able to adapt themselves to the new civilization, and he devotes a large part of his chapter on "The

[1] *The Descent of Man*, pp. 198–99.

Extinction of Races" to a study of this decisive factor.

Darwin points out that the effect of war would be a reversed selection, since the bravest men, who are always willing to come to the front in the war and freely to risk their lives for others, would on the average perish in larger numbers than others and would leave no offspring to inherit their noble nature. He even points out how militarism, by preventing co-operation and the formation of larger political units, may offset high intellectual powers, such as those possessed by the old Greeks. The true cause of their downfall he traces to the weakening of the moral bonds:

> The Greeks may have retrograded from a want of coherence between the many small states, from the small size of their whole country, from the practice of slavery, or from extreme sensuality; for they did not succumb until "they were enervated and corrupt to the very core." The western nations of Europe, who now so immeasurably surpass their former savage progenitors, and stand at the summit of civilization, owe little or none of their superiority to direct inheritance from the old Greeks, though they owe much to the written works of that wonderful people.[1]

And in a letter to his friend Lyell he emphasizes the fact that the history of the Greeks verifies his theories of social progress:

[1] *The Descent of Man*, p. 157.

. . . The high state of intellectual development of the old Grecians with the little or no subsequent improvement . . . harmonizes perfectly with our views. The case would be decidedly difficult on the Lamarckian or Vestigian doctrine of necessary progression, but on the view which I hold of progress depending upon the conditions, it is no objection at all, and harmonizes with the other facts of progression. . . . For in a state of anarchy, or despotism, or bad government, or after an irruption of barbarians, force, strength, or ferocity, and not intellect, would be apt to gain the day.[1]

This is a pellucidly clear statement of the true Darwinian theory that social progress depends, not upon force and collective homicide, but upon institutions and ideas.

Darwin's Theory of the Evolution of the Moral Law

Much light is thrown upon Darwin's theory of social progress by an analysis of his derivation of the moral law. The philosophy of force has much to say about the ethics of evolution, but in the true Darwinian theory the guiding principle is the evolution of ethics.

The moral sense, according to Darwin, is the greatest of all distinctions between man and the lower animals:

I fully subscribe to the judgment of those writers who maintain that of all the differences between man

---

[1] *Life and Letters of Charles Darwin,* vol. ii., p. 89.

and the lower animals, the moral sense or conscience is by far the most important. . . . It is the most noble of all the attributes of man, leading him without a moment's hesitation to risk his life for that of a fellow creature; or after due deliberation, impelled simply by the deep feeling of right or duty, to sacrifice it in some great cause.[1]

And again in the general summary of his theory at the end of the book he says:

A moral being is one who is capable of reflecting on his past actions and their motives—of approving of some and disapproving of others; and the fact that man is the one being who certainly deserves this designation, is the greatest of all distinctions between him and the lower animals.[2]

This moral sense which so clearly distinguishes man from the animal world, however, does not mark a break in the cosmic process, but is an inevitable result of the great principle of evolution which runs through the universe. The moral sense, according to Darwin, is the natural and inevitable development from the social instincts, and he lays down as the basis of his thesis the following proposition:

. . . Any animal whatever, endowed with well-marked social instincts, the parental and filial affections being here included, would inevitably acquire a moral sense or conscience, as soon as its intellectual powers

---

[1] *The Descent of Man*, p. 112.   [2] *Idem*, p. 634.

had become as well, or nearly as well, developed as in man. For, *firstly*, the social instincts lead an animal to take pleasure in the society of its fellows, to feel a certain amount of sympathy with them, and to perform various services for them. The services may be of a definite and evidently instinctive nature, or there may be only a wish and readiness, as with most of the higher social animals, to aid their fellows in certain general ways. But these feelings and services are by no means extended to all the individuals of the same species, only to those of the same association. *Secondly*, as soon as the mental faculties had become highly developed, images of all past actions and motives would be incessantly passing through the brain of each individual; and that feeling of dissatisfaction, or even misery, which invariably results from any unsatisfied instinct, would arise, as often as it was perceived that the enduring and always present social instinct had yielded to some other instinct, at the time stronger, but neither enduring in its nature nor leaving behind it a very vivid impression. It is clear that many instinctive desires, such as that of hunger, are in their nature of short duration; and after being satisfied, are not readily or vividly recalled. *Thirdly*, after the power of language had been acquired, and the wishes of the community could be expressed, the common opinion how each member ought to act for the public good would naturally become in a paramount degree the guide to action. But it should be borne in mind that, however great weight we may attribute to public opinion, our regard for the approbation and disapprobation of our fellows depends on sympathy, which, as we shall see, forms an essential part of the social instinct, and is indeed its foundation-stone. *Lastly*, habit in the individual would ultimately play a very important part in guiding the conduct of each member; for the social instinct, together with sympathy, is, like any other instinct, greatly strengthened by habit, and so consequently would be obedience to the wishes and judgment of the community.[1]

In other words, Darwin's thesis, expressed in the language used by the mathematicians, is that the social instincts are the necessary and sufficient conditions for the evolution of a moral sense.

The next step in the reasoning, namely that man possesses social instincts, hardly needs an elaborate proof. Darwin says:

Everyone will admit that man is a social being. We see this in his dislike of solitude, and in his wish for society beyond that of his own family. Solitary confinement is one of the severest punishments which can be inflicted. Some authors suppose that man primevally lived in single families, but at the present day, though single families, or only two or three together, roam the solitude of some savage lands, they always, as far as I can discover, hold friendly relations with other families inhabiting the same district. Such families occasionally meet in council, and unite for their common defence. . . . Judging from the analogy of the majority of the Quadrumana, it is probable that the early ape-like progenitors of man were likewise social.[2]

[1] *The Descent of Man*, pp. 113–14.
[2] *Idem*, pp. 123–24.

. According to the distorted social Darwinism, force is the basis of society, but in the true Darwinian theory the foundation of society is the moral law, derived from the social instincts. The purpose of the moral sense is to secure the welfare of the tribe:

We have now seen that actions are regarded by savages, and were probably so regarded by primeval man, as good or bad, solely as they obviously affect the welfare of the tribe—not that of the species, nor that of an individual member of the tribe. This conclusion agrees well with the belief that the so-called moral sense is aboriginally derived from the social instincts, for both relate at first exclusively to the community.[1]

And he points out that society, even on the limited scale of the tribes, could not exist without such a moral sense.

No tribe could hold together if murder, robbery, treachery, etc., were common; consequently such crimes within the limits of the same tribe "are branded with everlasting infamy."[2]

The contrast could scarcely be made more clear between Darwin's theory of society, held together from within by the cementing power of the moral sense and social instincts, and the theories of the philosophy of force, as represented in the sociology of Spencer, Ward, and Ratzenhofer, in which

[1] *The Descent of Man*, p. 134.   [2] *Idem*, p. 132.

society is held together only by the external force exerted by some other society, this other society having been constituted and held together in some miraculous way.

Darwin traces the evolution of the moral law with a master's hand. Analysing it down to its cosmic roots, he finds at the basis the element of love, and sympathy, which is distinct from love:

The development of the moral qualities is a more interesting problem. The foundation lies in the social instincts, including under this term the family ties. These instincts are highly complex, and in the case of the lower animals give special tendencies toward certain definite actions; but the more important elements are love, and the distinct emotion of sympathy.[1]

Darwin follows this element of love far down into the animal kingdom. From this element of love, through the channel of the parental and filial affections, have been evolved the social instincts, leading to mutual aid—the greatest factor of social evolution. The social instincts must have preceded association, just as the sense of hunger and the pleasure of eating were no doubt first acquired in order to induce animals to eat. He traces the first stages in the evolution of the social instinct as follows:

The feeling of pleasure from society is probably an extension of the parental or filial affections, since the social instinct seems to be developed by the young

[1] *The Descent of Man*, p. 634.

remaining for a long time with their parents; and this extension may be attributed in part to habit, but chiefly to natural selection. With those animals which were benefited by living in close association, the individuals which took the greatest pleasure in society would best escape various dangers; while those that cared least for their comrades, and lived solitary, would perish in greater numbers. With respect to the origin of the parental and filial affections, which apparently lie at the base of the social instincts, we know not the steps by which they have been gained; but we may infer that it has been to a large extent through natural selection . . . Parental affection, or some feeling which replaces it, has been developed in certain animals extremely low in the scale, for example, in star-fishes and spiders.[1]

From this extension of the filial and parental affections have come the important social qualities of sympathy, fidelity, and courage:

Turning now to the social and moral faculties. In order that primeval men, or the ape-like progenitors of man, should become social, they must have acquired the same instinctive feelings which impel other animals to live in a body; and they no doubt exhibited the same general disposition. They would have felt uneasy when separated from their comrades, for whom they would have felt some degree of love; they would have warned each other of danger, and have given mutual aid in attack or defence. All this implies some degree of sympathy, fidelity, and courage. Such social qualities, the paramount importance of which

[1] *The Descent of Man*, pp. 120–21.

19

to the lower animals is disputed by no one, were no doubt acquired by the progenitors of man in a similar manner, namely, through natural selection, aided by inherited habit.[1]

Darwin then proceeds to explain how, in response to the need for promoting the welfare of the tribe, the social virtues of truth, self-sacrifice, self-command, and the power of endurance are developed:

There cannot be fidelity without truth; and this fundamental virtue is not rare between the members of the same tribe: thus Mungo Park heard the negro women teaching their young children to love the truth. This, again, is one of the virtues which becomes so deeply rooted in the mind that it is sometimes practised by savages, even at a high cost, toward strangers; but to lie to your enemy has rarely been thought a sin, as the history of modern diplomacy too plainly shows. As soon as a tribe has a recognized leader, disobedience becomes a crime, and even abject submission is looked at as a sacred virtue.

As during rude times no man can be useful or faithful to his tribe without courage, this quality has universally been placed in the highest rank; and although in civilized countries a good yet timid man may be far more useful to the community than a brave one, we cannot help instinctively honouring the latter above a coward, however benevolent. Prudence on the other hand, which does not concern the welfare of others, though a very useful virtue, has never been

[1] *The Descent of Man*, p. 145.

highly esteemed.   As no man can practise the virtues necessary for the welfare of his tribe without self-sacrifice, self-command, and the power of endurance, these qualities have been at all times highly and most justly valued.   The American savage voluntarily submits to the most horrid tortures without a groan, to prove and strengthen his fortitude and courage; and we cannot help admiring him, or even an Indian Fakir, who, from a foolish religious motive, swings suspended by a hook buried in his flesh.[1]

This brings us to another problem.   How are actions which are useless for the welfare of the tribe, such as the self-torture by an Indian Fakir, to become immoral actions, while the moral sense gradually changes its character to meet changed conditions?   How can morality be made identical with the welfare of the community? Evidently some factor of reason and foresight must come in to direct the action of love and the social instincts.   This problem leads Darwin to the discovery of the second great root of the moral law in the desire for happiness and in the reasoning powers of the individual:

As all men desire their own happiness, praise or blame is bestowed on actions and motives, according as they lead to this end; and as happiness is an essential part of the general good, the greatest-happiness principle indirectly serves as a nearly safe standard of right and wrong.   As the reasoning powers advance and experience is gained, the remoter effects of certain

[1] *The Descent of Man*, pp. 133–34.

lines of conduct on the character of the individual, and on the general good, are perceived; and then the self-regarding virtues come within the scope of public opinion, and receive praise, and their opposites blame.[1]

Darwin finds the chief force making for moral progress in this love of praise and dread of blame, which acts through public opinion. He traces it back to the remote antiquity of the race and shows how it has become a highly complex sentiment in modern times:

We may therefore conclude that primeval man, at a very remote period, was influenced by the praise and blame of his fellows. It is obvious that the members of the same tribe would approve of conduct which appeared to them to be for the general good, and would reprobate that which appeared evil. To do good unto others—to do unto others as ye would they should do unto you—is the foundation-stone of morality. It is, therefore, hardly possible to exaggerate the importance, during rude times, of the love of praise and the dread of blame. A man who was not impelled by any deep, instinctive feeling to sacrifice his life for the good of others, yet was roused to such actions by a sense of glory, would by his example excite the same wish for glory in other men, and would strengthen by exercise the noble feeling of admiration. . . . Ultimately our moral sense or conscience becomes a highly complex sentiment—originating in the social instincts, largely guided by the approbation of our fellow-men, ruled by reason, self-interest, and in later times by deep religious feelings, and confirmed by instruction and habit.[1]

[1] *The Descent of Man*, p. 635.　　[2] *Idem*, pp. 147–48.

The causes of social progress Darwin finds in those factors which strengthen morality.

The more efficient causes of progress seem to consist of a good education during youth while the brain is impressible, and of a high standard of excellence inculcated by the ablest and best men, embodied in the laws, customs, and traditions of the nation, and enforced by public opinion. It should, however, be borne in mind that the enforcement of public opinion depends on our appreciation of the approbation and disapprobation of others; and this appreciation is founded on our sympathy, which it can hardly be doubted was originally developed through natural selection as one of the most important elements of the social instincts.[1]

Darwin recognizes not only reason, but also religion as a potent influence in moral progress.

The moral nature of man has reached its present standard partly through the advancement of his reasoning powers, and consequently of a just public opinion, but especially from his sympathies having been rendered more tender and widely diffused through the effects of habit, example, instruction, and reflection. . . . With the more civilized races, the conviction of the existence of an all-seeing Deity has had a potent influence on the advance of morality.[2]

He finds the great principle of reciprocity laid down in the Sermon on the Mount to be the foundation of the moral law, a kind of law of gravitation in human relations:

[1] *The Descent of Man*, p. 159.   [2] *Idem*, p. 636.

The moral sense perhaps affords the best and highest distinction between man and the lower animals; but I need say nothing on this head, as I have so lately endeavoured to show that the social instincts—the prime principle of man's moral constitution—with the aid of active intellectual powers and the effects of habit, naturally lead to the golden rule, "As ye would that men should do to you, do ye to them likewise"; and this lies at the foundation of morality.[1]

Darwin's genealogy of morals may conveniently be represented by means of a graphic illustration. At the centre of the process of evolution is the factor of mutual aid, going back on the one side through the social instincts and the parental and filial affections to its cosmic roots of love; and on the other side, through the desire for happiness and enlightened self-interest to reason and the first dawnings of intelligence in the scale of animal life. From this elementary need of mutual aid we may trace the causes of the advance of morality as summed up by Darwin:

The approbation of our fellow-men—the strengthening of our sympathies by habit—example and imitation —reason—experience, and even self-interest—instruction during youth, and religious feelings.[2]

The result of this evolutionary process, leading up to the moral law, is represented in the accompanying figure:

[1] *The Descent of Man*, p. 142.   [2] *Idem*, p. 153.

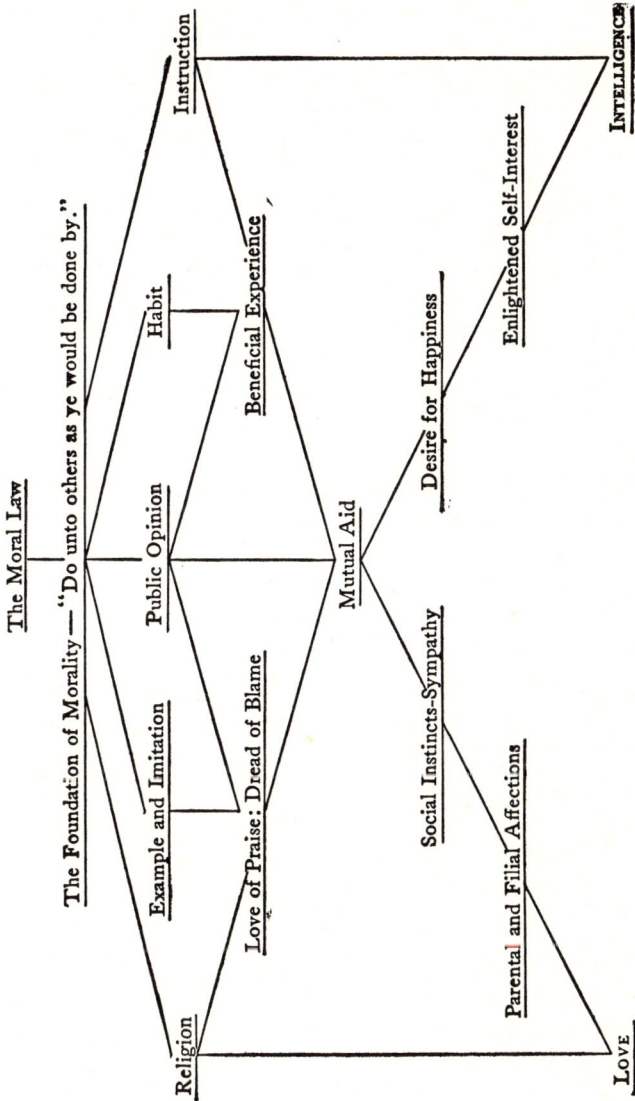

"Two things fill my soul with ever new and increasing wonder and awe the oftener and the more continuously I reflect upon them," said Immanuel Kant, "the starry heavens above me and the moral law within me."[1] Darwin's theory of social progress enthrones the moral law as the highest form of adaptation and brings it, as the nebular hypothesis has brought the starry heavens, within the cosmic sweep of the evolutionary process.

The Causes of Moral Advance

As social progress in the Darwinian theory is dependent upon morality, the causes of moral advance must occupy an important place in the social sciences. We have already noted[2] the effect of the factor of reason in contributing to the change of moral standards and especially in enforcing the observance of moral conduct, but the importance of the question justifies us in considering it in a little more detail.

Since the standard of morality is the general welfare of the community, a most important question is: How do these standards become changed to agree with more enlightened ideas as to what constitutes the welfare of a community? In a number of places Darwin considers the problem of the diversion of morality from the standards of true welfare and happiness of the com-

[1] Kant, *Kritik der praktischen Vernunft* (Conclusion), p. 205.
[2] See *supra*, pp. 291–93.

munity. The judgment of the community **is**
far from infallible; he says:

The judgment of the community will generally be
guided by some rude experience of what is best in the
long run for all the members; but this judgment will
not rarely err from ignorance and weak powers of
reasoning. Hence the strangest customs and superstitions, in complete opposition to the true welfare
and happiness of mankind, have become all-powerful
throughout the world. We see this in the horror
felt by a Hindoo who breaks his caste, and in many
other such cases.[1]

And in the summary of his theory he returns to the
same point:

But with the less civilized nations reason often errs,
and many bad customs and base superstitions come
within the same scope, and are then esteemed as high
virtues, and their breach as heavy crimes.[2]

Darwin finds the remedy for such wrong moral
standards in the reason and conscience of the
individual, who can thus rise above the current
standards of morality and aid in establishing
higher standards more in accord with the true
welfare of humanity. Thus he says:

. . . As love, sympathy, and self-command become
strengthened by habit, and as the power of reasoning
becomes clearer, so that man can value justly the
judgments of his fellows, he will feel himself impelled,

[1] *The Descent of Man*, p. 137.   [2] *Idem*, pp. 635-36.

apart from any transitory pleasure or pain, to certain lines of conduct. He might then declare—not that any barbarian or uncultivated man could thus think—I am the supreme judge of my own conduct, and, in the words of Kant, I will not in my own person violate the dignity of humanity.[1]

And in his general summary he adds:

Ultimately man does not accept the praise or blame of his fellows as his sole guide, though few escape this influence, but his habitual convictions, controlled by reason, afford him the safest rule. His conscience then becomes the supreme judge and monitor.[2]

He then describes the manner in which the higher moral standard, as embodied in some new virtue such as humanity, spreads to the other members of the community:

As soon as this virtue is honoured and practised by some few men, it spreads through instruction and example to the young, and eventually becomes incorporated in public opinion.[3]

The intellectual faculties and especially imagination are of fundamental importance for the high standard of conscience and morality. Imagination is one of the most powerful forces in creating a social conscience and Darwin advocates its cultivation as an important element of social progress:

[1] *The Descent of Man*, p. 125.   [2] *Idem*, p. 636.
[3] *Idem*, p. 138.

The moral faculties are generally and justly esteemed as of higher value than the intellectual powers. But we should bear in mind that the activity of the mind in vividly recalling past impressions is one of the fundamental, though secondary, bases of conscience.[1] This affords the strongest argument for educating and stimulating in all possible ways the intellectual faculties of every human being.   No doubt a man with a torpid mind, if his social affections and sympathies are well developed, will be led to good actions, and may have a fairly sensitive conscience.   But whatever renders the imagination more vivid, and strengthens the habit of recalling and comparing past impressions, will make the conscience more sensitive, and may even somewhat compensate for weak social affections and sympathies.[2]

It is largely because of this service as one of the fundamental bases of conscience and therefore of moral advance that Darwin finds that many of the mental faculties, such as the powers of the imagination, wonder, curiosity, an undefined sense of beauty, a tendency to imitation and the love of excitement or novelty, have been of inestimable service to man for his progressive advancement.[3] Even the æsthetic qualities, "the ability to admire such scenes as the heavens at night, a beautiful

---

[1] In a letter to John Morley in 1871, Darwin wrote: "When I speak of intellectual activity as the secondary basis of conscience, I meant in my own mind secondary in period of development; but no one could be expected to understand so great an ellipse." —*More Letters of Charles Darwin*, vol. i., p. 327.

[2] *The Descent of Man*, p. 636.   [3] *Idem*, p. 109.

landscape, or refined music," become important survival factors because of their contributions to the power of imagination, and it is through its contributions to a higher standard of morality that religion and the "ennobling belief in the existence of an Omnipotent God"[1] become important factors of social progress.

Among the most important contributing factors to moral advancement and therefore of social progress, Darwin emphasizes the extension of the recognized limits of association. He shows by numerous examples that the narrower are the limits of association the lower will be the standard of morality, and assigns to this factor the first place among the causes of the low morality of savages:

> The chief causes of the low morality of savages, as judged by our standard, are, firstly, the confinement of sympathy to the same tribe. Secondly, powers of reasoning insufficient to recognize the bearing of many virtues, especially of the self-regarding virtues, on the general welfare of the tribe. Savages, for instance, fail to trace the multiplied evils consequent on a want of temperance, chastity, etc. And, thirdly, weak power of self-command; for this power has not been strengthened through long-continued, perhaps inherited, habit, instruction, and religion.[2]

He traces the evolution of morality with the widening intellectual horizon of man as follows:

[1] *The Descent of Man*, p. 109.   [2] *Idem*, pp. 134–35.

As man gradually advanced in intellectual power, and was enabled to trace the more remote consequences of his actions; as he acquired sufficient knowledge to reject baneful customs and superstitions; as he regarded more and more not only the welfare, but the happiness of his fellow-men; as from habit, following on beneficial experience, instruction, and example, his sympathies became more tender and widely diffused, extending to men of all races, to the imbecile, maimed, and other useless members of society, and finally to the lower animals—so would the standard of his morality rise higher and higher.[1]

And he emphasizes especially the gradual widening of the limits of association, in spite of many obstacles, until the social instincts and sympathy are extended to include all humanity.

As man advances in civilization, and small tribes are united into larger communities, the simplest reason would tell each individual that he ought to extend his social instincts and sympathies to all the members of the same nation, though personally unknown to him. This point being once reached, there is only an artificial barrier to prevent his sympathies extending to the men of all nations and races. If, indeed, such men are separated from him by great differences in appearance or habits, experience unfortunately shows us how long it is before we look at them as our fellow-creatures.[2]

The inclusion of the entire human race within

[1] *The Descent of Man*, p. 140.   [2] *Idem*, p. 138.

the bounds of the moral law,—the federation of the world,—becomes, therefore, in the true Darwinian theory, the ultimate goal of human evolution. The federation of the human race under a system of justice and law will lead to the highest morality and will mark the greatest advance ever made in social progress.

Darwin's theory of social progress, approaching the problem from the point of view of biology, is in striking agreement with the newer school of history[1] which finds the key to evolution in the extension of the limits of association to include all humanity. It furnishes the scientific foundation for Kant's theory of universal history as the growth of a world community, reconciling the freedom of individuals and of individual nations with the accomplishment of a common aim for mankind as a whole. In the Darwinian theory of social progress, freed from the distortions of the philosophy of force, we have the clear guiding principle which seems to offer for the social sciences, something of the vitalizing organization and system which the discovery of the Newtonian law of gravitation gave to the physical sciences in the seventeenth century. The growth of a common humanity—this is the key to the synthesis of the humanities, whether we approach them from the science of biology, from history, from economics, from politial science, from ethics, or from sociology.

[1] See *supra*, p. 237.

CHAPTER X

MUTUAL AID AS A LAW OF NATURE

THE human race has had up to the present only a vague and intuitive comprehension of the advantages of association. Mutual aid constitutes the solid rock upon which all the great religions and systems of ethics are founded. The importance of mutual aid has been expressed in terms of modern scientific thought by Adam Smith, who based his epoch-making work on political economy—*The Wealth of Nations*—upon the great fact of the division of labour, and made the "consciousness of kind" the foundation of his *Theory of Moral Sentiments*. Bastiat gave an effective presentation to the advantages of association in his *Economic Harmonies* in the middle of the nineteenth century. Darwin made mutual aid, and the moral law which rests upon it, the central principle of his theory of social progress. Kropotkin in his *Mutual Aid a Factor of Evolution* has developed Darwin's thought further and has given us the classic work on the subject. The genius of Novikov recognized its importance and made it an integral part of all his scientific writings. Yet the work of creating a widespread understanding of the importance of this central fact of social evolution has hardly been begun.

Because men have not realized the benefits of association, those who affirm the existence of economic harmonies and the advantages of universal justice are considered idealists and visionaries. But when men comprehend scientifically that association results in life more abundant for the individuals who form the association, when they are intellectually convinced that in the end association *is* life and that mutual aid and the moral law alone make society possible, and are solely a means to the highest possible life for the individual, then those individuals who affirm the existence of these harmonies and the advantages of justice will be considered the true realists. The apostles of antagonism and the advocates of the philosophy of force will then be considered the visionaries, because they do not see phenomena as they exist in nature, but see them only darkly through a distorting glass of mediæval conceptions.

The philosophy of force, in assigning all progress to mutual struggle, ignores entirely association, although it is one of the most extended phenomena of nature. If progress results from struggle, it must result, in fact, from antagonism. But antagonism is opposed to solidarity and consequently to association. As a result it ought to follow logically that the less the association we have, the greater the progress. But this conclusion ignores the significance of one of the most general laws of the universe,—the law of progress and the intensification of life through association.

Association is a universal fact of Nature. From the highest form of life, the human body, with its thousands of billions of cells, down to the lowest forms of life, we find organisms created by the association of many small units. Even a chemical body is an embryonic association. In every rock and crystal of the mountains, in every drop of water in the sea, molecules have united in systems; and in the molecules themselves we find an assemblage of atoms more or less similar, held together by cohesion and forming a system in equilibrium, stable or unstable. The earth itself is a member of the solar system, held together by gravitation in a cosmic association. Nor is the phenomenon of mutual attraction limited to our system. It is found in many systems of double or triple stars moving about each other or around their common center. It may be traced back to the spiral streams of nebulæ, in which we can see the movement starting, with gravitation drawing thcm slowly together and globing them into new suns and solar systems. So does this law of attraction and union take various forms and pervade the entire universe. It is a cosmic principle.

But it is in the domain of biology that this law of association assumes its full power and undergoes an enormous extension. Life and association are synonymous terms. The simplest

20

cellule is an association of prodigious complexity. As soon as the microscope permits us to enlarge the cellule to a sufficient degree, we can see that it is a whole world in itself. And each element of the cellule, the nucleus, the chromosomes, are also associations of elements still more infinitesimal, which are beyond our vision. Strictly speaking there are no protozoas, because all living beings are associations. As for those organisms which are called metazoas, they are associations consisting of an enormous mass of smaller units. The body of man is a union of some 460 trillions of cellules.

The varieties of association which are found in biology are almost infinite. Biologists tell us that there are bonds of union, varying in importance from almost complete independence to absolute interdependence, between the various groups of protozas which form the cellules in related species. Lichens, for example, exhibit a form of association called symbiosis: they consist of a union of algæ and fungi. A still more mutually advantageous relation exists between certain algæ and radiolarians which are so interdependent that it is impossible for one to live without the other. The bonds which unite them are so intimate that they were for a long time considered a single organism.

In Nature the relationships between living beings are of infinite diversity, ranging from the most irreducible antagonism to the most complete affinity. If when two beings enter into contact their union has as a result a greater vital intensity for each of them, then union takes place. If antagonism would produce a greater vital intensity, antagonism results. The dominating principle in Nature is not struggle, nor is it association, although this is more important than struggle. The dominating principle of evolution is the expansion of life. When association favours this expansion, association takes place. When struggle favours it, struggle takes place. The entire universe is the result of certain general laws, and the expansion of life is one of the most important. For those beings between which association is the most advantageous combination, the vital intensity of the units composing this association is in direct proportion to the amount of their solidarity or interdependence. For those beings for whom it is not an advantage to unite, increase of vital intensity must be sought in other ways.

The philosophy of force has pictured the universe as a perpetual battle-field, and "the struggle for existence" has been worshipped as an idol,—a god, sombre, cruel, unpitying, omnipotent, omnipresent, and eternal. But really it does not deserve this worship. The struggle for existence is simply a law of Nature, like the law of gravitation; but no one proposes to worship the law of gravitation as a new divinity. Much more important than the law of struggle is the law of association—the law of mutual aid, which is the chief factor in evolution, —but the philosophy of force has ignored this more important law almost entirely because its advocates have concentrated their attention upon the combats between individuals which are of different and non-associable species and therefore naturally enemies.

As a result of this one-sided interpretation of evolution, a powerful support has been given to the pessimistic spirit which has characterized so much of nineteenth century philosophy. With the distortion of the Darwinian theory and the triumph of the philosophy of force, a great blight fell upon all Christendom in the last quarter of the century. In the intellectual life of the western world all generous impulses towards justice, humanity, and brotherhood, all the idealism which is based on the fundamental social instincts of the human race, and to a large extent all faith in religion, were crushed out by the resulting avalanche of materialism. Yet the doctrines of the philosophy of force are purely arbitrary and erroneous and their overthrow awaits only the rational and scientific study of the facts of that evolutionary theory which the philosophy of force claims for its scientific foundation.

In reality alliance and combat are parallel phenomena and in Nature that combination results, which in each case favours the maximum of vital intensity. Certain individuals and groups are able to associate with each other and certain others are not. The basic error of the philosophy of force consists in considering only the latter and forgetting entirely the former. Since the groups capable of association are at least as numerous as those which cannot associate, the basic error of the philosophy of force is one-sided reasoning. It sees Nature only from one point of view and therefore sees it falsely. As soon as we consider that association includes all living beings from the most invisible infusoria up to man, we can imagine what an enormous mass of facts it has completely ignored.

The philosophy of force describes dramatically the innumerable battles which have been fought since remotest antiquity and concludes, as a result of these conflicts, that superior types have been developed. But not the slightest allusion is made to the fact of association. The question is never raised, Why are certain types superior; why is man superior to the amœba? The superiority comes, of course, from the fact that man is an extremely complex association of trillions of cellules, while the amœba is a mono-cellular being. The philosophy of force, however, does not consider it necessary to dwell for an instant on the effect which association could have upon the perfection of the species. It is evident that even if mono-cellular beings had massacred each other with a hundred times the rapidity that we observe in Nature, they would not have made the slightest progress if they had not been associated. If the philosophers of force had not pretended to raise a scientific structure upon such a unilateral foundation, they would not have forgotten the phenomena of association at any of the phases of vital evolution and as a result they would have been compelled to perceive that the relations between associable beings are different from those between non-associable beings.

Although we live within an association, comparatively few persons comprehend its true nature. We always experience the greatest difficulty in observing in any scientific and objective manner the phenomena of which we are an integral part. The elementary truth is hardly recognized that *association is only a means serving to increase the vital intensity of the individual.* Society exists only for the benefit of its members, not its members for the benefit of society. This fact is ignored entirely by the philosophy of force. The error is emphasized in that theory of the State, which is set forth by von Treitschke and is common among all defenders of militarism. They forget entirely that great as may be the efforts made for the prosperity of the State, yet the claims of the State are nothing in themselves and become something only in so far as they embody the claims of its component individuals. This is the significance of the factor of mutual aid. It results in an increase of vital intensity for those who employ it. This is the reason that it is the chief factor of evolution among beings capable of association. Since the increase of vital intensity is the direct object of mutual aid, we can understand why evolution is so much more rapid in a society of associable beings, than it is among non-associable beings, where struggle is the dominant factor, and evolution only an accidental by-product of the process.

Association derives its importance from the fact that it leads not only to an *addition* of vital power but to a *multiplication* of this power. Ten men associated together do not produce ten times as much as the ten men separately, but produce a hundred or more times as much. The example given by the economist, Jean Baptiste Say, in regard to the manufacture of playing cards, is well known. He found that if every workman made the entire card himself, he could produce two cards a day, but thirty workmen, organized and dividing the labour, manufacture 15,000 a day, or 500 cards each. Association, therefore, increased the productive power of each workman 250 times.

In more complex processes of production the ratio is even greater. If one man had to manufacture an entire automobile alone, it would take him many years, possibly it might require a lifetime, yet 20,000 men in the Ford factory at Detroit, practising division of labour and specializing on the different processes of production, can produce more than 1,000 automobiles per day, or at the rate of one automobile every twenty days for each workman. This marvellous multiplication of productive power can be obtained only by association, because association although taking place under a thousand different aspects, is always a multiplication of vital power.

In the embryonic stage, when the germinal cellule divides itself into two, then four, then eight cells, and so on, in order to produce in the course of a few months the trillions of cellules of the human body, the multiplication of vital power which results is an effect of this same process of association. If these cellules separated from each other as fast as they were formed, as is the case among the protozoas, their vital power would not be increased, but by remaining united they produce a being whose vital power is enormous. As the result of this combination each cellule forming part of a very complex organization has a vital power infinitely superior to that of the mono-cellular organisms. In addition to his physiological growth, man can grow psychologically (increasing his knowledge) and economically (increasing his wealth) and go on until old age developing his vital powers. And the increase of intellectual and economic power is most rapid for the man who lives in the society which is largest and best organized, that is, for the man who is part of the most perfect association.

Darwin has shown that the cause of the low morality among savages is due to the narrow limits of association, and that a necessary condition for higher standards of morality is the extension of the area over which the moral law is applied. It follows from the law of acceleration, which comes into operation wherever a constant force acts in the same direction, that not only morality, but also the increase of intelligence and of wealth will be in proportion to the extent of the association. As long as man is a member of a small tribe, consisting of a score of individuals, the increase in his intelligence and his fortune must be slow. When the whole human race shall form a single organized group, the increase of the intelligence and the riches of each inhabitant of the world will be the most rapid possible. The problem of extending the limits of the moral law until it includes all humanity becomes therefore the central problem of all social progress.

Association and the intensification of life are identical facts. We can trace the process from the lowest to the highest ranges of life. In the vegetable and animal kingdom, cellules associate themselves into organisms. Then animals associate themselves into groups of varying extent. The biological and sociological processes are of exactly the same nature. One is the continuation of the other without the least trace of a break. One of the most difficult questions which the naturalist has to solve is to determine in certain cases whether a living organism is an individual or a collection of individuals, *i. e.*, a colony. The question of individuality is widely recognized as one of the most difficult in biology. However, all these phenomena which take on such extraordinarily complex forms are the resultants of a single effort and a single tendency: the exaltation of the vital intensity of the units which make up the association. Association is always a means. The vital intensity of the component units of the association is the end.

Association produces an exaltation of life because the functions are carried on simultaneously. At the same time that the lungs breathe air and the stomach digests food, the brain thinks. As the result of the association of cellules, each of them profits immediately from the favourable results of all three actions. It is as if each cellule accomplished at the same time the function of oxidation, assimilation, and cerebration. Since it accomplishes in this way and in an indirect manner a larger number of functions, the cellule which is part of a collective organism lives, naturally, with a greater intensity. Exactly the same results take place in society. Individually I may not have any direct part in the extraction of coal from the mines of the earth, or in the scientific researches which have for their object the discovery of a more perfect electric light, but as a result of human association and the division of labour, it is as if I had a part in the work, because in a certain measure I enjoy the advantages which they produce. Innumerable other concrete examples might be given to demonstrate that association is a process which augments the vital powers of the individual.

The philosophy of force fails even to comprehend the essential nature of struggle which it has made in theory the corner-stone of the structure of society. Struggle is not the object of life. The object is enjoyment, satisfaction, happiness. If association produces more enjoyment than struggle, association will take place. Nature is supremely indifferent in regard to the choice of processes. The advantage is found on the side of that process which favours most the greatest intensification of life. Struggle cannot produce as powerful an exaltation of vital force as that which can be produced by association. As a consequence we find that association dominates in an immense number of cases. It is estimated by the naturalist that there are on the earth 150,000 species of plants and 100,000 species of animals. When we consider the enormous number of individuals which constitute certain species, the number of associations which exist on the planet must be counted by billions of billions, since every metazoa is an association.

Kropotkin tells how his attention was called to the futility of struggle and the effectiveness of mutual aid as a factor of evolution, by his observations of the garrison of a city which had undergone a long and severe siege. As a result of this severe struggle, many of the garrison died during the course of the siege, and when they were at last relieved, instead of any progress taking place as a consequence of the prolonged struggle, all of the survivors were so greatly weakened by the privation and hardship which they had undergone, that they fell victims to disease and either died or suffered from a greatly weakened vitality for the remainder of their lives. It is evident that no advance over previous conditions could take place as the result of a struggle which means weakness and retrogression for all the individuals compelled to submit to this struggle. Whenever advance takes place it must be because of factors other than struggle. It must be as the result of an exaltation of life and well-being, and the most effective way of increasing this well-being and intensity of life is through mutual aid. At the very most then, struggle can only serve to select out advances which have been made as a result of other factors, especially mutual aid, and it is in this factor that the cause of progress must be found.

As a result of the exaltation of struggle as the *summum bonum* by its fervent and enthusiastic worshippers, the dominant philosophy of the Western civilization has tended to become largely a philosophy of despair, of pain, and of suffering. But with the scientific study of social facts, with the discovery that the rôle of association and mutual aid is much more important than that of struggle, and that both these are subsidiary to the great evolutionary principle of the expansion of life, will come a return to the philosophy of happiness, of hope, and of progress. This result in social theory will be one of the most important gains of the intellectual revolution.

Proceeding from the idea that struggle is the cause of progress, the philosophy of force has concluded that the greater the intensity of the struggle the more rapid will be the progress.[1] This conclusion neglects completely the phenomena of alliance, but alliance is a more universal phenomena than struggle. The philosophy of force thus represents a deviation from the truth on account of its unilateral point of view. It overlooks the fact that struggle must always take place between collectivities. The struggle between a man and a lion is in reality the struggle between some 460 trillions of cellules of the association man, and the 440 to 450 trillions of cellules of the association lion. In the same way in human relations the struggle of France against Germany is the struggle of two collectivities and implies the existence of these collectivities. From this point of view struggle is impossible if it has not been preceded by an alliance. It follows that association is the primordial, and consequently the most important phenomenon.

When association is recognized at all in the philosophy of force, its importance is belittled. Professor Lemeere, rector of the Free University of Brussels, represents a modification which the "social Darwinists" have been compelled to make in their views since the publication of Kropotkin's work:

[1] If we bring this theory to the test of concrete facts, the most rapid progress should be found in those nations where struggle is most intense, such as Turkey, Venezuela, and Mexico. But the accepted tests of social progress would hardly rank these countries ahead of nations like Switzerland or Sweden, which have not had a war, either foreign or civil, for more than a century.

The naturalists represent the earth to us as an immense battle-field on which all living beings struggle violently against each other, producing a frightful competition.   Reacting against such an assertion, Kropotkin has fallen into the opposite error, in wishing to make us believe that mutual aid is the law which rules the relations of organisms.   Mutual aid is a reality, but far from existing among all living beings, it is solely an appendage of a very small number of animals which have a complicated psychology, such as birds and the mammals, and it is also the common law of all the animal societies, in which progress is always accompanied by an evolution of solidarity.[1]

The law of mutual aid is certainly more than "the appendage of a very small number of animals." It is a universal fact in nature and is common to all living beings which are composed of more than one cell—all the metazoas.   Neither struggle nor mutual aid is "the law which rules the relations of organisms."   It is both struggle and mutual aid, each in proportion as it contributes to the increase of vital intensity.   Certainly the picture of Nature which the naturalists present to us is not an idyll.   A world in which millions of beings can only live as the result of the destruction of millions of beings of other species is certainly not the ideal world which our humanitarian impulses would lead us to construct if we had the

[1] Lemeere, Discourse at the opening of the Free University of Brussels, 1907, Oct. 14.

power. But when the philosophy of force draws the conclusion, "the world is not an idyllic place, therefore men ought to massacre each other until the end of time," this *therefore* causes a revolt in all persons with the scientific spirit. The struggle between individuals who are not associable does not prevent alliance between individuals who are associable from being a reality. Combats such as those between spiders and flies and millions of other similar forms of struggle which take place every minute do not prevent the federation of the human race, or delay it for an instant, any more than it is delayed by the continual killing of cattle and sheep which is carried on every day in the stockyards. In nature we see associations formed everywhere in order to combat disadvantageous conditions of the environment. And humanity is subject to the same imperious necessity as the other species. If the earth were a paradise, in which eternal spring reigned and ripe fruits fell into men's mouths, it might be possible for each individual to live isolated and enjoy the most complete happiness. But it is because the world is not an idyllic place that association with our own kind has become inevitable, since it is a question of life or of death. An environment in which 250,000 victims may be buried under ruins as the result of an earthquake, or in which millions of lives may be wiped out by a flood, with its ensuing famine and disease, is certainly not a world at the height of perfection, but it is precisely in order to gain the victory over these disadvantageous conditions that mutual aid is indispensable.

Of course struggle is a reality, but what astronomer would be so stupid as to affirm that the celestial systems are formed solely by centrifugal force? Scientific astronomy affirms, on the contrary, that the sidereal systems are the resultants of centrifugal and centripetal force, or rather of the proper equilibrium between these two.   In the same way evolution is the result of association between associable individuals as well as the struggle between species which are naturally enemies.   Association is life; dissociation is death.   Certainly death is a universal phenomenon, but so is life. To maintain that progress is uniquely the result of death and never of life, as is done in the philosophy of force, is unsustainable.

The philosophy of force is the negation of sociology because it denies that association is one of the fundamental phenomena of the science.   When it is affirmed that progress results from homicide, this amounts to the claim that progress results from dissociation.   Moreover, homicide is a physiological act; since it is the suppression of the life of an individual.   From this special point of view, therefore, the philosophy of force is the negation of sociology because it attributes all progress not to the complex play of social facts (which reduce themselves in the last analysis to interpsychic facts) but to a physiological fact.   In reality sociology is the science of human symbiosis—the science of men living together in society. The philosophy of force, in affirming that progress comes from the opposite of symbiosis, undermines the very foundations of the social sciences. The more closely we examine the actual facts of social life, the more difficult it is to understand, how sociologists like Spencer and Ward have been able to enlist themselves in support of the errors of the distorted "social Darwinism."

Since struggle is a universal phenomenon in nature the philosophy of force has concluded that it ought also to be found within human society. It has then established the fact that it is found there and from this it has proclaimed an irreducible antagonism between the interests of the individual and the interests of the collectivity, and also between the interests of the individuals and the interests of social classes. As we have seen in Chapter II. these doctrines of the philosophy of force are very old, but they have been greatly strengthened by the discovery of their apparently scientific foundation in "social Darwinism." The doctrines have been developed with especial power by German thinkers. In German philosophy we can trace clearly two important currents of thought proceeding from the philosopher Hegel. On the one side Treitschke applied the Hegelian philosophy to the theory of the State and created the intellectual foundation for what is becoming widely known as Prussianism, which regards the good of the State of as something quite apart from the welfare of the individuals who compose it.　On the other side, we may trace the influence of Hegel's philosophy, combined with the distorted "social Darwinism" in the so-called scientific socialism of Karl Marx.　The old Marxian school of socialism has made the struggle of the classes the very pivot of the evolution of the human race.　Moreover, the philosophy of force having proclaimed that the struggle is most severe when it takes place between the most nearly related individuals, the deduction has been drawn that the antagonism between men must be the most profound which exists in the. world.

The single fact which has been left out of account in all the theories of natural antagonism is the phenomenon, found throughout the universe, of association.　It may even be demonstrated that if there were a natural antagonism which is irreducible between men in society, there would not exist on the planet either a plant or an animal. For the assumption that antagonism is natural between men is equivalent to saying that association did not produce a multiplication of vital power or an enlargement of life.　If this were the case no biological association would have been able to form, since the object of biological association, as of human association, is the increase of vital power, the expansion of life.　Consequently neither plants nor animals would exist.　If the antagonism between men were inherent in the nature of things, if *homo homini lupus* were true, this would signify that the association of men did not produce the exaltation of life. Therefore no human association would ever have been formed, and society would not now exist.

If we consider the pretended antagonism between the individual and collectivity, we come immediately upon several contradictions. If this antagonism were real, evil for the individual would be equivalent to good for the collectivity. Therefore death, which is the supreme evil for the individual, would be the supreme good for the collectivity. In other words, a society or a State would attain the maximum of prosperity when all the individuals of which it is composed should cease to live. Or, if we consider it in the inverse direction, if there were a real antagonism between public interest and private interest, the day in which the community would suffer the greatest possible evil, total death, would be that on which the individuals would experience the greatest good. In other words, men would be most happy when they were all dead. This *reductio ad absurdum* shows the essential fallacy of the doctrine of the antagonism between individuals and the collectivity.

But, the philosophy of force maintains, we see the antagonism in operation everywhere about us. How is it possible to affirm at the same time that antagonism exists and that it does not exist? The Socialists claim that they do not strive to produce this antagonism, but simply draw aside the veil

and let the world see the antagonism which really
exists. What is the way out of this apparently
flat contradiction?

The explanation is very simple. There is no
opposition of interests between the individual and
society. The opposition is solely between that
which *appears* to be the interest of the individual
and that which is *really* his interest. It seems to
us that there is an antagonism between the individual and society because we see falsely. If we
could see the *truth*, this imaginary antagonism
would disappear immediately. The opposition
is not between interests; the opposition, in the last
analysis, is between error and truth. When an
elementary knowledge of social science becomes
the common possession of all men, when the advantages of association and the object of the
moral law as the basis for the expansion of the life
of the individual are generally understood, the
identity of the interests of the individual and of
society will be universally realized and the way
will be open for the greatest advance in the history
of the human race.

The same reasoning concerning the relations
between the individual and the collectivity holds
for the relations between individuals. This follows from the fact that the relations between the
individual and the collectivity reduce themselves to
the relation between the individual and a great
number of his own kind. A real antagonism is
established between two men, Peter and Paul,

only when Peter wishes to commit an act which is contrary to his true interests, and therefore solely from the moment when Peter wishes to commit an act which he *believes* is in accordance with his own interests, but which is not so in reality. As long as men wish to act in conformity with their real interests, no antagonism can arise between them from the social point of view. This follows from the law of nature that association augments the vital intensity of the units of which it is composed. A real antagonism between individuals within an association could only take place in a case where the association did not increase the vital intensity of the individual.

It is well known that both Darwin and Wallace have stated that they were indebted to Malthus for the idea of the struggle for existence as a factor in natural selection. Spencer took over much of his philosophy of struggle unchanged from the Malthusian theory also, including his opposition to charity and the poor laws. The significant fact in this connection is that Malthus ignored completely the phenomena of association and mutual aid in human relations. In his chapter entitled "General Deductions from the Preceding View of Society," Malthus sums up his theory in the statement:

That the checks which have been mentioned are the immediate causes of the slow increase of population and that these checks result principally from an insufficiency of subsistence. . . .[1]

But what causes insufficiency of subsistence? According to Malthus the ultimate limit of subsistence is lack of space on the earth upon which food can grow; but the earth has never yet been populated to its limits and this cannot be the ultimate limiting factor which has operated in the past or which operates at the present time. Malthus devotes a chapter to the study of the checks to population among the American Indians and says:

> Under such circumstances, that America should be very thinly peopled in proportion to its extent of territory is merely an exemplification of the obvious truth that population cannot increase without the food to support it.[2]

But the same continent which supported with difficulty a few thousand Indians, now supports more than one hundred million people, still increasing without any indications of pressing upon the limits of subsistence. What is the essential difference between the wandering tribes of Indians who peopled this continent a few centuries ago, and the present civilization, which produces not only enough foodstuffs for its own use, but exports

[1] Malthus, *An Essay on Population*, Everyman's Library, vol. i., p. 304.
[2] *Idem.*, p. 26.

several hundred millions of bushels every year to Europe? Evidently it is not a difference in space. The limits of the continent are the same as when it was inhabited by the Indians. The difference is in the institutions of the two civilizations, and these reduce in the last analysis to a difference in ideas. Instead of being divided into hundreds of petty tribes, each making war upon the other, the present population of the North American continent forms practically one great association, practising mutual aid and the division of labour upon an enormous scale. It is the same with all the other cases considered by Malthus. Everywhere he neglects the effects of institutions and of association as the chief factors in determining the productivity and the amount of subsistence available for any given society.

Malthus emphasizes repeatedly the fact that population tends to increase in a geometric ratio, but he fails entirely to note that association also increases productivity in the same geometric ratio, so that until the world is populated up to its limit (a condition which will probably never be reached, on account of the declining birth-rate which everywhere accompanies advancing civilization), the productive power and the means of subsistence of the human race will always keep ahead of the population. This fact of association which Malthus ignores, completely shatters his whole theory. According to Malthus the means of subsistence can only be increased in an arithmetic ratio while population increases in a geometric ratio, so that he gets the following series of numbers[1]:

Population	1	2	4	8	16	32	64	128	256
Subsistence	1	2	3	4	5	6	7	8	9

But the true theory, if we take into account the law of acceleration whereby ten men working together and practising the specialization and the division of labour, produce not ten times as much as each one separately, but one hundred times as much, would be as follows:

Population	1	2	3	4	5	6	7	8	9	10
Productive power	1	4	9	16	25	36	49	64	81	100

According to Malthus every increase of population results in a decrease of prosperity and a scarcity of foodstuffs. According to a true theory of society, which takes into account the universal fact of association, an increase of population within the limits of an association should result in an increase of productive power and therefore in an increase of wealth, and this is what we see actually happening in all civilized countries.

Malthus was the first to propose the hard and pitiless doctrine afterwards adopted by Spencer and the other worshippers of the anti-social, anti-Christian philosophy of force, that all charity should be abolished and the unfit should be allowed to go to the wall. He states his conclusion as follows:

[1] T. R. Malthus, *An Essay on Population*, vol. i., pp. 10, 11.

I feel persuaded that if the poor-laws had never existed in this country, though there might have been a few more instances of very severe distress, the aggregate mass of happiness among the common people would have been much greater than it is at present.[1]

This doctrine has been especially widespread among those who are only too ready to evade their social responsibilities in the matter of poverty, and have found it a convenient means for quieting restless consciences. The full doctrine has been stated by Hobhouse as follows:

The true problem of social betterment was to determine the conditions under which the better qualities are propagated and the worse repressed. As to the general nature of these conditions, indeed, there could be no doubt for the biologist. . . . The best was that which survived, and the persistent elimination of the least fit was the one method generally necessary to assure the survival of the best. . . . Life was constantly and necessarily growing better. In every species the least fit were always being destroyed, and the standard of survivors proportionately raised. No doubt there existed even in human society many features which are at first sight objectionable. But here again the evolutionist was in the happy position of being able to verify the existence of a soul of goodness in things evil. Was there acute industrial competition? It was the process by which the fittest came to the top. Were the losers in the

---

[1] T. R. Malthus *An Essay on Population*, Everyman's Library, vol. ii., p. 51.

struggle left to welter in dire poverty? They would the sooner die out. Were housing conditions a disgrace to civilization? They were the natural environment of an unfit class, and the means whereby such a class prepared the way for its own extinction. Was infant mortality excessive? It weeded out the sickly and the weaklings. Was there pestilence or famine? So many more of the unfit would perish. Did tuberculosis claim a heavy toll? The tuberculosis germs are great selectors, skilled at probing the weak spots of living tissue. Were there wars and rumours of wars? War alone would give to the conquering race its due, the inheritance of the earth. It would maintain the efficiency of the stronger and erase the less fit from the roll of nations. In a word the only blot that the evolutionist could see upon the picture was the misguided enthusiasm, the "maudlin sentiment," to use a favourite expression, which seeks to hold out a hand to those who are down, and to prolong the life of those who are proved unfit to exist by the fact of their ill success in the struggle.[1]

The fallacy in this harsh reasoning has been exposed by Darwin. Mutual aid is the great survival factor in human society and the possibility of mutual aid is due to certain social qualities, without which it could not exist. Any action which tends to weaken these qualities, by hardening the sympathies of the individual and lowering the moral standards of society, interferes with the action of association and prevents the benefit

[1] L. T. Hobhouse, *Social Evolution and Political Theory*, pp. 20–21.

which might be derived from mutual aid, so that the loss to society is much greater than any possible gain through the killing off of a number of the physically weak. Darwin emphasizes the importance of these charitable actions, which tend to take the form in modern legislation of old age pensions, mothers' pensions, sickness and accident insurance, and other social measures, as follows:

The aid which we feel impelled to give to the helpless is mainly an incidental result of the instinct of sympathy, which was originally acquired as part of the social instincts, but subsequently rendered, in the manner previously indicated, more tender and more widely diffused. Nor could we check our sympathy, even at the urging of hard reason, without deterioration in the noblest part of our nature. The surgeon may harden himself while performing an operation, for he knows that he is acting for the good of his patient, but if we were intentionally to neglect the weak and helpless, it could only be for a contingent benefit, with an overwhelming present evil.[1]

The same failure to understand the significance of the change from the individual to the group as the survival unit, and the resulting paramount importance of mutual aid as the dominant factor of social progress, constitutes the fundamental error in the writings of Nietzsche. He recognizes that Darwin has discarded struggle as the chief factor of his social theory, and failing to

[1] *The Descent of Man,* p. 150.

understand the importance of mutual aid, he accuses him of cowardice. Thus in *Beyond Good and Evil* he says:

All modern moralists after and including Darwin are afraid to establish a moral code of life out of their concepts of struggle, and the privileges of the strong and fit. Like Kant, when it comes to practical morals they construct systems quite independently of the question, What is our conception of the universe? They are cowards.

Nietzsche's ideal of a race of supermen, of the ascent of humanity from species to super-species, possesses an irresistible attraction for the human spirit. But in disregarding the fact of association and relying entirely upon struggle he built his edifice, as all the social structures of the philosophy of force are built, upon foundations of sand.

To those who know Darwin's devotion to truth and his courage in standing by his convictions during the long warfare which raged between science and the old traditional theology, it must be clear that it was not cowardice which prevented him from basing his theory of social progress upon struggle. As we have seen, it was his realization of the new factors of evolution, intellectual and moral, which entered into play and assumed the dominant rôle when he passed from the biological to the social realm.

One of the most important results of the return to the true Darwinian theory of social progress will be the establishment of democracy and religion upon new and unshakable scientific foundations. The philosophy of force, which is anti-democratic, anti-social, and anti-Christian, has fallen like a blight upon the intellectual life of Christendom during the past half-century, but its effects have been almost entirely confined to the aristocratic, intellectual, and governing classes. The growing democratic forces of the labour movement, the social democracy of the European countries, and the great potential forces of the rise of woman in all countries of the world, represent irresistible social and moral forces to which the future in great measure belongs, and which are still largely untouched by its devastating influence. With the rise into intellectual and political power of these groups, bringing with them traditions of the practise of mutual aid and the intuitive knowledge of its advantages, we may expect also a great impetus toward the establishment of a sounder social philosophy, which will prepare the way for a renaissance of idealism and a reconstruction of society on a truly democratic basis.

Kropotkin, in his conclusion, has traced with rare insight the manner in which the mutual-aid tendency has triumphed over all the crises and obstacles of the past, and its promise for the future of the race:

The mutual-aid tendency in man has so remote an origin, and is so deeply interwoven with all the past evolution of the human race, that it has been maintained by mankind up to the present time, notwithstanding all the vicissitudes of history.   It was chiefly evolved during periods of peace and prosperity; but when even the greatest calamities befell men—when whole countries were laid waste by wars, and whole populations were decimated or groaned under the yoke of tyranny—the same tendency continued to live in the villages and among the poorer classes in the towns; it still kept them together, and in the long run it reacted even upon those ruling, fighting, and devastating minorities which dismissed it as sentimental nonsense.   And whenever mankind had to work out a new social organization, adapted to a new phase of development, its constructive genius always drew the elements and the inspiration for the new departure from that same ever-living tendency.   New economical and social institutions, in so far as they were a creation of the masses, new ethical systems, and new religions, all have originated from the same source, and the ethical progress of our race, viewed in its broad lines, appears as a gradual extension of the mutual-aid principles from the tribe to always larger and larger agglomerations so as to finally embrace one day the whole of mankind, without respect to its divers creeds, languages, and races.[1]

And he shows the vital importance of mutual aid as the foundation of ethics and of all religions:

However, it is especially in the domain of ethics that the dominating importance of the mutual-aid

[1] Kropotkin, *Mutual Aid a Factor of Evolution,* chapter vii., "Mutual Aid Amongst Ourselves," p. 223.

principle appears in full. That mutual aid is the real foundation of our ethical conceptions seems evident enough. But whatever the opinions as to the first origin of the mutual-aid feeling or instinct may be,—whether a biological or a supernatural cause is ascribed to it,—we must trace its existence as far back as to the lowest stages of the animal world; and from these stages we can follow its uninterrupted evolution, in opposition to a number of contrary agencies, through all degrees of human development, up to the present time. Even the new religions which were born from time to time—always at epochs when the mutual-aid principle was falling into decay in the theocracies and despotic States of the East, or at the decline of the Roman Empire—even the new religions have only reaffirmed that same principle. They found their first supporters among the humble, in the lowest, down-trodden layers of society, where the mutual-aid principle is the necessary foundation of every-day life; and the new forms of union which were introduced in the earliest Buddhist and Christian communities, in the Moravian brotherhoods and so on, took the character of a return to the best aspects of mutual aid in early tribal life.

Each time, however, that an attempt to return to this old principle was made, its fundamental idea itself was widened. From the clan it was extended to the stem, to the federation of stems, to the nation, and finally—in ideal at least—to the whole of mankind. It was also refined at the same time. In primitive Buddhism, in primitive Christianity, in the writings of some of the Mussulman teachers, in the early movements of the Reform, and especially in the ethical and philosophical movements of the last century and of our own times, the total abandonment of revenge, or of "due reward"—of good for good and evil for evil— is affirmed more and more vigorously. The higher conception of "no revenge for wrongs," and of freely giving more than one expects to receive from his neighbours, is proclaimed as being the real principle of morality—a principle superior to mere equivalence, equity, or justice, and more conducive to happiness. And man is appealed to, to be guided in his acts, not merely by love, which is always personal, or at the best tribal, but by the perception of his oneness with each human being. In the practice of mutual aid, which we can retrace to the earliest beginnings of evolution, we thus find the positive and undoubted origin of our ethical conceptions; and we can affirm that in the ethical progress of man, mutual support—not mutual struggle—has had the leading part. In its wide ex- tension, even at the present time, we also see the best guarantee of a still loftier evolution of our race.[1]

[1] Kropotkin, *Mutual Aid a Factor of Evolution*, pp. 299–300.

PART III

JUSTICE AS A PRIME SOCIAL NEED

CHAPTER XI

THE RELATION OF MORALITY AND SELF-INTEREST[1]

IN the Darwinian theory of social progress morality is synonymous with the welfare of the community and therefore with the greatest expansion of life for the individual. For one of its roots it goes back through the social instincts and the parental affections to the great fundamental factor of love, but it has also another root in intelligence, which brings to morality a powerful reenforcement by showing that it is identical with the highest self-interest of the individual.

But the belief is almost universal that morality and self-interest are opposed, not only in the case of individuals, but in the case of groups of individuals or nations. A moral action is considered to be an action in which the individual sacrifices his own welfare for that of others, and is therefore an action which is diametrically opposed to his own highest interest. Lord Hugh Cecil has clearly

[1] Novikov has replied at length to the various objections raised against this view of enlightened self-interest as the rational basis of morality in his *La morale et l'intérêt dans les rapports individuels et internationaux.* (Alcan, Paris, 1912).

339

stated the doctrine in its international form as follows:

Some good men seem inclined to maintain that the action of a state towards other states ought to be the same as the action of an individual towards other individuals. But this contains a fallacy which, one might think, it should not be difficult to discern. We personify a state, but a state is not a person. It contains a vast number of persons, and those who speak in its name and determine its policy act not for themselves but for others. It follows that all that department of morality which requires an individual to sacrifice himself to others, everything which falls under the heading of unselfishness, is inappropriate to the action of a state. No one has a right to be unselfish with other peoples' interests. It is the business of every ruler to exact to the utmost every claim which can both justly and wisely be made on behalf of his country. He is in the position of a trustee of the interests of others and must be just and not generous.[1]

This idea of the essential opposition between morality and the highest interest of the individual or the nation, characterizes the philosophy of force in all countries. Prof. R. Broda sums up Bismarck's attitude thus:

Bismarck declared that a powerful nation could not bind itself to a sentimental policy, but that it ought to obey solely its own interests, in other words that it is necessary to put aside all those things which individuals

[1] Lord Hugh Cecil, "*Conservatism*," pp. 200–202.

and peoples consider as sacred, everything which re-
sponds to their superior instinct of justice.[1]

And General von Bernhardi repeats the same
idea, in a quotation from von Treitschke:

" The individual must sacrifice himself for the higher
community of which he is a part, but the state is the
highest conception in the wider community of man
and therefore the duty of self-annihilation does not
enter into the case."[2]

These quotations could be multiplied by a score,
all of them showing that action in accordance
with justice, that is to say with morality, appears
to be contrary to self-interest.   Since a sacrifice
is made in acting in accordance with morality,
since justice is opposed to self-interest, men prefer
not to sacrifice themselves, and when a choice
must be made they prefer to abandon morality
in order to follow their own self-interests.   And
when we come to international relations, morality
is not considered to be applicable because in these
relations the safety of the State and the interest of
the people for whom the statesman is acting as
guardian, must take precedence over everything
else.   From this point of view then, it becomes the
highest duty of a statesman to act in an immoral
fashion, because only in this way can he serve the

[1] *Les documents du progrès*, September, 1910, p. 193.
[2] Treitschke, *Politik*, vol. i., § 3, quoted by Bernhardi in
Germany and the Next War, Powles' translation, 4th ed., p. 46.

highest interests of the people for whom he acts as trustee. From the practical point of view also, the belief in the irreducible antagonism between morality and the highest interests of the nation, makes it necessary for the statesman to act in an immoral fashion, under penalty of being dismissed from office and being replaced by a statesman who will serve what appear to be the highest interests of the people.

When Bismarck concluded the Treaty of Frankfort, which gave to Germany Alsace-Lorraine and imposed a huge war fine of $1,000,000,000 upon conquered France, he knew that he was not acting in accordance with the moral law "Nations should do unto nations as they would be done by." Certainly Bismarck would not have wished to put himself in the place of Jules Favre. It is even stated that Bismarck was unwilling to impose these unjust terms upon France and that he only consented under pressure. What impelled Bismarck to act in this immoral fashion? The general belief that the interests of his country were opposed to the moral law, and that in this conflict the moral law ought to give way. Confronted with the alternative of conducting themselves in an immoral fashion or conducting themselves in conformity with their highest interests, most men shape their conduct to conform with their own interests and sacrifice morality.

But was there any real opposition between the highest interests of the German people and the

moral law? If we follow the inevitable consequences of the Treaty of Frankfort, we find the
answer to this question. We can see how the
injustice committed upon France led to the formation of the *Revanche* party, how it led to the
Franco-Russian Alliance, to forty-four years of
insane armament competition on the continent of
Europe, and how it led finally to the breakdown of
civilization in August, 1914. In the face of such
an inevitable chain of retribution it is clear that
in 1871 there was no conflict between the moral
law and the highest interest of the German people,
but that these were identical.

Let us take another example. In 1878 Lord
Beaconsfield went to the Congress of Berlin and
brought back what he called "peace with honour."
At this Congress Lord Beaconsfield forced the
diplomats to tear up the Treaty of San Stefano,
which had regulated the boundaries of the Balkan
States in accordance with the principle of nationality, and to thrust the Balkan peoples back under
the yoke of Turkey. Certainly Lord Beaconsfield knew he was not acting in accordance with
the Golden Rule. He would not have wished
any nation to do unto England what he did unto
the Balkan peoples, but he considered that the
interests of England demanded that there should
be a strong Turkey holding the Dardanelles and
preventing Russia from getting access to warm
water and menacing the route to India. In other
words, he considered that the highest interests of

the British people were in conflict with the moral law and in this conflict the moral law had to give way.

Was this conflict real?   If we follow the inevitable chain of consequences, we can again find the answer.   We can see how the Treaty of Berlin, by thrusting the Balkan peoples back under Turkish rule, led to all the years of massacres and atrocities in the Balkans, how it led to the First Balkan War, to the Second Balkan War, and to the world war which began in August, 1914, and which has aptly been called the Third Balkan War. And we find hundreds of thousands of the flower of the British Empire laying down their lives in the Balkans and the Gallipoli peninsula, and billions of treasure poured out in the attempt to open the Dardanelles for Russia, after Great Britain had fought the Crimean War with Russia to keep this passage closed. Was there any conflict between the moral law and self-interest, and would not Lord Beaconsfield have been serving the highest interests of his people if he had followed the Golden Rule and allowed the Treaty of San Stefano to stand, based as it was on the principle of nationality, to which sooner or later the European nations will have to come as the ultimate settlement of the Balkan problem.

Or let us consider an example from the western hemisphere. In 1883, after the war in which Chile was victorious over Peru, a treaty was signed according to which Chile should retain possession of the conquered provinces of Tacna and Arica for a period of ten years, at the end of which time a plebiscite should be taken in the two provinces to determine to which of the two countries the inhabitants preferred to belong. When the time arrived for taking the referendum, the Chileans refused to carry out their agreement. They said in effect, "Might makes Right: we have possession and do not propose to sacrifice the interests of our nation. In the conflict between self-interest and morality, morality must give way."

When we follow the inevitable train of retribution from this immoral act, we find the same answer to our question. The result of this act of injustice has been to blacken the whole subsequent history of the western coast of South America. The armament competition between Chile and Peru has cost a hundred times over the value of the conquered provinces, and conditions are so bad today that a Chilean ship cannot stop at a Peruvian port or a Peruvian ship at a Chilean port without the bitterness and hatred breaking out into open hostilities. The conditions on the west coast of South America are in striking contrast to those on the east coast, where the Argentine statesmen, after the victorious war with Paraguay, recognized the identity of morality and the highest self-interests of the nation in the statement of Argentine policy "Victory gives no right."

A growing recognition of this identity between morality and the highest self-interests of a nation can fortunately be traced in the international relations of the past few years. The action of the United States in returning a large part of the Boxer indemnity to China, and President Wilson's declaration in his Mobile speech on October 27, 1913, that "the United States will never again seek one additional foot of territory by conquest," are illustrations of this tendency. And even the traditional orthodox diplomacy of Europe is beginning to recognize the true relations between morality and self-interest. Thus Winston Churchill, a member of the British Cabinet, declared in an address reported in the London *Times*, of September 12, 1914:

Now the war has come, and when it is over let us be careful not to make the same mistake or the same sort of mistake as Germany made when she had France prostrate at her feet in 1870. (cheers) Let us, whatever we do, fight for and work towards great and sound principles for the European system.

But in the relations of individuals, this identity of morality and self-interest is far from being recognized. For nearly twenty centuries it has been repeated that we should love our neighbours as ourselves, but very few persons apply this precept. Why? Because it is not believed to be advantageous. What purpose would it serve to love one's neighbour as one's self? What benefits could be derived from this? And because we have not been able to see any possible benefits, we now find more than one half the world's population engaged in collective homicide and wholesale destruction, while even in times of peace, in Europe alone more than four millions of men are constantly under arms ready to attack their neighbours at the first favourable opportunity, to massacre them and to seize their territory.

The blight which fell upon Christendom in the latter part of the nineteenth century, which was marked by the triumph of materialism, the disappearance of the great idealistic forces from public life, and the disintegration of religious faith, may be traced in large measure to the gulf which was created between reason and morality by the development of pseudo-scientific "social Darwinism." As the result of the triumph of true Darwinism and of the real scientific spirit, all other realms of human life and activity have been rationalized and given a scientific foundation. Religion and morality alone remained upon the old basis of authority and divine command, and the belief in the fundamental contradiction between morality and the highest self interest became almost universal.

Various methods of escape from the dualism created by the rise of the philosophy of force have been sought. For a great number of modern men, educated in scientific thinking, the path opened by the monistic movement under the leadership of Haeckel, which rejects religion and morality and takes reason and science as the sole

guide, has constituted a solution. The traditional moralists like G. K. Chesterton, representing
the view of the orthodox Catholic Church, have
sought to find a solution in a return to the Middle
Ages, frankly rejecting the discoveries of modern
science and calling Darwin a charlatan. And even
enlightened spirits like Tolstoi, breaking away
from the orthodox Christianity of creeds and dogmas, compelled to face the conflict between deep-
lying social instincts and intellectual convictions,
have been able to find a solution only by abandoning reason as a guide and relying solely upon
intuition and faith. Tolstoi has stated the
dilemma clearly as follows:

Would reason ever have proved to me that I ought
to love my neighbour instead of choking him? I
was taught it in my childhood, but I believed it gladly
because it was already existent in my soul. Reason
discovered the struggle for existence,—that law which
demands the overthrow of every obstacle in the way of
our desires; that is the result of reason; but reason has
nothing to do with loving our neighbour.[1]

From this accepted antagonism between morality and interest arises the pronounced current of
hostility against the moralists. They are considered as theorists—visionaries living in the clouds
far above the practical realities of life. What they
preach is admitted to be very beautiful, but only
when it has no direct application. When the

[1] Tolstoi, *Anna Karénina*, p. 750.

moralists repeat their precepts, practical men listen with impatience, and say, in effect, "the same eternal outworn old sayings which have been repeated from time immemorial and which mean nothing." They shake their heads and pass on. And when the moralist, convinced of the disastrous effect of the appeal to the instrument of force, redoubles his efforts, and goes on to declare, "If you are struck upon one cheek, turn the other also," then with the evidence of such folly before them it is no longer good-natured intolerance which is expressed, but open hostility and hatred. Morality is regarded in this case as an obstacle to our happiness. It becomes an enemy. As a result of the conviction of the fundamental opposition between morality and self-interest, men who act in accordance with the moral law are looked upon with disdain and are considered as feeble and timid, while those who, like Napoleon and Bismarck, placed self-interest beyond all ethical considerations are regarded as political geniuses and heroes.

The supposed opposition between morality and self-interest results from the failure of the human race to understand the advantages of association and the importance of the factor of mutual aid in increasing the vital intensity of the individual. The chain of cause and effect which proceeds from the moral action of the individual to the welfare of the society or community of which he is a part, and then returns to increase the fulness of his own life, has never been worked out rationally in sufficient detail, and the elementary facts of social science are known only in a vague and intuitive manner.

A logical analysis will prove that there is no contradiction between morality and self-interest. The result of a moral action must be one of three things. Either it is a benefit for the individual who acts morally or it is indifferent and has no result or it is injurious. In the first case the moral action is in accord with the self-interest of the individual and the supposed opposition is untrue. The second possible case reduces, on analysis, to the third, because indifference is an abstract state which does not exist when we consider concrete realities. An action without any consequence is time lost and therefore disadvantageous, if for no other reason than because it prevents the achievement of the good which might have been attained in the time lost. If then an action does not have a useful result, by this very fact it has an injurious result. The whole problem reduces then to the last case. If morality and self-interest are not identical, then all moral action is injurious to the individual who performs the action.

But this last case leads to a direct contradiction of terms. If a moral action could have an injurious result for those who commit it and if under these conditions all men were moral, they would constantly be injuring themselves by their moral actions and would ultimately perish. Morality would consist in the sacrifice of the interests of individuals; a moral society would be one in which every individual sacrifices his own interest; and the maximum of morality would be reached in a society in which the sacrifice of the interests of the individuals resulted in the destruction of the individuals and of the society itself. The result would be that morality would have as its object the suppression of life. When we are told then that a moral action cannot have an advantageous result for the one who commits it, it is as if we were told that life can have as its object its own destruction, or in other words that non-being is the condition of being. This is the *reductio ad absurdum* to which the supposed opposition between morality and the highest interest of the individual logically leads.

It is only because of the widespread ignorance of the true nature and advantages of association that this disastrous belief in the opposition between morality and the interests of the individual has become established. Many persons are able to see so far as to understand that morality is identical with the highest welfare of society, but few persons are able to see the final link in the chain of cause and effect whereby the welfare of society is identical with the highest self-interest of the individual. This is because of the failure to understand the true object of association and mutual aid, namely, to increase the vital intensity of the units which compose the association.

As soon as the true nature and object of association is understood, the supposed opposition between morality and self-interest will disappear. It will then be understood that every action is moral which increases the sum of enjoyment of those who commit this action. But sum of enjoyment and self-interest are equivalent terms, and this amounts to saying that all action is moral which is in accord with self-interest and all action is immoral which is contrary to self-interest. From a negative point of view the proposition may be stated thus: All action is immoral which does not have as a consequence an increase of enjoyment for those who commit this action, or in other words, those acts alone are immoral which are contrary to self-interest and because they are contrary to self-interest. If after the most penetrating analysis it is found that an action is injurious to the one who commits it, this action is immoral. If, after no matter how long a circuit, an action causes harm to its author, this action is immoral, but solely on account of the fact that it causes harm to its author. This reasoning can be made clear by applying it to the rules of moral conduct in the light of the current facts of existence in society.

If we analyse the mechanism of association, we find that if one man kills another, he kills himself in a certain measure. It is because the murderer harms himself that murder is a crime and therefore a supremely immoral action. Suppose that murder were truly in accord with the interests of the individual, murder would tend to become a moral act.   It would be practised universally in society. The life of each individual would become less secure and finally society, including the individual murderer, would disappear.   The commandment, "Thou shalt not kill," is a law of morality solely because it is in accord with the self-interest of the individual.

Not only is it immoral to destroy the lives of one's fellow-men, but there are cases in which it is immoral to destroy an animal.   A man who kills an ox without any purpose, even if the ox belongs to him, acts in an immoral manner, but if the same man sends a certain number of oxen to be killed at the public slaughter-house every day, he does not commit an immoral action.   Why?   Because the killing of the first ox does not have as a result the increase of his own well-being in any permanent fashion, while the regular sending of the other oxen to death at the slaughter-house has these advantageous results.

The same reasoning holds in the economic field. A workman who produces a piece of bad workmanship acts in an immoral fashion.   Why?   Simply because in reality he injures himself by this act. If it were possible to increase wealth indefinitely by bad workmanship, this would be moral.   The same exact analysis of the facts of the social mechanism shows that it is impossible to exploit one's neighbour without exploiting one's self.   It

is for this reason alone that the act of exploitation
is a reprehensible act. If exploitation could be
incontestably advantageous for those who practise it, it would be moral. A man may produce
fabulous wealth and still remain moral. He ceases
to be moral, however, from the moment when he
destroys wealth or when he prevents its most
rapid increase by resorting to exploitation, to
privileges, or monopoly. But he is immoral solely
because the man who retards production dimin-
ishes in reality the sum of his own wealth. If
stealing, fraud, exploitation, and banditism, practised universally, could really increase the wealth
of those who commit these actions, they would be
perfectly moral and legitimate.

Slavery and conquest are immoral actions in
the same way, because slavery is injurious to the
masters and conquest to the conquerors. If the
violent conquest of Alsace-Lorraine was immoral,
it was because this conquest was contrary to the
true interests of Germany. The political measures of repression applied by Germany and Russia
in Poland are immoral because they are injurious
to the whole of the German and Russian nations.

If we examine each moral quality in detail we
see that each reduces itself to interest, or in other
terms, to the maximum of enjoyment.

Chastity and temperance are moral because
they render possible a more intense and prolonged
happiness. Intemperance is immoral because it
leads to satiety, to disgust, to disease, and to short-

ness of life, and, therefore, in all these cases produces a diminution of happiness.

Envy is immoral because it causes those who
experience it to suffer.　Emulation, however, is not
immoral even though it proceeds from an impulse
related to envy, because it is different in its nature.
The person who is envious suffers from seeing in
the possession of another an advantage which he
himself does not possess.　The person animated
by emulation does not experience the evil feeling
in regard to the individual who possesses a good
which he does not possess, but on the contrary
he attempts to procure this same good or a still
greater good if it is possible.　In the desire to sur-
pass his neighbour he does not experience any
suffering, but, on the contrary, a greater intensification of mental activity, and therefore enjoyment.
This is why envy is immoral and emulation is not.

Among the moral qualities which are most
precious are always arrayed the following: gentle-
ness, benevolence, kindness.　However, it is easy
to demonstrate that if these qualities are so prized
it is because they bring with them the greatest
happiness.　The gift of inspiring sympathy is the
greatest which exists in human personality.　He
who knows how to make himself loved is a king
upon earth, he obtains all that he desires, he brings
all under his rule.　And this is true not only of
individuals, but still more of collectivities.

What greater happiness can be found upon earth
than to be loved?　However, that which procures

us this immense advantage is exactly the possession of those moral qualities, affability, righteousness, and kindness, which men estimate so highly
and with so great reason.

The satisfaction of the social instincts is of
course one of the most important elements of
happiness, and no conception of enlightened self-
interest would be complete which did not recognize
the fundamental importance of psychological
factors. Darwin has emphasized the importance of
the psychological element of self-interest repeatedly. The following quotation will illustrate his
view:

. . . Even at an early period in the history of man,
the expressed wishes of the community will have
naturally influenced to a large extent the conduct of
each member; and as all wish for happiness, the
"Greatest happiness principle" will have become a
most important secondary guide and object; the social
instinct, however, together with sympathy (which
leads to our regarding the approbation and disapprobation of others), having served as the primary impulse
and guide. Thus the reproach is removed of laying
the foundation of the noblest part of our nature in
the base principle of selfishness; unless, indeed, the
satisfaction which every animal feels, when it follows
its proper instincts, and the dissatisfaction felt when
prevented, be called selfish.[1]

In the true Darwinian theory, morality is deduced
from the principle of association. Mutual aid is

[1] *The Descent of Man*, p. 136.

the biological process by which the parts composing the association obtain the maximum of vital
intensity.   Everything which contributes towards
the re-inforcement of association is moral because
association is life.   Everything which makes for
dissociation is immoral because dissociation is
death.   In consequence of this the breaking of the
bonds of association is a crime solely because it is
disadvantageous for the individual.   If the rupture of association could be useful for the individual,
this rupture would cease to be a crime immediately.
The triumph of right and the maximum of vital
intensity are synonymous terms.   My right is the
totality of the acts which my fellows ought to
perform in order to permit me to attain the maximum of vital intensity.   But, from another point
of view, my right is also the totality of the acts
which I ought to perform in order not to diminish
the vital intensity of my fellows, because this
intensity of life for others is the indispensable condition of vital intensity for me.   To respect the
rights of others then (that is, to act according to
morality) is my fundamental interest,—morality
and self-interest are identical.

It is necessary to understand this clearly.   In
many cases the impulse which leads a man to act
morally cannot be self-interest.   This is not in
contradiction to the statement that the action can
only be beneficent if it conforms to his interest,
because if the impulse to do good results in evil
for the individual who commits an action, this

action is evil, however pure the intentions of its author may be.   A public official might be honest on account of simple instinctive horror of stealing, but this does not contradict the truth that to steal from a state is an evil action only because it is contrary to the interest of this official. If his corruption did not cause him any evil, direct or indirect, it would not be immoral.

To sum up, if it is not morality which produces the happiness of the individual, can it be immorality which produces this happiness? It is impossible to sustain such a paradox, for it amounts to saying that in order to be happy one must be vicious. To affirm that an action is moral which results in evil for its author is to maintain that living beings do not seek pleasure and avoid suffering. This is to affirm that death is life. These suppositions are so contradictory that we are compelled to adopt the conclusion that morality and self-interest are identical.

The supposed antagonism between morality and interest has brought morality into derision and even aroused hatred against it in our otherwise scientific age. A greater calamity can scarcely be imagined, for it leads in the last analysis to complete confusion in making nations and individuals accept evil for good. It results in plunging the human mind into the most despairing anarchy. With the disintegration of the old basis of authority as the sanction for morality, which resulted from the rise of the modern scientific spirit, and with no rational or scientific substitute adopted in place of authority, the human race has become like a ship without compass or rudder, tossed about at the mercy of every shifting wind and wave.

In the book in which Benjamin Kidd has tried to prove by means of reason that reason is a dangerous guide in human relations, he has included the following definition of religion:

A religion is a form of belief, providing an ultra-rational sanction for that large class of conduct in the individual where his interests and the interests of the social organism are antagonistic, and by which the former are rendered subordinate to the latter in the general interests of the evolution which the race is undergoing.[1]

Mr. Kidd is wrong in two respects. There is no conflict between the interests of the individual and the interests of the social organism of which he is a part any more than there is a conflict between the interests of the human brain and the human body, of which it is a part. The antagonism appears to exist because of the elementary state of our social thinking. Nor is religion an ultra-rational sanction for social conduct, for Mr. Kidd uses rational processes in the attempt to convince us that social conduct is desirable and has apparently reached this conclusion for himself by a rational process.

[1] Benjamin Kidd, *Social Evolution*, Macmillan & Co., 1895, chapter v.

Morever, the theory of association shows us that social evolution is the process of the expansion of life for the individual, and expansion of life means, not the subordination, but the realization of the interests of the individual. The true statement should be: religion provided a *pre*-rational sanction for the conduct of the individual where his interests and the interests of the social organism *seemed* to be antagonistic. The real opposition is not between morality and interest, nor even between the interests of the individual and the interests of the society. These are always identical. The opposition, as in all problems of human misery, is that between *error* and *truth*.

The establishment of the true Darwinian theory of social progress opens the way for the reconciliation not only of morality and self-interest but of science and religion. With the overthrow of the philosophy of force will disappear the apparent conflict between reason, groping in the darkness of a pseudo-science, and intuition, made up of primordial inferences based on the social instincts of human nature.

The triumph of the Darwinian theory will mark the conquest of reason over the only remaining area of irrationality—the realm of human relations and morality. Religion gives us eternal truths, but, in order that they may be effective, these eternal truths must be expressed in terms of the thought of each generation, and the spirit of our age is essentially rational and scientific. When the great truths of religion shall receive their new expression in terms of modern scientific thought, when morality is given its scientific foundation in the highest self-interest of the individual and the nation, when it is realized that the central principle of religion is the same as that of biological and social evolution—the principle of the "life more abundant" for the individual—then the blight of materialism which has darkened the past half-century of human history will disappear. Religion will become again a vitalizing power in human life. Idealism and creative art will reappear with a new confidence, and the way will be open for the redemption and reconstruction of human society upon the great principles of humanity and justice.

CHAPTER XII

JUSTICE AND THE EXPANSION OF LIFE[1]

MORALITY and justice are identical in their essential nature, but they employ different processes. To be moral is to practise justice without constraint, solely under the influence of internal impulse. Since the internal process is more rapid than external pressure, morality is superior to justice, but if on account of wrong social thinking and failure to realize the identity of morality and self-interest, the internal processes are not sufficient, the less effective external processes must be employed. If the moral man is he who practises justice of his own free will, justice in its turn is a means which has for its object the morality of society. Since morality in the Darwinian theory is synonymous with the life more abundant for the individual, the passion for justice, which is inherent in every human heart, is essentially a passion for the expansion of life.

The failure to understand the real meaning of justice and injustice, like the failure to understand

[1] For a more complete treatment of this subject, see Novikov, *La justice et l'expansion de la vie.*

362

the advantages of association and the relation of morality and self-interest, has been the cause of an incalculable amount of evil and suffering for the human race.   In its essence, justice is synonymous with expansion of life; injustice with its limitation, or in other words, with partial death.

Suppose a skilled workman can make seventy-two pieces of pottery a week, for which he receives twenty-five cents each.   Then suppose a new tariff limits his market so that he can sell only forty-eight pieces of pottery a week.   The result to him is the same as if two of his fingers had been cut off so that he could make only forty-eight instead of seventy-two pieces a week.   In other words, injustice is equivalent to a mutilation.

Suppose a lecturer delivers ten addresses a month and receives fifty dollars a lecture.   Suppose the government refuses to allow him to speak in certain public buildings, or otherwise restricts freedom of speech, so that he is able to lecture only five times a month.   His annual income is reduced one-half.   The result to him is the same as if a nervous breakdown had limited his activity.   It is, figuratively, a mutilation.

This illustrates what has been called *passive* injustice.   But active injustice is an equally injurious mutilation of the one who inflicts it.

Suppose Paul is a weaver and earns two dollars a day.   With it he can buy each day, let us say, ten commodities.   But one day all the other members of Paul's group are accidentally stricken by paralysis. Paul works as before and produces as much, but he cannot exchange it. He can buy no commodities, no bread, no butter, no shoes. They have not been made. If the paralysis is partial, so that only half as many commodities are produced as before, then Paul can get only approximately half as much bread, butter, shoes, etc., in exchange for the cloth which he weaves in a day. And if the paralysis were not accidental but due to wounds inflicted by Paul, he would be just as ill situated. *On account of the interdependence of human society every mutilation is in the last analysis an auto-mutilation.* From whatever aspect it is viewed, injustice is a limitation of life.

We can now better understand altruism. In so far as altruism serves to increase the welfare of the society of which I am a part, it is simply enlightened self-interest. It is to my interest to love my neighbours as myself—and myself as my neighbours; in other words, to be just. If I go further, and sacrifice my real interests as a member of society, I lose and society loses. Not altruism, but justice is the solution of the social problem.

This is equally true of political relations. A State is just when it assures its citizens full liberty. Then each individual can attain his or her fullest physical and intellectual development. To be unjust is to inflict on them a series of mutilations. To censor a writer's book is equivalent to rendering him physically incapable of writing it. In individual relations this is called a crime. When a government limits the activity of a number of people, it is a case of social pathology. When the biological units of which society is composed are mutilated or diseased, society itself is diseased.

Despotism is a violation of the rights of the governed by the governing. In a despotism citizens who seek the best interests of the State are considered criminal and are punished for it. Hence they lose interest in the State; and patriotism disappears. A large part of the world has already learned that despotism is unprofitable. The cases of despotism which still remain are striking illustrations of its failure. Although the Sultan of Turkey levied taxes of thirty per cent. on his twenty-four million subjects, he received less revenue than the Queen of Holland with only six million subjects and a lower tax rate. Every diminution of the vital intensity of the governed is a diminution of the vital intensity of the governing. Turkey is reactionary and hence unproductive. Despotism mutilates not only the governed, but the governing as well.

Despotism is the use of brute force to compel citizens to do that which is contrary to their own interests, for the supposed profit of their masters. War is the process by which international despotism is established; and internal despotism is essentially a latent and perpetual war between the governed and the governing. War like despotism is a violation of the rights of others, a mutilation.

When a government, in order to impose its will on others, sends forth its citizens to kill them, it is obvious that it is violating justice most flagrantly. Defence obviously presupposes such aggression, and it is absurd to discuss war solely in terms of defence. Aggression is always precedent.

The reaction of injustice is a universal phenomenon. A conquering government may wish to censor all separatist discussion. It cannot tell by their bindings what books contain separatist ideas. It must appoint censors to read all books published, even those by its own citizens. That is, it must limit the rights of its own citizens. The injury cannot be confined to the conquered people. Who knows what the Balkans might have produced but for Turkish misrule? Had Russia allowed Polish education, who knows but a Polish doctor might have discovered a cure for cancer that would have saved millions of Russians?

The prosperity of our neighbours is essential to our own. The widespread delusion to the contrary has caused centuries of bloodshed. Only the persistence of the old mercantilist illusion, which ignored the advantages of association and the division of labour, can account for the belief that the prosperity of one country can be promoted by injury to its neighbours. What is true economically is true intellectually. Intellectual development in Germany never hampered intellectual life in France; there was rather a reciprocal stimulation. The thought and energy given to military defence and preparation, whether in time of peace or in war, is a loss, a mutilation, of the constructive and productive thought not only of that country, but also of the neighbouring countries, which, under the system of international anarchy, make this preparation necessary.   As soon as it is realized that each nation has an interest in the intellectual and economic health of its neighbours, the pathological condition of international anarchy will disappear.

It is of little importance to the happiness of one individual whether there are fifty-two or 520 countries in the world.   It is important that the number correspond to the needs and wishes of the peoples, that is, to justice; for only then will each enjoy all the possible advantages of political association, of division of labour and exchange.   The principle of national autonomy is an essential condition for the highest development of life, not only for the people of the nation directly concerned, but for all the members of the human race.

Every injustice is then a limitation of the full exercise of his faculties on the part of both victim and victimizer.   It is really a diminution of life. The converse is obvious.   Justice is synonymous with the greatest possible expansion and expression of life.

Most modern nations are composed of provinces which were once independent states.   Germany, Italy, France, England, and the United States are all products of such unions of states which formerly held their interests to be opposed. The establishment of justice has made it possible for them to live together, just as the establishment of universal justice, *i. e.*, the juridical association of all mankind, will make it obvious that the interests of present-day nations are in reality one, and war will become a thing of the past. Then human life will be able to expand as far as the natural limitations of our planet will permit.

Expansion of life depends not only on the number of men associated together, but on the intensity of their activity, and this too is a function of justice. When every citizen's rights are respected and each enjoys the full fruits of his labour, activity is most intense. In Turkey the poor peasant does not dare increase the yield of his garden for fear of tempting the cupidity of brigands and tax collectors, and in America and England the factory worker who feels that he is being exploited and believes he has no interest in increased activity, often deliberately limits his output. The fact of injustice leads to conscious limitation of the fulness of life.

We cannot abolish earthquakes or cyclones, and the injury caused by them is beyond our power to prevent. We cannot give men more inherited intelligence. But we can cease massacring and despoiling one another. The forms of suffering and unhappiness due to injustice we can prevent.

If every injustice is a mutilation, obviously injustice and unhappiness are synonymous. No one will deny this from the point of view of the victim of injustice. Everyone realizes that subject peoples, such as Filipinos, Armenians, Finns, and Poles, in asking for their rights, are impelled by the desire to escape from unhappiness. But the tableau changes when we pass from injustice suffered to injustice inflicted. If all men understand that it is disastrous to be victims, most men still think that it is advantageous to be victimizers; they think it is unfortunate to have one's watch stolen but fortunate to be the thief. The thief is of course the better off of the two—but that is not the question. It is no real gain for either an individual or a nation to become relatively three feet higher than another, if in the process both sink six feet below the ground.

It was long ago observed that slavery often demoralized the masters even more than the slaves. Now slavery is simply a series of spoliations; it is continuous theft. And the result was what we should expect. The old slave states of America are still industrially far behind those that were free. The South does not yet fully realize that "if you want to keep the negro in the ditch, you must stay in the ditch with him." But it is a necessary consequence from the nature of injustice as an act of auto-mutilation.

The existence of conscience is an evidence of the identity of justice and the expansion of life. Conscience is really a lightning calculator of enlightened self-interest. Just as the human spirit has replaced the image with the word, it has replaced calculation of interest by the love of good and hatred of evil. Self-interest is no longer consciously present, but the good is synonymous with enlightened self-interest, as we have seen in Chapter XI. Now conscience has become one of the great factors in human happiness. When a man commits an act which he knows is evil, he feels himself degraded and disgraced: he is unhappy. So too with nations. The oppression of subject peoples causes something like a series of permanent cerebral lesions in the oppressors. The Russians oppressing Poles and Finns; the Germans oppressing Poles, Danes, and Alsatians; the Magyars, Serbians and Roumanians; the English, the East Indians; and the Americans, the Filipinos, ought to feel themselves disgraced and degraded. Unfortunately the masses do not feel so; that is because the general public has not yet a sufficiently keen insight into far-reaching social phenomena. But in every civilized country there is a growing group who feel such shame. The day will come when collective crimes will appear to the masses as odious as individual crimes do today. It will then be realized that happiness without justice is for nations as for men the most chimerical of dreams.

Happiness and justice are then synonymous. All the goods of the world without sympathy profit a man nothing. Hatred contracts the soul as cold contracts a metal. Could the nations of the world but realize this! It is only injustice that keeps them apart. For centuries statesmen have believed the violation of their neighbours' rights to be sage wisdom and good politics, and the memory, conscious or unconscious, of these accumulated injustices, has given rise to national hatreds that seem ineradicable. But as surely as injustice has produced hate, just action would provoke respect and sympathy.

Association is another synonym of justice. Universal justice and universal association are one and the same. My happiness is in direct proportion to the number and power of my associates. It is to my interest that they attain their maximum vital intensity. I do not attain my maximum development by violating their rights. I attain it by co-operation. Imagine a world in which every man was hostile to every other: *bella omnium contra omnes*. Each individual would have to devote a large share of his time to fighting the others; the total production and the individual production would be correspondingly lessened. History is a record of increasing solidarity. Man has felt himself a part of ever larger groups—of the horde, the clan, the tribe, the city, the state, and nation. And always his interests have in reality been identical with a larger group than that of which he was consciously a member. The people of New York and Virginia, of Breton and Provençal know it is not to their interests to violate each other's rights. Some day the people of Germany and England will know it too. Universal happiness is impossible without universal justice and universal association.

The biological analogue of justice is organization. Organization begins in multi-cellular bodies by differentiation of function and division of labour. Obviously division of labour involves exchange. But equity is an essential condition of exchange. If the service rendered and the service received are not equivalent, one part is hypertrophied and the other atrophied; association ceases. In sociological terms exchange without justice is exploitation. And just as equity of exchange is one of the first conditions of life, so justice is the necessary condition for society.

Similarly we may compare justice with health. A person or a state is healthy when vital intensity is at its maximum. Justice produces that condition. If we compare Russia with Switzerland, we note that political assassinations are every-day occurrences in Russia; the most extreme precautions must be taken to preserve the life of the Czar. In Switzerland peace reigns and disorder is unknown, which amounts to saying that Switzerland is socially healthy while Russian injustice has led to social disease.

Unemployment is another form of social disease, due to injustice. There is work enough to be done. The Russian soil is perhaps the richest in the world, but is unexploited because foreign citizens and foreign capital do not feel sufficiently secure there. Australia makes slow progress because labour, as the party in power, has made laws unjust to capital. In many countries lack of access to the land results in widespread unemployment and suffering. All over the world the barriers to commerce prevent a rational development of resources and the employment of labour in those activities in which it would be most productive. Rapid increase of population should increase the demand for commodities, and labour-saving inventions go hand in hand with new needs. The pathological situation of inadequate demand for labour is always a direct product of injustice.

Since, then, happiness can only be attained by universal justice, and universal justice means the organization of all mankind, such organization must be the most immediate and most imperative need of our age. But most men act on precisely the contrary principle. Even politicians and statesmen consider perpetual anarchy the supreme good and cry, "My country right or wrong." Is it not true that the highest patriotism demands justice? That the interest of States is not to preserve their "sovereignty," nor to prolong the reign of anarchy, but to advance the federation of the world? It is not an impracticable vision. All that is needed for its realization is an appreciation of its actual advantages. The eight great Powers dominate the world. If they once lead the way, the others will follow. If they once resolve no longer to tolerate military aggression as they no longer tolerate piracy, the rest of the world

374 Justice and the Expansion of Life

must follow. All that is needed is that the statesmen and the governing classes realize the necessity
of international justice, and mankind will be
organized.

When will organization come? No one can tell.
But in our day he who cannot see that the union
of civilized peoples is the most urgent of all necessities, is truly blind.

Only through organization can the nations obtain absolute security—only by the establishment
of world-justice. War is the greatest possible
violation of right. It begins with homicide (total
suppression of life), continues with a series of
spoliations (partial suppression of life), and ends
in despotism (diminution of the intensity of life).
Men have believed brute force the best means of
avoiding war, and they have piled armament on
armament. In 1868 France could mobilize three
hundred thousand men in three months; in 1914,
three million in fifteen days. Yet she was no
more secure. Germany too had increased her
armament. The risks of war were not decreased
by the increase in military defence. Absolute
security can be obtained only by being stronger
than all possible rivals, and the failure of Napoleon's attempt proved that to be an impossibility.
As long as there is no guarantee, such as a League
of Peace alone can give, that armaments created
ostensibly to establish security will not be used
for aggression, coalitions of nations will always
arise against any one nation or alliance, that

assumes so dominant and threatening a position. Such an attempt is obviously incapable of general realization: a very one-sided reasoning is behind it. Every nation cannot be stronger than every other. Brute force alone cannot give security. Only a world federation, representing a world public opinion, can be stronger than any possible enemy. There can be no security without justice and organization.

Liberty, too, the guarantee against violation of rights by individual or by government, is conditioned by justice. Individuals as well as social groups can be free only if they respect the rights of other individuals and of other groups. Peter is not completely free until all men respect his rights. And Paul, Peter's cousin, can be free only on this same condition. So when Peter fails to respect the rights of Paul, Paul is no longer free, and *vice versa*. When Bodin speaks of the freedom and sovereignty of the State, he usually means not the right to determine its own destiny, but the possibility of determining that of others. It often means an assertion of the right to steal. It is the right to attack a neighbour on any pretext and at any moment, that is, to maintain perpetual anarchy, which is called "sovereignty." But it is truly kindergarten logic to see the palladium of liberty in the maintenance of anarchy. Liberty means, essentially, security, and security comes from respect for law, not from its violation. The masses have no interest in the maintenance of anarchy, and the great democratic forces oppose it. Only an infinitesimal minority can gain by anarchy, but in the absence of an enlightened public opinion, this infinitesimal minority controls the destinies of nations.

One more synonym for justice: equality. Political equality requires strict respect for the rights and liberties of compatriots, equal justice for rich and poor, equal security for all. It is the natural system, for the history of dynasties proves that political aptitudes are not inherited. If inequalities were inherited and permanent, aristocracy might be justified. If it could be proved that mental qualities were racial and not individual, that, for instance, all negroes were stupid and all white men wise, overlordship might be justified. But there are Booker T. Washingtons and there is "white trash." An inferiority which instead of being congenital is the product of adverse historical environment cannot justify the refusal of the right to liberty and independence. If the juridical equality of the races of man is not made a fundamental principle of international law, human happiness will remain a dream, for without equality there will be no justice, and without justice, no happiness.

Security, liberty, equality—these are conditions of the greatest expansion of life.

Social phenomena are inextricably interwoven. The marvellous civilization displayed in the magnificent beauty of the French Riviera is a product of the last century. Why? Because only within the last century has there been security from Saracen pirates, in other words, justice. Now barbarism is the social condition which allows a minimum of pleasure; civilization that which permits a maximum. And since every individual seeks to avoid suffering and tries to find happiness, the impulse towards a higher civilization is rooted deep in human nature. Barbarism and injustice are synonyms whether used internationally or within a nation. One of the principal factors in the high Sicilian criminality is the absence of prompt expeditious justice. And, similarly, we call that State civilized, whose citizens enjoy to the full civil and political liberty; that is to say, where justice reigns.

Democracy and conquest are at opposite poles. Conquest is a form of exploitation which cannot coexist with true democracy. To die for king and country has meant but too often to die to despoil a neighbour, in other words, to perpetuate international anarchy.

We still live in an era of illusions. We condemn petty brutalities, but when they exist on a vast scale we call them inevitable and honour them. For centuries men have dimly guessed what justice meant, they have had vague intuitions that it was the goal of human progress. In large measure it was the need of justice that inspired the idea of God and gave man this belief in a future life. As Renan says:

A single thought sums up the history of the Hebrew prophets during a thousand years: The day will come when justice will reign upon the earth.[1]

Every social reform is based upon the demand for justice. Yet, knowing this, men act on the principle that the way to avoid submission to injustice is to practise injustice to others. Reprisal follows retaliation, leading to a cumulative use of force in ever-increasing destruction.

But we have moved forward. Tacitus tells of a slaughter of four hundred slaves. In 390 A.D. Theodosius had seven thousand Thessalonians killed in the public theatre because they had protested against one of his decrees. In times of peace such things are no longer possible. With the sole exception of international war we have advanced far beyond our position of even a century ago. We are developing a new type of social legislation which represents a new social conscience, awakening to the need for a larger conception of social justice.

History is a lesson in the evolution of law—first within small units, then within larger and larger areas. Despotism served its term in extending the sphere of law. The mediæval dream of a universal monarchy was an imperfect image of a world of law. The whole history of political evolution is a record of the extension of the area of justice. Today the human species is broken up

[1] Renan, *Histoire du peuple d'Israel*, Paris, 1893, vol. v., p. 132.

into a multitude of independent states. Federation must and will come. It is for the good of each and every one of these States. Humanity still has far to travel, but the road lies clear before us.

Biologists speak of positive and of negative selection. The one strengthens a trait and a race; the other weakens it. War, as Darwin has pointed out, acts as a negative selection. So long as international anarchy persists, the negative selection of war will continue.

Justice is the prime condition of positive selection. It alone permits the highest development of human life. Life and justice—these are identical terms. Expansion of life, happiness, association, order, organization, health, security, liberty, equality, material well-being, civilization, justice —all are synonyms. What a pity that the world has not realized it; what a calamity if it does not soon realize it! The form and aspect would remain the same; but a world animated by the spirit of justice would, in its life more abundant, seem to be peopled by a new and higher species.

CHAPTER XIII

WORLD FEDERATION AND SOCIAL PROGRESS

THE goal of social evolution, in the true Darwinian theory, is the federation of the entire human race.[1] This is an essential condition of the highest development of man, for only thus can moral progress, the highest welfare, and the largest life for the individual, the nation, and the entire race be attained. The federation of the world is the unifying thesis of all social progress.

The chief obstacle in the way of world federation is the philosophy of force. As long as nations believe that military force can be used aggressively to promote national welfare, they will be unwilling to give up the right to declare war whenever they wish to do so. But the Great War itself may be a powerful factor in bringing about the intellectual revolution which is the necessary condition for the abolition of our present system of international anarchy. The disappearance of the belief in the advantages of aggression on the one hand, and the common need of all nations for

[1] See *supra*, pp. 299–302.

security on the other, is bringing the project for a League of Peace down from the realm of academic discussion into the region of practical politics.

Such a League of Peace, even though it be limited to an agreement of the signatory powers not to begin hostilities before the question in dispute has been referred to an International Court of Justice or an International Council of Investigation and Conciliation, will lay the secure foundations upon which the structure of world organization may be built. The creation of such an agreement inevitably involves the establishment of a World Court of Justice. It involves creating the international law which this court shall administer, and some method for enforcing the agreement in case it is violated by any of the signatory powers. In other words the establishment of a League of Peace leads inevitably to the development of all three elements of world government, the judicial, the legislative, and the executive functions.

Such a League of Peace would not abolish force as a factor in human relations, but it would profoundly modify the conditions under which force is used, transforming it from the violent part it plays under the present conditions of international anarchy into a true police force used under the direction of law and in behalf of a universal conception of justice. Even though the force employed may be composed at first of co-operating national armies and navies, its essential characteristics would nevertheless be those of an international police force. The essential function of a police force is to prevent aggression and compel the parties to a dispute to bring their case into court. It does not itself commit aggression or attempt to establish justice. The disastrous defect of rival armies and navies under the present system of international anarchy is that each nation, disregarding the universal principle that it should not be a judge in its own case, attempts to impose a one-sided conception of justice by physical force, and constitutes itself, not only judge, but also advocate, sheriff, and executioner, in the dispute to which it is a party. The result is necessarily to base the decision on Might instead of Right, and to employ a maximum of force where a minimum would be more effective.

Still less would such a League of Peace abolish struggle from human relations. This is, of course, one of the chief militaristic objections to world federation. For example, General von Bernhardi says:

To expand the idea of the State into that of humanity, and thus to entrust apparently higher duties to the individual, leads to error, since in a human race conceived as a whole, struggle, and by implication the most essential vital principle, would be ruled out. Any action in favour of collective humanity outside the limits of the State and nationality is impossible. Such conceptions belong to the wide domain of Utopias.[1]

[1] Bernhardi, *Germany and the Next War*, p. 25.

After our analysis of the errors of the philosophy of force, it is unnecessary to demonstrate again that even after the federation of the world has been created, men will continue to compete with each other, that the different social classes will desire to secure certain privileges, that men will not cease to be divided into political parties, that the language frontiers will continue to be displaced, that struggles will continue between the various philosophic and scientific systems, and between the different literary and artistic schools, and that the limits of the different groups of civilizations will continually undergo change,—in other words that struggle under its most diverse aspects will not be ruled out. The only difference will be that these struggles, instead of resulting, as now, in collective homicide on the battle-field, will take place by processes which, in those fields of human life where anarchy has been abolished, are called legal. Only the lowest and least effective form of struggle, that which proceeds by physiological processes, will be minimized, and struggle as a factor in human relations will rise to the higher and more fruitful stages of economic, political, and intellectual struggle.

Nor is it necessary to change human nature in order to establish world federation. The Americans who united the thirteen original colonies and the Swiss who united their cantons into a federation were not angels. In order to form a federation of the world, it is indispensable, not that men should become more moral, but that they should become more intelligent. It is not necessary that men or nations be asked to sacrifice their interests, but only that they shall recognize what are their true interests.

The obstacles in the way of world federation are undoubtedly formidable. Among the most important obstacles, besides those produced by the prominence in the minds of men of the philosophy of force, are: land hunger and desire for territorial conquest; the spirit of jingoism and the desire for national expansion; the enormous financial interests involved in the private manufacture of armaments; the special interests created by militarism; a distrust and even defiance of the principles of international justice; race prejudice and race hatred, egotism and social myopia of the nations; national illusions; the powerful effect of inertia and indifference; traditions and old routines; and the poverty of imagination which results in social fatalism—the belief that federation is impossible or impracticable.[1]

The advantages of world federation will be irresistible to overcome all obstacles once they are known. The economic advantages alone are fraught with the highest significance for the future welfare of the human race. It offers the only

[1] Novikov has devoted a chapter to the analysis of each of the chief obstacles to world federation in his *La fédération de l'Europe* (Paris, 1901), and reaches the conclusion that they are all based upon illusions due to ignorance and the absence of an enlightened public opinion in regard to international relations.

possibility of a solution of the problem of poverty by increasing production and diminishing enormous waste. The problem of misery cannot be solved simply by a redistribution of wealth. Any plan for abolishing poverty by redistribution without increasing production would be but a drop in the ocean. Out of every ten inhabitants of the world, nine never have enough to satisfy their hunger. And the same proportion lack shelter meeting the most elementary requirements of decency and sanitation. Income tax statistics of all countries show that out of every 10,000 persons in the world, 9999 are unable to spare as much as twenty dollars per year for the satisfaction of their intellectual or artistic life, and millions of men even in the richest countries are not able to buy as much as a single book a year.

A study of the fundamental statistics of wealth and production shows that humanity considered as a whole is plunged in the deepest misery. The average income per person and per day for the whole human race has been calculated by Jean de Bloch to be about ten cents.[1] But if all the fortunes in excess of $2000 should be confiscated and given to the poor it would add only ten per cent. to their income. The most elementary analysis of the statistics shows that no plan for redistribution can solve the problem of poverty.

When we consider the increase of prosperity in France, which resulted from its unity and the

[1] See Jean de Bloch, *The Future of War*, 1898, volume iv.

removal of the obstacles to commerce and the
division of labour within its boundaries, and
the similarly great increase of prosperity which followed the formation of the German Customs Union
in 1866 and the German Empire in 1871, we can
realize what enormous possibilities for increasing
human welfare will be the result of the federation
of the world. Jean de Bloch has estimated that
world federation, with the formation of a world's
customs union, would increase the average income
from its present value, about fifty-two centimes
per person and per day, to between twenty-eight
and thirty-three francs per day for each family of
five which included three workers. In other words,
the average standard of living for the human race
would be raised to ten times its present height as
the result of world federation.

Nor is the money cost the chief waste of the
present system of international anarchy. Much
more important is the diversion of the energies
and thoughts of men from productive to unproductive purposes. Projects for social legislation
must be indefinitely postponed because all the
governments are forced to devote more than two-
thirds of the entire national revenue to war purposes. At present the activities of all men are
divided into three parts:

(1) The production of wealth (*i. e.* the adaptation of the planet to their needs); (2) the preparation of a formidable military force for the purpose
of making conquest and despoiling their neigh-

bours; and (3) the preparation of another huge military machine in order not to be despoiled in their turn.

The problem of misery will be solved only when men renounce the last two modes of activity, in order to concentrate solely upon the first. There is no other way of procuring the welfare of humanity, except to cease massacring and despoiling and focus all our energies upon production. But this means replacing international anarchy by juridical relations, that is to say, forming a League of Peace as the first step towards world federation. In its essence this implies the substitution of solidarity for hostility because solidarity and federation are synonymous terms. Solidarity is, of course, an empty word unless it is translated into action; and such action must consist in due respect for the rights of all members of our human society, which is to say,—world federation under a system of justice.

The political advantages of federation are almost equally important. The object of political organization is to obtain for the individual security for his life and his property. The federation of the world will mark the first time in the history of the human race when political security has been complete. The attempt to obtain security by sheer bulldog piling up of armaments on the basis of the unilateral aberration has broken down completely in Europe, where casualty lists running into the millions, and national debts of tens of billions of dollars, with income taxes exceeding in many cases thirty-three per cent., have demonstrated the logical results of the system of international anarchy as the method of obtaining security for life and property. But federation and political organization, which are based on a universal instead of a unilateral point of view have, wherever they have been instituted, produced security except against attack from the outside. With the federation of the human race there will be no "outside" left, and political security for the first time in human history will be complete.

Other political benefits of world federation will be no less important. The political institutions of all States have been deeply affected by the condition of international anarchy. It is clear that the greater the social insecurity, the more it is necessary to surrender powers and rights to the central government, and this political centralization has at least three disastrous consequences: bureaucracy, the destruction of individuality, and the non-differentiation of social functions. With the disappearance of the imperative need for centralization in governments, the way will be open again for individual initative to replace the deadening hand and red tape of bureaucracy. The principle of home rule and local self-government can be extended to its widest limits and differentiation of social functions can be carried on until the central power is relieved of all functions except its essential duties of the protection of life and property (police and justice).

One of the most important results of this differentiation of social functions will be the complete separation of Church and State. Without war the necessity for a state religion would never have arisen. In the past the State has been a group of institutions combined for the purpose of attacking other States or for defence against such attack. In order to render these institutions more effective, they were placed very early under the all-powerful protection of the religious spirit. The union of Church and State which resulted and which still continues in many parts of the world has been one of the chief obstacles to social progress and a source of misery for a large part of the human race. Religious beliefs have been largely fashioned by the anarchy of international relations. Primitive ideas of a tribal god have persisted into the twentieth century. The early representations of the gods as battling together in heaven just as warriors battle upon the earth led to the development of the idea of God as a man of war. The worship of the God of War is a direct result of international anarchy and reveals itself in religious intolerance with all its train of evils. From the moment when God becomes a national divinity, religion loses the character of an ennobling universality. It ceases to represent the worship of the truth. After federation, the chief reason for the union of Church and State will disappear and a true religion, freed from the chains of political reaction, will at last be possible. In

Christendom federation will make possible a religion of the New Testament with its God of Love in place of the religion of the old Testament with its God of Battles.

The advantages of federation for the cause of education will be far-reaching. As in the case of the Church, public instruction has been used as an instrument for strengthening the centralized power of the State. In France public instruction was introduced by Napoleon Bonaparte as a measure for increasing its military power. In many countries the schools have been used to teach a narrow idea of patriotism, based on a distorted interpretation of history and a hatred of the "hereditary" national enemies. In the midst of an anarchistic environment, the ideal of the school has been the regiment, with its mechanical automatism. In the environment of federation the ideal will be the most complete diversity and the development of individual character. For the first time adequate funds will be available to reduce the number of pupils per teacher so that there will be a possibility of giving sufficient attention to each child to develop his own individuality. As long as the reign of international anarchy continues, armaments must consume all the fruits of progress and there can be no hope of providing adequate funds for social welfare, education, science, art, or any of the higher purposes of civilization.

The subjection of women, as we have seen in

Chapter VIII., has been the result of militarism and the dominance of brute force in the world. With the triumph of federation the chief reason for denying justice to women will disappear and the contribution of the moral and spiritual power of womanhood to social progress will be of immense importance.[1]

The effects of federation upon social theory will be epoch-making. As long as the philosophy of force is writ large in international relations, it is hopeless to expect that the human race will have a true theory of human society, but with the establishment of federation in place of anarchy, the way will at last be open for the establishment of a sound social philosophy of mutual aid and justice.

World federation will make possible the establishment of a new individualism to replace the older anti-social individualism of persons and of nations —a new individualism founded upon the knowledge of the advantages of association in procuring the maximum of vital intensity for each individual. The true interests of each individual, arranged in the order of their importance, are—

[1] Mme. Emma Pieczynska has expressed the relation of the rise of woman to the establishment of justice as follows: "It is always brute force which covets domination or which wishes to maintain it: it is moral force which refuses to permit it. The defenders of justice under all its forms serve in reality under the same banner; their causes, in appearance diverse, are in reality one."—*Revue de la morale sociale*, 1899, March 1st, p. 10.

1. To live in a world which is rationally organized and most perfectly adapted to the needs of the human race;
2. To form a part of the most perfect society within this larger association;
3. To occupy as high as possible a position in this society.

This classification of the interests of each individual is in the order of importance, but unfortunately it is the reverse of the order in which these interests are presented to his consciousness. Every person in seeking his own personal welfare (wealth, position, honor) tends directly toward the third object. Patriotism is a means by which all citizens, or groups of citizens, who contribute their services to advance the welfare of their country, tend toward the second. But that larger patriotism, embracing all humanity and indispensable alike for the highest development of the individual and the nation, has become conscious in the minds of only a few men, and can become a vital force only with the growth of such political institutions as a world court, a world parliament, and a world executive.

Social theory, then, after advancing from individualism through nationalism to internationalism, returns again to the individual as the object of the highest development of the process of evolution. The first condition for the maximum enjoyment and the greatest expansion of life for the individual is the perfect adaptation of the planet to our needs. When we shall draw from the earth all the resources which it is capable of furnishing us, wealth will attain its highest point. Then, since intellectual development follows economic development, and depends upon the latter for its indispensable instruments, the greatest sum of wealth will give the greatest amount of intelligence and the maximum opportunity for a larger life. The organization of the world, therefore, ought to be the first interest of every individual, to which all other interests are subordinated. The process of the expansion of life through association, which has been a process of evolution from the family to the horde, the tribe, the city, the state, the nationality and the group of civilizations, can attain its logical culmination only through the federation of the world.

Such are some of the advantages which make world federation the unifying thesis of social reform. We read often of an army of social workers. But if we analyse the facts more closely, we find that they constitute, not an army but rather a number of guerilla bands, working at cross purposes and often fighting each other instead of the common enemies of the human race—ignorance, disease, vice, greed, poverty, and misery in all its forms. When it is realized that the key to the solution of all social problems is the establishment of justice, social and international, these guerrilla bands of social reformers, now struggling ineffectively because of their lack of a common aim and of organization on the basis of mutual aid, will become an irresistible army victorious in the struggle against one after another of the foes of humanity.

Many factors favourable to federation are already powerful and are steadily growing in strength. In many respects the world is even now a unity and the task of federation is to give open political recognition to the economic, social, and intellectual facts of vital interdependence. As the result of the advance of science and the conquests of engineering, the earth has become smaller every year, so that division of labour is now established upon a planetary scale. Capital has become international and by means of the telegraph and cable, stock exchanges in all the financial centres of the world have established a sensitive nervous system by which an injury to any part of the social fabric is felt by all the other parts. The migration of labour is taking place upon a scale unknown since the folk wanderings of primitive times, and as a result all the problems of social welfare and of attaining high standards of life and civilization have become international problems. In many cities of the United States two-thirds of the inhabitants are foreign-born or children of foreign-born parents, and the solution of the immigration problem goes back to its roots in wrong social conditions, absentee landlordism, and other forms of injustice in Italy and South-eastern Europe.

So completely have all the interests of men become internationalized that more than six hundred
international associations, ranging from organizations of workmen to scientific associations, have
been formed to carry out on a world scale, the objects which they found it impossible to achieve on
a national scale. Intellectually the unity of the
world is almost complete, in science, literature, and
art. By all the tests of economic, social, and intellectual reactions of one part upon another, the
human race already forms a single social organism,
and it is only because of the backward condition
of the social sciences that political unity has not
long since been achieved.

The extension of the mental horizon, which has
resulted from the telegraph, the newspaper, and
the moving-picture, is a powerful factor making for
world unity. The extension of the limits of the
moral law, which is an indispensable factor of a
larger association, has proceeded very rapidly in
recent years, so that group interests tend increasingly to cut across national boundaries. The
socialists of different nations have much more in
common with each other than they have with
capitalists in their own country, and the same is
true of the capitalists. These ethical factors will
naturally suffer a severe reaction as the result of
the war, but the forces which have produced them
in the past are indestructible and the process of
horizontal instead of vertical stratification of social
interests will go on irresistibly.

Paradoxical as it may appear, the perfection of military organization and its instruments must be counted as one of the most powerful forces making for world federation. Although militarism is to a certain extent a cause of international anarchy, it is still more important as a symptom and effect of this anarchy. Political leaders in all countries, alarmed by the growth of military budgets, have tried in vain to reduce these expenses. "There is some deep underlying cause for the continued growth of armaments," said Sir Edward Grey; and the British Chancellor of the Exchequer, Lloyd George, has referred to the armament competition of the nations as "organized insanity." The national debt created by the Great War will produce almost unsupportable burdens of taxation, and any attempt to maintain the old system of international anarchy will result in a renewal of the armament competition which can have only one of two possible outcomes—bankruptcy or revolution.

Since there is no possible way of stopping the increase of armaments except by international agreement to surrender the right of conquest and aggression, the pressure of the burden of armaments themselves, which caused the Russian Czar to call the First Hague Conference, will lead inevitably to the next step of world organization, the formation of a League of Peace. From this step, once taken, the road leads straight on to the realization of the goal of evolution and the highest aspirations of the human soul, the perfection of the species, and the life more abundant for the individual through the establishment of world federation under the reign of justice.

INDEX

Aberration, unilateral, 120–4
Absorption and elimination, 79–82; death by, 185
Abyssinians, 147
Adaptation to environment, 29, 56; constant, 54, 62; obtained by economic work, 63; rapid in economic processes, 189
Adriatic, 127
Affection, parental and filial, 288–9
Africa, 48, 100, 144. *See also* South Africa
Aggression, dangers of, and motives for, 110; military force and, 113; social reactions from, 119; armaments for, 176; futility of, 177–8, 222; "sovereignty" implies right of, 179; motives for, 179; best means of defence, 180; inevitability of war and, 182–3; key to problem of force, 184; unprofitable, 213; repudiated by public opinion, 220; always precedes defence, 366; changing attitude towards, as result of war, 380; preparation for, diverts large part of energies of men, 386; calls forth preparations for defence, 387; *see also* Conquest, Defence, War
Algerians, 102
Alliances, national, 102; absence of war between members of, 194

Allies, 226
Alps, 114
Alsace-Lorraine, 125, 128, 145, 150, 204, 223, 225, 354
Altruism and enlightened self-interest, 364
America, *see* United States
America, North, 103, 130, 179
America, South, philosophy of force in, 44; part of international credit system, 100; Jesuits in, 204; international conditions on east and west coasts of, 345
American Indians, 326–7
Americans, xi
Analogies, doctrine of definite, 65–71; biological and social, 85–6; in science, 119, 120
Anarchy, of wars of religion, 36; international, 37, 112–13, 129, 178, 375, 387–8; a social disease, 109
Angell, Norman, 184, 190, 253 note
Anglo-Saxon, 128, 145
Animism, 133
Annexation, lust for, 226
Antagonism, between different species, 66–7; in elimination by absorption, 80; artificial national, 102–3; fallacies underlying belief in, 236; supposed, between individual and society, 324; supposed, between individuals, 324–5; supposed, between morality and self-interest, 348; *see also* Struggle

399

The History
of the Child in
Human Progress

By George Henry Payne

8°. Many Illustrations

The treatment received by children in the
past was, until Mr. Payne started on his
work, left out of consideration; children of the
present have been studied and written about
as inefficiently as might be our law, were no
consideration given to the past experience of
men wherein its traditions are rooted.

Having established the status of the child
in what is wrongly called "the prehistoric
period" by showing its status among races
now on earth but "co-eval with the neolithic
age," he shows with great clearness the successive steps which have been taken since
the days of Tyre to the founding of child-
welfare societies during the present generation.   The result is a faultless background
for all literature on child-welfare.

G. P. Putnam's Sons
New York   -::-   London

INEQUALITY

OF THE

HUMAN

RACES

By Count Arthur de Gobineau
Author of " The Renaissance "

◎

Edited by Dr. Oscar Levy
Translated by Adrian Collins, M.A.

8vo. $2.00 net

The author shows the philosophical
foundations upon which his brilliant
studies of the Renaissance are based,
and provides the historical student
with a totally new standpoint from
which to view his subject.

G. P. PUTNAM'S SONS
New York ∴ London

DATE DUE

DE 12			

DEMCO 38-297